I've DIBEL'd, Now What?
Designing Interventions With DIBELS® Data

By Susan L. Hall, Ed.D.

SOPRIS WEST EDUCATIONAL SERVICES
A CAMBIUM LEARNING COMPANY

BOSTON, MA • NEW YORK, NY • LONGMONT, CO

Printed in the United States of America
Published and Distributed by

SOPRIS
WEST™
EDUCATIONAL SERVICES

A Cambium Learning™ Company

4093 Specialty Place ■ Longmont, Colorado 80504
(303) 651-2829 ■ www.sopriswest.com

253LINK/BAN/10-05

Dedication

To my husband, David, who is an ever-present source of encouragement to me.

To my children, Brandon and Lauren, who have sacrificed countless family hours together so this book could be written.

To all the teachers I've worked with in Indiana, Louisiana, and Illinois who have taught me so much.

Acknowledgments

I would like to thank several people who spent countless hours reviewing this book:

Roland Good and Ruth Kaminski
Louisa Moats
Linda Farrell

Thanks to all of them for their insightful comments.

About the Author

Susan Hall, Ed.D., is a reading consultant specializing in teacher training in early reading. Dr. Hall is president and founder of an educational consulting and professional development company called the 95 Percent Group Inc. The company provides consulting and teacher training to districts and schools in how to use early literacy assessment data to inform data-driven small-group tiers of intervention to address specific skill deficits. Clients of the 95 Percent Group include the New Orleans Public Schools, Baltimore City Public Schools, Jamestown New York Public Schools, as well as schools in Parsons and Emporia Kansas, Lake Station and Knox Indiana, and others. Susan is a Sopris-certified trainer of DIBELS and LETRS. Dr. Hall was appointed by the U.S. Department of Education as a member of the Reading First Review Panel to review state grants. She served for two years as a consultant to the Louisiana Department of Education in the implementation of professional development associated with the Reading First program. Dr. Hall has presented to the Reading Coaches for Reading First in many other states, including Arizona, Connecticut, Michigan, New Mexico, Utah, Kansas, and Oklahoma. Susan is coauthor with Dr. Louisa Moats of two books, *Straight Talk About Reading* and *Parenting a Struggling Reader*. Susan can be reached at her Web site www.95percentgroup.com.

Contents

Foreword From the DIBELS Research Team

As we travel around the country, we are often asked about how to analyze DIBELS data to differentiate instruction once students have been assessed. As far as we are aware, this book is the first of its kind and it meets a pressing need. It provides answers to that important question, "I've DIBEL'd, now what?" It's exciting to see so many teachers and schools assessing their students with DIBELS. Yet, if we don't also provide assistance for teachers so that they use the data to inform instruction, the opportunity to change the trajectory for struggling readers will be lost. In this book Susan Hall provides guidance for teachers on how to interpret the data to group students who have similar instructional needs. She also provides a process for analyzing error patterns on the DIBELS scoring pages, along with other sources of data, to inform decisions about where to begin instruction. Additionally, teachers will appreciate the instructional strategies and activities provided in the second half of the book. Based on Susan's insights from many years of working in schools, *I've DIBEL'd, Now What?* provides a practical approach to using DIBELS data. We wholeheartedly recommend this book.

Roland Good, Ph.D.
Ruth Kaminski, Ph.D.

Part I

About Intervention Instruction

This is an exciting time to be involved in the field of early reading. We know more than ever about how students learn to read, and what happens when reading doesn't come easily. We also know about effective procedures to determine which children are at risk of experiencing reading difficulties, and how to intervene early to help avert later trouble. Early literacy assessment instruments have played a significant role in preventing problems because they enable schools to screen all students for signs of delay as part of a Preventive approach. By providing good core reading instruction along with differentiated intervention instruction to small groups of struggling readers, many students will avoid the major problems they would have faced if the reading difficulty had been dealt with much later.

The Preventive approach is based on several important premises about early reading. First, all but a few children can be taught to read proficiently. Second, prevention of reading difficulties in kindergarten through third grade is far more cost effective and efficient than remediation in later grades. Third, relying upon research findings about assessment tools and the components of effective instruction can prevent reading failure. There is no question that the research about reading has brought critical insights about the process of learning to read.

Yet in order to put research into practice, a school will need to implement three things:

- A systematic process for periodically screening all students in kindergarten through third grade to determine which students are not meeting critical milestones in early literacy

- Procedures to provide data-informed intervention instruction in small groups when a student's scores on the screening indicate he is at risk for later reading difficulty, or already experiencing difficulty

- Continued monitoring to ensure that the instruction is helping and that the struggling student stays on track once he reaches benchmark

Increasing numbers of schools have initiated the first part. They are diligently training teachers and aides in how to administer an early literacy assessment instrument.

Success is more than simply having the tool, or even being required to administer it. What is often lacking are the second and third components. Too often the scores are sitting on the shelf. Merely assessing and not using the data to inform instruction is a waste of time. Teachers need to know how to use the data, including making decisions about how to place students in small groups and to determine what instruction is appropriate to address the students' deficits.

The research findings about the effectiveness of early identification and intervention to prevent reading difficulties are extensive. The challenge now turns to how to implement research into practice. The purpose of this book is to help teachers learn how to interpret and use data from one early literacy screening instrument called the Dynamic Indicators of Basic Early Literacy Skills (DIBELS). Although many of the procedures included in this book may apply to other screening instruments, explaining how to make that translation is beyond the focus of this book.

The title of this book reflects the topic. This book is for teachers who are wondering what to do after they have completed administering and scoring the DIBELS assessment. There are three main topics covered in this book. First, a process is provided for how to place students in groups based on the data. Second, a detailed step-by-step process for analyzing a single student booklet is included to help teachers look for error patterns. Third, information is provided about how to match groups to appropriate programs and strategies.

This book contains a unique approach to grouping based on analyzing all the data about a student and considering what he needs and the instructional focus of the group. Some schools group students by randomly assigning students with others who have received the same instructional recommendation provided by the DIBELS or m:class data management system. That is, the students in the "intensive" category are grouped together and those in the "strategic" category are grouped together. While it may work in some cases, this approach ignores some of the information available. Better placements are possible by analyzing the data for each indicator in a more systematic way. In this book, a different approach to grouping is provided, one that has been field-tested by several thousand teachers throughout the United States already.

Another unique feature in this book is that a step-by-step approach to analyzing an individual DIBELS student booklet is provided. There is more information available to inform instruction than the number or score alone. By analyzing the error patterns and reviewing the scoring page on each indicator, it is possible to see whether the student has specific gaps in his knowledge or if his deficits are more pervasive. On each measure, you can see if fluency or accuracy is the issue, or both. There are many other specific observations for each measure. For example, on Phoneme Segmentation Fluency (PSF), it is possible to observe if the student understands the concept of segmentation, and whether he is partially or completely segmenting the sounds in words. On the Nonsense Word Fluency (NWF) indicator, you can see if the student is reading sound-by-sound or whole word. Is the student equally strong at reading consonants and short vowels? On the Oral Reading Fluency (ORF), did the student accurately read phonetically regular words, multisyllable words, and nonphonetic sight words?

After using the DIBELS data and other information to place a student in a group with others whose deficits are similar, the last step is to select the appropriate programs or strategies for instruction. There are more than 200 published intervention programs available today. Many of these programs are excellent, and schools often select several different ones so that they have a portfolio of materials for use in small intervention groups. My recommendation to schools is that some groups should be placed in programs and other groups would best be served by teacher-designed lesson plans to teach specific missing skills. Part II of this book contains activities and strategies that teachers can use when designing lesson plans for groups.

Regardless of whether teachers design intervention lessons or use purchased programs, professional development is the key to success. Even when teachers are using program materials, instruction must be differentiated in response to the errors each student makes. Intervention instruction should be focused and provide immediate feedback and error correction, along with opportunities for extensive practice. A key piece of implementing intervention instruction is learning how to use the progress monitoring data to increase the intensity of instruction until the student's scores indicate he will achieve benchmark.

A reasonable goal is that 95% of all students will reach DIBELS benchmarks with the instruction they receive in the core program during the language arts block and small group intervention instruction. To achieve these results, schools need to implement systematic procedures to screen all kindergarten through third grade students and intervene intensively with instruction that is data-informed. This goal is achievable when teachers receive sustained professional development and coaching to learn to interpret DIBELS data to inform intervention instruction for the struggling readers. We must set our goals high and be relentless in our determination that all students will read.

Susan Hall, Ed.D.

Chapter 1

The Importance of Prevention

> *For the past 3–4 years, I have been pleading our case for early intervention. Last year I started working with kindergarten. This year, with DIBELS, our kindergarten and first grade interventions are the best I've seen in my 14 years at our school. We are teaching the things that students need in order to be good readers. We finally have a systematic plan (based on sound research) that works. I still service 67 students (K–4), but with this new emphasis, I hope in a few years our numbers will go down.*
>
> Title I director

A New Model to Avert Reading Difficulties

One of the most important changes in education this decade is the realization that early identification and intervention can prevent reading problems for many students. New screening instruments make early intervention possible because they identify those kindergarten through third grade students who are at risk for, or are already experiencing, reading difficulties. Schools can provide intervention instruction immediately after a student is identified as at risk, sometimes before a student has even begun formal reading instruction. With early intervention, many students will avoid the major problems they would have faced if the reading difficulty had been dealt with much later. That is why the early identification and intervention approach is called the "Preventive Model," as opposed to the model that schools are increasingly abandoning, which is sometimes referred to as the "Wait-to-Fail Model."

The Preventive Model (American Federation of Teachers 2004) is based on three important premises about early reading. First, all but a very few children can be taught to read proficiently. Second, prevention of reading difficulties in kindergarten through third grade is far more cost effective and efficient than remediation in later grades. Third, relying upon research findings about assessment tools and the components of effective instruction can prevent reading failure. These premises convey high expectations for all children in reading and a sense of urgency for them to have a strong start in early reading.

In contrast to the Preventive Model, the Wait-to-Fail Model is based on the premise that children who experience reading difficulties in the early grades are experiencing developmental delays and will catch up. Schools using this model generally keep struggling readers in regular reading instruction without providing special help, and they do not test for reading deficiencies until students are in third or fourth grade, or later.

The New Preventive Model

The Preventive Model requires the school to have three essential practices in place:

- A systematic process for periodically screening all students in kindergarten through third grade to determine which students are not meeting critical milestones in early literacy skills

- Procedures to provide data-informed, differentiated intervention instruction in small groups when a student's scores on the assessment indicate he is at risk for later reading difficulty, or already experiencing difficulty

- Continued monitoring to ensure that the struggling child is making progress, and that he stays on track once he reaches benchmark

The development of new screening measures over the past 15 years has become a major reason that a preventive approach is possible today. Screening all kindergarten through third grade students multiple times each year with a research-based early literacy screening instrument makes it possible to determine which students are not meeting critical milestones in early literacy skills. Some of these milestones must be met before most children begin formal reading instruction.

Screening assessments in kindergarten and early first grade measure proficiency in skills such as letter naming, letter-sound relationships, and phoneme identification. Screening for students in late first grade, second grade, and third grade includes having students read grade-level passages and demonstrate comprehension of the material read. The best screening instruments are very accurate at predicting which children are at risk for later difficulty based on missing critical milestones in earlier developing literacy skills.

Accurate identification of at-risk students is merely the first step in preventing reading difficulties. Screening is meaningless without targeted intervention that changes reading outcomes for children. Therefore, schools need an organized approach to providing all students who miss milestones with effective and immediate intervention instruction. The Preventive Model assures that each child who lacks any critical reading skill is immediately placed in a small group and given instruction targeted toward developing the weak or missing skill. Intervention instruction is most effective when delivered in small groups of three to five students who are working together because of the similarity of their instructional needs. The teacher or aide working with the small group targets specific skills, provides extensive opportunities for practice, and gives immediate corrective feedback to the students.

A defining characteristic of the Preventive Model is that it is informed by data. Data from the screening assessment not only identify those students who need extra help, but also help teachers determine specifically which skills are lacking and require intervention. Data help teachers form groups that are homogeneous with regard to skill deficits.

Assessment data also reveal whether the intervention instruction is effective in raising the student's abilities in specific areas. This is why it is important to select an assessment tool designed for repeated administrations. If the student's rate of progress isn't adequate for him to reach benchmark by year-end, changes can be made immediately, within a few weeks of initiating intervention. Teachers need to be relentless in their determination to catch a student up, and data play a critical role in helping with this effort.

An assessment tool designed for repeated administrations enables teachers to determine who needs to be in what group. Progress monitoring data show within weeks of placement in an intervention group whether the student is making enough progress to be on the trajectory toward achieving benchmark in a particular skill by year-end. This means that intervention groups need to be flexible. A student moves out of one group as soon as he reaches benchmark. Conversely, a student whose skills are not improving fast enough can be moved to another group or the intensity of her intervention can be increased immediately, with continued monitoring to ensure that the student will reach grade-level benchmarks.

The Outdated Wait-to-Fail Model

The Wait-to-Fail model refers to a lack of institutional processes designed to look for, and respond to, early signs of delay in reading progress. I've worked with many teachers who report having expressed concerns about a kindergarten through second grade student, only to be told by their administrators that it's too early to recommend testing. In contrast, the Preventive Model completely avoids having to convince administrators to test a student since all children are routinely screened. Additionally, help is not tied to a legal qualification process, as with special education.

Waiting to respond to delays may be an approach to allocate testing dollars, or a belief that children with reading difficulties in the early grades will "catch-on" as they get older. However, multiple scientific studies show that children who get a slow start in learning to read are not simply experiencing a developmental lag, but are unlikely to catch up. The two most often cited studies on this topic publish these findings:

- The probability of remaining a poor reader at the end of fourth grade, given a child was a poor reader at the end of first grade was .88 (Juel 1988)

- 74% of children who are poor readers in third grade remain poor readers in ninth grade (Francis et al. 1996)

The Wait-to-Fail model has failed too many students.

Until the late 1990s, almost no schools had systematic screening procedures or a program of intensive intervention at the kindergarten level. If schools did have a program to address reading delays, it was a one-on-one, 30-minute daily tutoring session taught by a reading specialist trained in the program for a set number of weeks of first grade. Children typically qualified for entry into these programs based on teacher referral and a qualification screening by a reading specialist. The problems with these first-grade tutoring programs are numerous, including their expense, their ability to serve far too few children, their relatively lower effectiveness than kindergarten interventions, and their failure to target specific skills with adequate data about what is causing the students' reading difficulties.

Many schools now are abandoning their one-on-one programs in which a teacher or reading specialist served only 16–20 first grade students across the year and are establishing programs to provide early intervention to small groups, beginning with kindergarten students. Each interventionist can work daily with about 30–45 students, assuming that she sees nine small groups of three to five students each for 30-minute time blocks. Additionally, more children are served when students are moved in and out of groups across the year. Other schools are restructuring their Title I programs around the Prevention Model, or supporting classroom teachers in establishing small group intervention instruction within the day.

Informal Assessment Compared With Research-Based Screening

Most schools have had informal kindergarten screenings for many years, but these screenings are not at all similar to the new research-based early literacy screening tools that are instrumental in the Preventive Model. The informal screenings that are common practice in kindergarten typically evaluate a child's knowledge of the alphabet, his book and print awareness, and sometimes letter sounds. These informal screenings are not as reliable or valid as a screening instrument that has been proven to accurately predict if the student will have trouble meeting later milestones.

The use of nonscientific, informal screenings is often sporadic and does not allow the user to compare a child's results with indicators of future success. Without research-based benchmarks, it is difficult for informal assessments to determine whether a student's performance is at a low enough level to cause immediate concern. Even in schools that have established benchmark expectations, very rarely is the informal screening related to an intervention approach designed with specific intervention goals in mind.

Many times teachers who have used a valid and reliable early literacy screening instrument become the strongest advocates for its use. Once they have seen not only its effectiveness in identifying students who need help, but also the amount of information it provides about what to pinpoint and how to help, they argue to keep this assessment over other types of assessment in the school. In one district I work with, teachers at a school that piloted early identification and intervention held before-school meetings to inform teachers at the other seven elementary schools in their district about the success they were having. It was amazing to see teachers passionately advocating for their colleagues to try the approach.

Prevention vs. Special Education

Schools currently using the Wait-to-Fail model for dealing with reading difficulties often do not have an extensive formal program of special help in reading until a student is accepted into special education. Without an early intervention program in place, the teacher's only course of action is to refer the struggling reader for testing to determine if he qualifies for special education services.

Although the reauthorization of IDEA promises reforms, the most recent system by which children were qualified for special education required them to fail for months or years. Often it took that long for a student to show a large discrepancy between potential and achievement. In most states the discrepancy was measured by the difference between a child's score on an IQ test, which represents a measure of potential, and a standardized achievement test. Since children are generally not taught to read passages until first grade, failure to read is not visible until second or third grade. Even if a problem surfaces early, the procedures for testing and evaluation for special education often take months to establish qualification and decide upon remediation services before help is provided.

The Preventive Model avoids relying on "special education" services and the need for expensive and time-consuming diagnostic testing for many students. Prevention and special education are, in fact, inversely related. When the Preventive Model is well implemented, referrals for special education evaluations decline. No special education label is necessary before students are eligible to receive early intensive intervention instruction. Formal, standardized diagnostic testing and referrals for special education are given only to those few students who show persistent weaknesses in skills after receiving small group intervention instruction.

The Preventive Model is also distinct from special education in that it is primarily a general education initiative administered and controlled by the classroom teacher. The classroom teacher, not a psychologist, generally administers or participates in the screening of students. School psychologists may participate on assessment teams with classroom teachers, reading specialists, specially trained aides, speech and language pathologists and others, but the assessments used for screening do not require a psychologist's training to administer. After assessment occurs, the classroom teacher, not a special education teacher, is intimately involved in providing the intervention or supervising others who provide this special instruction. Additionally, intervention instruction does not replace the core classroom instruction in reading as it often does for children on an IEP (Individualized Education Plan), but rather is in addition to the core program.

In the Preventive Model, students targeted for early intervention are served outside the special education venue. Teachers and aides generally provide intervention instruction in groups of three to five students in a classroom or classroom-like setting, rather than in a resource room setting. Intervention groups are formed to combine children with similar needs so instruction can be targeted to address particular early reading skills. Children move in and out of flexible intervention groups on a fluid basis without any need for staffing meetings, IEP meetings, or parental permission. Children are referred to special education only when their skills don't respond well to intensive and systematic intervention instruction.

Why Screening Instruments are Critical to Ensuring Reading Success

In order to assure that every student is progressing well in early reading skills, all kindergarten through third grade students must be screened regularly. Routine screening of *all students* two or three times a year for essential early reading skills ensures that no student compensates for a weak skill by using a strong one. An example of this would be the student who memorizes many words in kindergarten, first and second grades, but cannot sound out longer words introduced in third grade. Without early screening, this student would not be "discovered" to have a reading difficulty until third grade, when the words in reading material are more numerous and longer, preventing the student from being able to rely on his memorization skills.

Early and routine screening has two particularly attractive features. First, early identification enables schools to provide intervention before deficits become a major problem. Second, early screening avoids an extended or agonizing qualification process before a student receives instructional help. This means that neither the teacher nor the parents have to move heaven and earth to defend why a student should be tested. Screening occurs routinely for *all* students.

Research Basis for the Preventive Model

The Preventive Model is based on extensive critical findings from scientific research. Over the past two decades scientific research has led to major revelations about how expert readers read, how children learn to read, and what goes wrong when children fail to read easily. One of the most significant findings is how important early intervention is to averting later problems for students at risk of reading difficulties (Torgesen 2004). It is considerably more efficient and effective to deliver intervention earlier rather than later in the elementary school years. According to the NICHD (National Institute of Child Health and Human Development) branch of the National Institutes of Health, it takes four times as long to remediate a student with poor reading skills in fourth grade as in late kindergarten or early first grade (Lyon & Fletcher 2001). That means that the earlier we can provide reading help to a student, the less time that student will need to catch up.

Researchers also have informed the educational community of the importance of assuring that children get off to the right start in reading. What has been learned repeatedly in multiple studies is that children who get a slow start in learning to read aren't simply experiencing a developmental lag, but lack critical early reading skills that they will not learn without targeted intervention instruction. If students don't learn these critical early reading skills, they may never catch up. As mentioned above, the longer we wait to provide intervention, the more time the intervention takes to be successful. This finding, replicated numerous times, helps teachers confirm that it is critical not to allow a student to get behind in reading.

Schools need practices that ensure students get off to a strong start and stay on track. In an article titled "Early Warning System," Dr. G. Reid Lyon and Dr. Jack Fletcher, two reading research experts, advocate for schools to adopt early identification and intervention systems. They question why so many more students today are being identified with learning disabilities (LD), particularly older students, and why the gap isn't closed by special education instruction.

> "Early intervention can greatly reduce the number of older children who are identified as LD. Without early identification, children typically require intensive, long-term special-education programs, which have meager results. Early intervention allows ineffective remedial programs to be replaced with effective prevention while providing older students who continue to need services with enhanced instruction so they can return to the educational mainstream." (Lyon & Fletcher 2001, 24)

In this article they explain the rise in the incidence of LD as the result of three factors:

1. Current measurement practices work against identifying struggling readers before second grade.

2. It is more difficult to get results when remediation is started after second grade.

3. Federal and school policies allow ineffective assessment and teaching practices to continue.

They describe problems related to the definition and diagnosis of learning difficulties, and argue for discontinuation of the discrepancy formula for justifying that a student is eligible for special services. They suggest "it makes no sense to wait for a discrepancy to reveal itself" (Lyon & Fletcher 2001, 27).

Children identified as reading disabled after second grade rarely catch up to their peers. One of the most cited longitudinal studies is the Connecticut Longitudinal Study directed by Dr. Sally Shaywitz of Yale University (Shaywitz 1996). Children were studied from kindergarten through grade 12. The children in the study who were determined to have a reading disability made some progress in reading from ages six to twelve. Yet they never closed the gap and furthermore, they reached a plateau near age 12, after which their rate of growth leveled off and they fell further and further behind. These meager outcomes were found even though over half of the children in this group were receiving special education services (Lyon & Fletcher 2001, 27).

While researchers find that children who get behind generally stay behind, what evidence is there that it is possible to identify those who will struggle and thus avert failure? Researchers have confirmed that it *is* possible to predict which children will struggle and then actually change the trajectory for these students. A longitudinal study followed 201 children randomly selected from five schools that served children from mixed socioeconomic status and ethnic backgrounds where 28% received free and reduced lunch. These students were followed from the beginning of first grade through the end of fourth grade.

In this study, the researchers followed the students to validate whether their prediction of which students were at risk was accurate. Based on measures of phonemic awareness and letter knowledge at the beginning of first grade, children were divided into two groups: those at risk, and those thought to be at low risk of difficulty. Both groups of children had roughly equivalent levels of overall ability, as measured by IQ. The at-risk group was in the bottom 15% in phonemic awareness and letter knowledge. By the end of fourth grade, the at-risk students had achieved only a mid-second grade level in reading, as measured with a combination of reading accuracy and comprehension. The group considered at low risk finished fourth grade reading at the beginning of fifth grade level. This research project is known as a "passive observation study," which means that the researchers didn't provide any intervention once they determined which children might be at risk. The purpose was to validate that the screening instruments could effectively predict which children were at risk.

The researchers who conducted this study then received funding to go back to the same five schools (see Table 1.1). The mission of their second study was to see if they could act upon their predictions to prevent a new group of at-risk students from following this trajectory of failure. Two changes were implemented: the schools adopted a new research-based comprehensive core reading program, and children from the bottom 15% in phonemic awareness and letter recognition were randomly assigned to two groups. One group served as the control group, and they received only the new core reading program. The second group got the new core reading program plus intervention instruction delivered in small groups during first and second grade. The new core reading program produced slightly better outcomes, with a 3.2 reading level. The group that got the intervention plus the new core program reached a 4.9 reading level by the end of fourth grade, nearly closing the gap and reaching their not-at-risk peers at 5.2 (*The Reading Leadership Academy Guidebook*; U.S. Department of Education 2002).

Table 1.1

Comparison of Core Reading Program Alone Versus Core Plus Intervention Instruction (U.S. Department of Education 2002)

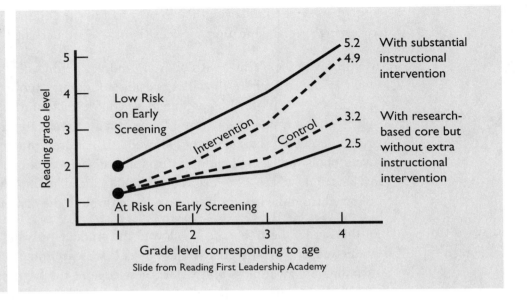

Slide from Reading First Leadership Academy

A series of research studies validates the effectiveness of early identification and intervention. In a series of five studies, students were identified through screening assessments and received intervention instruction, varying from 1:1 tutoring to intervention instruction in groups as large as eight students (Denton & Mathes 2003). In these five studies, between .7 and 4.5% of the total students in the schools did not achieve benchmark levels in early reading indicators (see Table 1.2). Most researchers now assert that effective early intervention practices can bring the percent of struggling readers down to the 2–5% range.

Table 1.2

Summary of Studies About Preventing Reading Problems (from Denton & Mathes 2003)

Percent of Children Scoring Below the 30th Percentile After Intervention

Study	Hrs. of Instruction	Student/ Teacher Ratio	Reading %ile for Initial Identification of Risk Status	% of Lowest Readers Reading Below 30th %ile After Intervention	% of Students Reading Below 30th %ile After Intervention Extrapolated to the Total Population
Felton 1993	340 hrs.	1:8	16	24%	3.4%
Vellutino et al. 1996	35-65 hrs.	1:1	15	30%	4.5%
Torgesen et al. 1999	88 hrs.	1:1	12	23%	4.0%
Torgesen et al. (Manuscript in preparation)	92 hrs.	1:3	18	8%	1.0%
Torgesen et al. 2002	80	1:3	18	4%	.7%

How to Implement the Preventive Model

Many times when teachers and administrators hear about the effectiveness of early identification and intervention, they want to establish this practice in their school. Often their question is, "But how do we get started?" Schools that succeed with the Preventive Model have strong leaders in both administration and among the teachers. These leaders help to bring about the cultural change that leads to better reading performance for almost all students.

Cultural Change May Be Necessary

In most schools, a cultural change occurs when the Preventive Model is implemented. Teachers must view early identification and intervention as so important that they are willing to change practices in a number of ways. First, teachers have to invest the time and energy to learn to administer and score an early literacy assessment instrument. Next, they need to learn to use data to group students with similar deficits and to analyze the student scoring booklets to discover error patterns that inform intervention instruction. One of the greatest challenges for some teachers is organizing centers or preparing independent work for benchmark students so they can teach a small group of intervention students. Sometimes teachers arrange for other teaching staff to work with one small intervention group so that their attention can be devoted to instructing another small group of struggling readers. Finally, teachers must make instructional decisions based on student data, not solely on their "gut" feeling about students. Teachers are accustomed to looking at data to measure outcomes such as year-end data, but don't have as much experience in using data to make ongoing decisions about students and instruction.

It is interesting to observe how readily teachers learn that data can be a friend. They look forward to receiving the next progress monitoring data because they know there will be celebration. Often teachers have not had such clear evidence that their struggling students are making progress. One teacher who had just started using this approach wrote in her journal:

> *This has given me more things to celebrate through repeated progress monitoring and testing. I have a chance to celebrate even the little gains. It also gives me direction and focus for my teaching and for grouping.*
>
> Classroom teacher

A principal in a school that implemented early literacy assessment and intervention spoke in a focus group setting about how her teachers know their students better by using this type of data. Teachers also reported feeling more credible in speaking with parents about delays they observe when they have assessment data to share. At the end of the first year of implementing early intervention, a group of 50 classroom teachers and aides strongly agreed (4.8 on a 5-point Likert scale) with a statement that they would recommend their school continue providing small group interventions next year (Hall 2004).

How Can I Begin to Visualize the Preventive Model?

One of the best ways to develop a vision for what is possible is to hear about successful implementations in other schools. Teachers are accustomed to observing other teachers and talking to them about what they do. There is no better way to communicate what the Preventive Model looks like than to describe how schools have implemented it. These descriptions of schools serve as "success stories" that show us different ways the Preventive Model can work.

Hearing what other schools have done helps principals and other instructional leaders establish realistic goals for their schools. When teachers can visualize the end results of their work, they are more easily motivated to administer the assessments, spend time learning to analyze the data, and put in the extra effort to prepare lesson plans for intervention groups. Studying other schools' successes to learn from their experiences also avoids reinventing the wheel.

There are many alternate models for organizing intervention instruction groups. The possibilities are limitless, and making decisions about how to organize groups can be overwhelming. Even with a vision for the outcome, schools are not always clear about how to realize their vision. By observing other schools, looking at models they use to organize their staff for group instruction, and seeing what they were able to achieve in the first and second year, it is easier to get started.

Three Success Stories

I have worked with many schools that experienced outstanding success using the Preventive Model. While the following stories are typical of the many schools I have worked closely with over the past four years, I selected these three schools because they implemented early screening and intervention in unique ways, and they all experienced rapid and remarkable improvement in their reading scores.

Two of the schools participated in a program called the Early Intervention Program (EIP). The third school implemented an early intervention model through the vision and determination of the superintendent and the principal, and by the successes of some teachers serving as models for the rest.

The Early Intervention Program

The Early Intervention Program (EIP) is a professional development program to help teachers learn how to administer DIBELS, a research-based early literacy assessment instrument, and establish differentiated small group instruction for children who show signs of being at risk for reading failure. A series of eight workshops spread throughout the academic year serve as the foundation for building deep content knowledge about:

- Scientifically based reading research (SBRR)

- How children learn to read

- What goes wrong for those who struggle

- Instructional strategies and practices that help prevent reading difficulties

- How to administer, score, and interpret the DIBELS early literacy screening assessment

Schools in the EIP are supported by an EIP reading coach who provides follow up between workshops and visits each of the schools in the program at least a half-day weekly. The reading coach assists teachers as they learn to administer DIBELS, interpret the data, and implement instruction for intervention groups. One of the most important duties of the reading coach is to work with aides and teachers to help them plan instruction, including modeling and demonstrating teaching strategies and activities. From time to time, the reading coach works with students in order to provide advice on instruction.

EIP focuses on the intervention component of instruction and how to incorporate the use of data to plan differentiated instruction for those children who are struggling with early reading. In spite of the focus on the instruction for students in intervention groups, most teachers have imported the research-based instructional strategies they have learned during the professional development and coaching into their core classroom instruction, as expressed by this first grade teacher who participated in the EIP program:

I have incorporated many "short" activities in between other parts of our daily schedule.

First grade teacher

Early literacy assessment and intervention practices are most effective when embedded in a school where scientifically researched instruction is delivered to students not only in small intervention groups, but also through the core instruction provided during the language arts block.

Five schools participated in the EIP during the 2002-03 school year. Fifty-five teachers and aides who serve kindergarten and first grade students attended eight workshops. During the first EIP workshop, teachers were taught how to administer DIBELS. Immediately after the workshop, they returned to their schools and screened their students. The content at the remainder of the workshops taught teachers how to use DIBELS data as well as deep content knowledge about reading development from *LETRS (Language Essentials for Teachers of Reading and Spelling)*, a professional development program written by Dr. Louisa C. Moats.

All five schools that participated in the first year of the EIP improved their reading scores. Two schools were so successful that they have not only served as models for other schools that joined the EIP in subsequent years, but also for schools in the region that have learned of their success. Their implementations of the Preventive Model are described below, along with the unique reasons these schools had such outstanding results so quickly. A third school in Northern Illinois equally successful in achieving student results is also described below. It achieved these results with a far less extensive professional development initiative.

Success Story No. 1—Lilly School

Lilly School[1] is located in Northwest Indiana on a two-lane country road surrounded by farmland. This one-story elementary school has four classrooms at each grade level. During the 2002-03 academic year, Lilly School voluntarily participated in the EIP because the demographics of the community were changing, the number of children from homes below the poverty line was increasing, and the principal foresaw that the shift to greater numbers of children qualifying for Title I assistance was likely to continue. This principal was a visionary thinker; she talked about the big picture and clearly articulated her goals for improving reading instruction in her school.

One requirement for a school to join the EIP program was that the kindergarten and first grade teachers attend a meeting to hear about the commitment required for participation, and then they must decide to enter as a complete

---

[1] All names have been changed to protect the privacy of schools and participants.

team. Not only must all the kindergarten and first grade teachers participate, but instructional aides, Title I teachers, speech language pathologists (SLPs), and others involved in reading are all invited to attend the workshops. One benefit of including the entire team is that everyone has a common language and common goals, expressed succinctly by this comment that the Title I supervisor at Lilly School wrote in a journal:

> *I'm so excited that we're all "talking the same talk" now.*
>
> Title I director

Lilly School's organization for intervention instruction. After the fall benchmark scores were available, the EIP project director and reading coach met with the teachers and Title I director to find out how many students needed extra help and to group all the students who did not meet benchmark in DIBELS measures. They made a quick calculation that revealed the number of intervention minutes that would be necessary to provide daily intervention for all below-benchmark students. During this meeting, the teachers learned that each classroom needed two or three intervention groups and that intervention for students in each class would take more time than the teacher could provide. Faced with this problem, the teachers determined that the best approach would be for the Title 1 teachers to meet with groups in the classrooms during a specified half-hour per grade level each morning. This key decision led to a restructuring of the Title I program and also contributed to the great success that Lilly experienced.

Under the teachers' plan, a Title I teacher was paired with each of the four first grade teachers from 10:00 to 10:30 to work with one group in the classroom, while the teacher worked with another intervention group. The choice of the first-grade time block was significant because during that time there was already a high school cadet in the room who could work on a literacy activity with the normally progressing students under the supervision of the teacher. Every day at 10:00 a.m., the first grade students broke into groups. About ten to twelve on-grade-level students went to one corner to work with a high school cadet, and four or five at-risk students worked with the teacher. Another four or five students worked in a different corner with the Title I teacher. One or two of the strongest readers from each first-grade room went to the library to work on enrichment activities with the librarian. One or two other students per class who had difficulties with attention went to the multipurpose room to participate in gross motor activities and to develop phonemic awareness with a special education aide.

Changes in the Title I schedule to provide group intervention enabled all at-risk students to receive intervention because the classroom teacher could work with one intervention group while the Title I teacher worked with another group that contained Title I eligible students. Classroom and Title I teachers now collaborate in ways that never existed previously. The integration of Title I teachers into the Early Intervention Program also gave clear and measurable structure and purpose for Title I.

In addition to the importance of the teacher-designed plan that integrated Title I and classroom instruction, two teachers played significant leadership roles. First, the incredibly strong interpersonal skills of the Title I director were instrumental in effecting the change in roles of Title I educators. Second, one first-grade teacher enthusiastically embraced the effort and her leadership impacted her fellow grade-level teachers. She not only embraced the plan and modeled its success in her own classroom, she also organized a meeting one Saturday in October to assemble materials for intervention activities. The team also developed a system for logging specific activities used with each instructional group. Organization of materials and a record-keeping system created a huge impetus for successfully launching the intervention groups. The Saturday meeting and its results created ownership among the teachers for the early intervention concept.

Another important part of organizing intervention procedures was that teachers monitored the progress of all intervention students every three weeks using DIBELS measures. The progress monitoring scores were entered in a set of Excel spreadsheets and used to follow the results for each group. Teachers created their own charts and graphs from these spreadsheets and used them to analyze whether students would benefit by moving between groups.

Results at Lilly School. The progress at Lilly School was evident in many of the scores. Since this was the first year of the Early Intervention Program, many students entered first grade behind in the skills that DIBELS measures. Phoneme Segmentation Fluency (PSF) is a skill that is measured in DIBELS and is supposed to be established by the end of kindergarten at a level of 35 phonemes per minute. Only 36% of first grade students entered the year at the established level of 35. By January, 99% were established in this skill with all but one of the 67 students reaching benchmark. However, because the students were delayed in reaching the PSF benchmark goal, they were also delayed in achieving the Nonsense Word Fluency (NWF) benchmark. Although they didn't achieve benchmark in NWF as early as hoped, the progress was evident, as illustrated by the numbers shown in Table 1.3.

Table 1.3

Student Results at Lilly School

First Grade 2002–2003

DIBELS Nonsense Word Fluency (NWF)

% of Students Achieving Each Level

	Fall	Winter	Spring
At Risk/ Deficit	49%	27%	7%
Some Risk/ Emerging	15%	39%	33%
Low Risk/ Established	36%	34%	60%

The kindergarten teaching team also worked very hard to reduce the number of students at risk. By mid-year, only 45% of 56 students were "low risk" on the Phoneme Segmentation Fluency (PSF) measure, or considered at an appropriate interim level to be on track to make the year-end goals. This increased to 71% by year-end.

One of the most important changes that occurs when a school implements early intervention practices is that the strong instructional foundation provided in kindergarten is translated into higher skills for the students as they enter first grade. The first-grade teachers in Lilly School commented at the beginning of the second year that the students entered their classes with stronger skills than in previous years. This enables the first grade scores to be substantially stronger in the second year of the program.

Conditions that led to success at Lilly School. Analysis of Lilly School's first year of implementing the Preventive Model suggested that two critical components were present in this school that contributed to its success:

1. *The principal's visionary leadership.* The principal is a very experienced and effective leader in this building. She has outstanding communication skills that enable her to get the most possible from each teacher. The principal's subtle, but ever-present, oversight ensures that the school runs well. She also controls the political infighting among teachers that is so prevalent in many schools. Perhaps most importantly, the principal developed a vision to improve children's early reading skills, and she clearly articulated the vision to her teachers.

2. *Two very strong teacher-leaders.* Once the principal explained her goal, she stood back and let the teachers figure out how to implement assessment practices and intervention groups. She gave room for teacher leaders to step forward and take an active role. One first grade teacher became instrumental in getting the intervention organized. The Title I director was the other key leader in the success of the initiative in this school by encouraging the Title I aides to try the new approach and often working closely with the aides in the classroom to help them develop the skills and the confidence to carry out their new roles.

In summary, the principal does not establish a Prevention Model in the school simply by articulating a vision for the school. Teachers can push for the Prevention Model, but without the principal's support, successful implementation is very difficult. The best implementations have both an engaged and effective principal and one or more teacher-leaders who build enthusiasm among other teachers, most often by demonstrating how to implement early intervention in their classroom.

Success Story No. 2—Simon School

Simon School is another outstanding school that participated in the Early Intervention Program. Like Lilly School, Simon School is located in rural Northwest Indiana, but it is about half the size, with only two full-day kindergartens and two first grade classes. The principal is an effective leader, always interested in constant improvement, and the EIP had her wholehearted support. At the teacher meeting required before any school is accepted into the EIP, the teachers shared their observations that students were entering K with lower and lower prereading skills. Simon School was extended an invitation to join the EIP. The principal and staff immediately accepted the invitation.

Simon School's organization for intervention instruction. Simon School's model is different from Lilly School, yet was just as successful for bringing the skills of the students up to benchmark level. During the second workshop, and just two weeks after administering the fall DIBELS benchmark screening, the team of teachers from Simon School began grappling with the implications of how low their students' scores were. Until this meeting, they had no data that compared their student population to benchmarks at the kindergarten and first grade level. Only students in third grade and above had been given state assessments that provided teachers with data.

Once the Simon School teachers absorbed the magnitude of the low scores for the entering kindergarten class, they began to share ideas about possibilities for providing the intervention time that would be needed to bring all at-risk students to benchmark. One first grade teacher looked at her colleagues, looked at me, and asked if we could train the aides to help with intervention. After I endorsed her idea, this first grade teacher offered to give up her classroom aide to help with kindergarten intervention groups. She reasoned that if the intervention didn't begin in kindergarten, those students were going to enter her first grade classroom the next year with minimal early literacy skills. After a bit of squirming, the other first grade teacher also reluctantly agreed to give her aide to the intervention efforts.

The model created that day at the end of the second workshop is still in place today at Simon School. At Simon School, the role of the aides was restructured so that aides provided small group intervention instruction. Previously, the two half-time aides had worked with kindergarten and first grade in a variety of roles. The aides had copied papers, graded papers, organized materials for the teachers, and helped students in various ways, most of which were non-academic in nature. Now the aides would no longer be in an assigned class-room; instead they would provide intervention instruction in small groups.

The teachers created a plan and schedule for how the aides could provide intervention to all the at-risk students during the mornings. One aide was asked to work with kindergarten groups and the other one would work with first grade groups. They sketched out a rough schedule for how to avoid any special classes such as physical education and art, and still make maximum use of the aide's limited morning availability. The aides took responsibility for planning and implementing the intervention, under the guidance of the EIP project reading coach and the classroom teachers. The aides also organized an empty classroom in the kindergarten and first grade hallway by dividing it in half with an old cubicle wall, and began setting up materials. One of the kindergarten teachers had a student teacher for the fall semester, and she used her freed-up time to create a lot of materials from a phonemic awareness activity book. The most important thing that the kindergarten teacher did was to organize the activities by skill addressed through a categorization system using color-coded dots.

It is critical to note that the teachers were responsible for overseeing the intervention instruction, and they conferred with the aides at least weekly about each group. As one kindergarten teacher wrote in her journal during the year:

The "partnership" aspect of this experience has been one of the best things about it. Having someone with lots of experience directing our path, and having

In addition, three of the four teachers integrated some of the same instructional strategies and activities into their classroom. Both kindergarten teachers, including the one who had coordinated the creation of the materials, increased the amount of phonemic awareness teaching for the entire class.

Conditions that led to success at Simon School. At this school the aides were a key component to success. Neither was a certified teacher but both were experienced and talented with children. Both are mothers whose children had attended this school. Their work was closely supervised by the classroom teachers. In addition, the EIP reading coach taught them new activities and helped them learn how to select activities appropriate for each group. This degree of training, along with seven full days of workshops and the materials from LETRS and DIBELS, provided the equivalent of a graduate course in early reading.

Although the aides were crucial to the effort at Simon School, aides cannot always provide as much of the instruction with the intervention students. These aides were exceptionally talented and received extensive training and supervision. Normally we recommend that the most needy students receive intervention instruction from the most qualified and experienced teachers, and the least experienced aides work with the benchmark students during that time.

The other two factors that led to success at Simon School are the same as those at Lilly School — strong and effective leadership from the principal, and teacher-leaders. At Simon School, the aides took a leadership role in implementing this program. They were very tentative at first, but grew into this role beautifully. By spring they were asking the principal if the following year their intervention work would not only continue, but be expanded to include assessment and work with second and third grade struggling readers. During the second year of the program, a kindergarten teacher was appointed the "DIBELS Coordinator."

Success Story No. 3—Gamma School

Gamma School is located in a small community north of Chicago. There is a significant Hispanic population, and the 2002 Illinois School Report Card showed that 25% of the school was "low income." The mobility rate of 25% was a particular concern. While 89% of third graders met the Illinois standards in mathematics, only 68% met standards in reading. Only 49% met reading standards by fifth grade.

At Gamma School, the initial driving force for early intervention came from the superintendent, who was newly appointed in this district. "Ms. Thompson" brought with her not only commitment and vision, but knowledge and information about early reading gained from a very informed and bright teacher at her former school.

In her new role as superintendent, Ms. Thompson clearly articulated that reading must improve, and she talked extensively with the principals at the elementary buildings about early reading. "Mr. Girth," an elementary school principal, was not intimidated by data; actually it was through the data that he learned a great deal about the milestones to early reading.

Gamma School's organization for intervention instruction. When Gamma first became interested in early intervention, a small assessment team, including a few teachers, a district psychologist, and a speech teacher, was trained to administer and score the DIBELS. The fall screening scores revealed that over half of the kindergarten and three-fourths of the first grade students were below benchmarks that would predict success on the third grade "high stakes" test. In mid-October a former kindergarten teacher was hired for the position of interventionist and began training in how to provide intervention instruction.

All the below-benchmark students were placed in small groups of three to four students, based on their DIBELS data and the focus of their needs. For some kindergarten groups it was sounds in words and letter naming. For others, it was sounds only. Some more advanced groups knew many of the initial sounds and were ready for ending and middle sounds. The less advanced groups were still struggling with many initial sounds, so their intervention started with initial phoneme identification.

A schedule for the intervention teacher's day was created based on student need and student availability. Based on the number of students in each classroom who needed extra help, the interventionist was scheduled to spend 30, 45, or 60 minutes with students from each classroom. All the groups met at least fifteen minutes daily, with the students whose scores were the lowest receiving thirty minutes daily in a small group.

Results at Gamma School. Eighty-four percent of first graders were considered at risk for reading difficulty at the beginning of the year, as measured by the DIBELS assessment. All at-risk students received core classroom instruction plus either small-group or one-on-one intervention instruction for as long as needed until they reached benchmark. At the April DIBELS assessment, the average score on the phoneme segmentation test (PSF) increased from 11 to 46 for the intervention students, above the target of 35, as a consequence of the instruction.

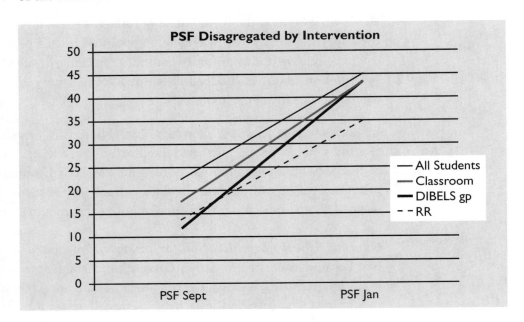

Table 1.4 shows the DIBELS results of the first year of implementing intervention groups. The children who received only classroom instruction made progress across the year with the core reading instruction only. The at-risk students who received core and intervention instruction nearly caught up with the classroom-only group. The students who received individual tutoring along with the core instruction made improvements that kept them up with the pace of the non-intervention students, but didn't close the gap on as many measures as the small-group intervention groups.

At year end, data helped the staff determine that the kindergarten curriculum was not meeting the needs of the majority of students. More children were slipping below benchmark at the beginning of first grade than in the fall of kindergarten. The district decided to purchase a new reading program for kindergarten.

At the beginning of the second year of implementation, the principal waited for the results of the fall screening to see if students who had received small-group intervention during kindergarten would regress over the summer.

Fortunately, there was only a 2% regression in scores among the intervention students over the summer break. This was a huge relief given all the hard work to put the intervention program in place.

During the second year of implementation the district also decided to expand the intervention program to the second and third grade.

Conditions that led to success at Gamma School. The principal's leadership and conviction helped in the implementation. Mr. Girth stood firm when doubters and naysayers on the staff attempted to undermine the initiative. He decided that teachers could not prohibit their students from receiving intervention, but he gave them choice about where it occurred. At the end of the first year of implementing early intervention he made some additional tough decisions that involved staffing. He reassigned the best teachers to kindergarten and first grade so that children would get a strong start in reading. Lack of receptivity to change among some first grade teachers made implementation more difficult. He moved a newer teacher into first grade who was less likely to follow the others. He also used kindergarten end-of-the-year DIBELS data to place students who were still weakest in phonemic awareness with a teacher whose instruction in this area was strong.

What Does It Take to Implement Early Intervention Procedures in a School?

Although early literacy screening tools have become increasingly available since the mid-1990s, school-wide implementations are occurring principally in schools that are required to assess as part of receiving a grant. Far too often, even when staff is administering the assessments, teachers are stopping short of reaping the full benefits of their efforts. They are doing the screening but not using the data to drive decisions about instruction.

Success involves more than simply having the tool or being required to administer it. Success requires professional development for teachers that is sustained and job-embedded, including coaching and discussions at grade-level meetings, if at all possible.

Teachers need to learn how to use a data-informed approach to small group intervention instruction. They need professional development to learn how to decide which data are most critical in forming groups, how to analyze whether a child is struggling with accuracy or fluency in a skill area, and how to use the student booklets to determine what a student already knows and what skills he lacks.

Some of the most effective approaches to professional development combine workshop days with follow-up coaching and discussions at grade-level meetings. Case studies of sample students are analyzed during the workshop, followed by teachers analyzing a scoring booklet for a student in their class. Learning becomes grounded for a teacher when his or her own student's data are involved. An expert facilitator can engage teachers in discussions about observations that are not only factual, but also require inference and interpretation. A trained reading coach can help teachers engage in dialogue about their students' data.

In addition to helping teachers learn to use data to inform instruction, two additional factors help ensure success in implementation of the Preventive Model approach. Effective administrative leadership from the principal allows teachers to focus on reading and provides time in the schedule for intervention instruction. Principals need to organize the building and the schedule of the day so teachers have help through additional staffing and prioritized blocks of time for reading. Scheduling grade-level planning time is critical for teachers to learn to implement these new practices. Teacher leadership is also important for modeling for others effective small-group instruction in the classroom.

Conclusion

The research findings about the effectiveness of early identification and intervention to prevent reading difficulties are extensive. The greatest challenge remaining is how to implement research into practice. The only way that students will receive early intervention in reading is if schools routinely provide screening on early literacy skills, and then have a process in place to intervene immediately if any student is below benchmark. The research is clear about what practices will benefit children. Schools need a process to help teachers learn how to use a screening instrument and to plan intervention, and that process will most likely include some form of professional development. Teachers need workshops with planned follow-up that includes support, modeling, and opportunities to learn how to use this data in a collaborative community with their colleagues. This cultural change in the way a school uses assessment data may not be easy, but it is well worth it given the hundreds of students per school each year whose reading difficulties will be averted by implementing procedures for early literacy screening and intervention instruction.

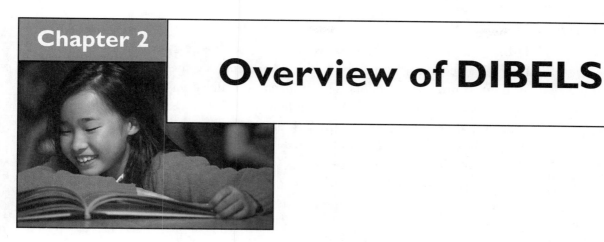

Chapter 2

Overview of DIBELS

Having used DIBELS, I know better how to give strategic support more effectively and efficiently. One of the most useful things I've learned is to identify at-risk students early in the year and to be consistent with intervention groups. DIBELS has helped me to teach more strategically to students at the lower end of the learning profile. The most dramatic impact on my teaching has been the realization of the importance of fluency—not just knowing letters and sounds, but knowing them rapidly and accurately. I don't feel that anyone is getting left behind.

Kindergarten teacher

Selecting an effective assessment instrument for routine screening of students in kindergarten through third grade is a critical step in implementing the Preventive Model for averting reading difficulties. The most effective screening instruments have four critical characteristics: (1) they have met minimum research criteria as valid and reliable in identifying at-risk students, (2) they are teacher-friendly, (3) they provide valuable information, and (4) they take the shortest time possible to administer. If the screening assessment isn't efficient as well as effective, then the entire Preventive Model may fail in the implementation stage.

Efficiency is critical because teachers do not want to spend any more time than necessary screening their students. Teachers today have many demands and are pressed for valuable instruction time. Most good screening assessments in kindergarten and first grade are administered one-on-one with students two or three times a year. Unfortunately many popular screening assessments take between 20 and 45 minutes per student to administer. Adopting an instrument that takes so long to administer and score can be a recipe for teacher reluctance and misuse of the screening process.

DIBELS is one of the best early literacy assessment instruments available today. It is efficient to deliver, taking approximately five to ten minutes per student. It provides teachers with information that is easy to understand because it assesses five essential components of effective reading instruction. In addition, alternate forms of DIBELS measures are available to reassess students periodically if they are below the "grade level" benchmark and their progress needs to be closely monitored. At this time, no other instrument provides alternate forms for progress monitoring. As one experienced first grade teacher who had used DIBELS for about a year said:

> *I'm pleased with the DIBELS program because it is the <u>most</u> reliable way of assessing first graders that I've used in 30 + years of teaching.*

DIBELS is a screening, outcome, and progress monitoring instrument and is not a formal diagnostic tool, although teachers feel that DIBELS scoring booklets contain the kind of information that helps them figure out where to start intervention with at-risk students. Many research reviews demonstrate that DIBELS is reliable in predicting whether a child is on track to becoming a reader by the end of third grade (Good, Gruba & Kaminski 2001). DIBELS does this by assessing whether students are achieving critical milestones along the way to proficient reading.

What Is DIBELS? (and Why Does It Have Such a Funny Name?)

DIBELS is an assessment instrument that measures how successfully a child is progressing in the critical skills that underlie success in early reading. This tool assesses several early reading skills and uses the child's status in these areas to predict how likely it is that he will read fluently. A student's score in each skill falls into one of three levels—benchmark, at risk of reading difficulty, or somewhere in between. These three levels indicate if the student's skill is developing on track at a given time, compared to the scores of a large pool of children in the same grade. Yet identifying whether a single student is at benchmark is not the only use for data from this assessment instrument.

DIBELS has three primary uses:

- It is a screening instrument that determines whether all the major skills are in place for a student to read on grade level by the end of third grade.

- It offers progress monitoring assessments that measure whether intervention instruction is effective.

- It is used as an outcome assessment that measures the effectiveness of a school's reading instructional program.

In practice, the data are used for many more purposes. For example, principals use DIBELS data to:

- Examine reading progress of their school over time

- Observe whether the lowest readers are improving at the same pace as the highest readers

- Follow progress of the school's intervention program in closing the gap for struggling readers

- Ask questions about the effectiveness of the core reading curriculum in helping all students achieve reading goals

District administrators use DIBELS data to evaluate district needs for professional development and district staffing needs for reading coaches and specialists. Having an assessment tool and this type of data help administrators drive reading reform at the building level and can be invaluable in establishing district and school goals for yearly progress in early reading outcomes for students. This data can become a centerpiece of district conversations with principals about their building goals, interim successes in implementing early intervention programs, and identifying additional needs to continue improvements. When administrators have data that indicates success in getting students off to a strong start in reading, they are better able to hold schools accountable for this all-important goal of the early elementary years.

While data from DIBELS is important for principals and administrators, this book focuses on how teachers can use the data to make informed decisions about students. Teachers are increasingly finding the information in the benchmark and progress monitoring scoring booklets useful for spotting students' error patterns and planning intervention instruction. Although using DIBELS data to more specifically group students and analyze error patterns to inform instruction has not been specifically researched, it is consistent with research that supports the use of data to inform small-group instruction as described at the end of Chapter 1.

Now, About That Name...

DIBELS is an acronym for **D**ynamic **I**ndicators of **B**asic **E**arly **L**iteracy **S**kills. Each word is significant.

- **D**ynamic—The instrument is dynamic because the measures change over time to match the evolving developmental progression in early reading. Different skills are assessed at each grade, based upon which skills are most highly predictive of reading success and failure at that particular grade level. There are seven indicators, some of which are administered only in kindergarten, others primarily in kindergarten/ first grade, and additional ones in grades one, two, and three.

- **I**ndicators—The subtests in DIBELS are referred to as "indicators" because they quickly and efficiently provide an indication of a child's performance and/or progress in acquiring a larger literacy skill. For example, the number of segments a student produces per minute on Phoneme Segmentation Fluency (PSF) is an indicator of a child's development of the larger construct of phonemic awareness.

- **B**asic—The skills that are assessed are basic in that they are early to develop and critical to accurate and fluent reading and to comprehension.

- **E**arly—DIBELS only assesses skills critical to early reading.

- **L**iteracy—DIBELS doesn't address skills in math or other academic domains.

- **S**kills—The indicators in this assessment are targeted at key underlying skills that are important in learning to read.

The DIBELS assessment is short and administered one-on-one, typically by a teacher or aide. Schools administer the DIBELS assessment three times a year—fall, winter, and spring—to all students. A student's scores are compared to empirically derived benchmarks based on a large national sample of students. Additionally, DIBELS provides 20 alternate forms of the critical indicators which can be used to frequently measure the progress of students who are receiving intervention instruction.

What Is the Purpose of DIBELS?

Understanding the purpose of an assessment instrument helps protect against confusion over what conclusions can be drawn from the data and how to use that information in decisions about the curriculum to teach students.

Assessment instruments meet one or more of four purposes (Reading First Academy Assessment Committee 2002[1]).

Outcome—Assessments that provide a bottom-line evaluation of the effectiveness of the reading program.

---

[1] Based on materials developed for the Secretary's Reading Leadership Academies, January and February 2002, U.S. Department of Education, slide 2 of Assessment Overview.

Screening—Assessments that identify which children are at risk for reading difficulty and need additional intervention.

Diagnosis—Assessments that help teachers plan instruction by providing in-depth information about students' skills and instructional needs. Some instruments may also help determine the presence of a developmental disorder that requires specialized treatments and interventions.

Progress Monitoring—Assessments that determine if students are making adequate progress or need more intervention to achieve grade level reading outcomes.

In 2002, eight researchers were appointed by the U.S. Department of Education to serve on the Reading First Assessment Committee. The task of this peer review committee was to evaluate early literacy assessment instruments for Reading First. For each instrument submitted for review, they determined whether there was an adequate body of research to meet minimum criteria for validity and reliability for use for one or more of the four purposes.

DIBELS was submitted for review and the committee found it to be valid and reliable as a screening, progress monitoring, and outcome measure, but not as a diagnostic measure.

To see a complete list of the assessment instruments that were validated by the Reading First Assessment Committee, visit Web site http://idea.uoregon.edu.

Instruments may not be on the list for reasons other than their failure to meet the criteria, one of the most common reasons being simply that they were not submitted for review. The committee's analysis and subsequent report provide excellent information for schools evaluating assessment tools, whether or not the school is eligible for Reading First funding. This list can help you select from among the best early literacy instruments available today.

DIBELS as a Screening Instrument

The assessments administered in the fall, winter, and spring are called "Benchmark Assessment Screenings." The Benchmark Screening is given to all students to determine whether they are on track or at risk for reading difficulty. Benchmark Screening assesses whether the students are achieving certain critical milestones that good readers achieve. Students who do not achieve these benchmark scores are placed in intervention groups after confirming the need for intervention through teacher observation and other data.

Many times teachers ask how to describe a screening instrument to parents. Here's an analogy that may be helpful. When someone goes to the emergency room of the hospital, what does the triage nurse do (after asking for a health insurance card)? The triage nurse takes the patient's temperature, listens to his heart, and takes his blood pressure. Why does the nurse do this? These vital signs are *indicators* of the patient's overall state of health. The triage nurse is responsible for determining who needs immediate service and who can wait a bit longer before seeing a doctor. Skyrocketing blood pressure or an accelerated heart rate may be an indication that the patient is experiencing a serious immediate health risk, such as a heart attack or internal bleeding. The nurse uses this data, along with information from the patient and her own observations of the patient's behavior and speech, to decide the severity of the patient's injuries.

The vital signs don't tell the doctors everything they need to know, but they help. Just as with vital signs, DIBELS doesn't tell you everything there is to know about the student's reading development and skills, but it does give you vital information about the overall progress the student is making toward becoming a proficient reader.

DIBELS as a Progress Monitoring Instrument

The progress monitoring capability of DIBELS is perhaps the most important characteristic of this assessment instrument. With DIBELS, educators can conduct frequent, repeated administrations of the same indicators by using one of twenty alternate forms. This is possible because DIBELS indicators are sensitive to change over a short period of time. Repeated administration helps monitoring the progress of students receiving intervention instruction.

DIBELS Progress Monitoring assessments are administered primarily to students whose benchmark screening indicated that they were at some level of risk, and therefore they are receiving intervention instruction. DIBELS can be repeated as often as weekly, although most teachers assess their intervention students every two to three weeks. Some teachers choose to strategically monitor any student for whom additional information is desirable, such as a student who was on track at the beginning of the year but has missed a lot of days of school.

It's very difficult to know exactly which instructional strategies will lead to success with each student. Matching the right materials with the right child at the right time for the appropriate duration of time is a complex task. If the research enabled teachers to prescribe exactly the right instruction for every individual child, then reading difficulties might not exist. Teachers need knowledge of the development of reading skills and effective research-based practices. They also need to match that knowledge with their insights about the needs of the particular student. One of the beauties of using DIBELS progress monitoring data is that teachers can know in a timely manner whether the instruction selected is effective for the student.

DIBELS Progress Monitoring data help teachers in making professional judgments about whether the intervention instruction should be continued or changed. Teachers feel relieved that they have a tool to help them determine, within weeks of beginning special instruction, whether the strategies and materials they selected are helping the student succeed. If intervention is not working, then the teacher can make adjustments right away, without waiting until the end of the school year to measure the level of success. Being able to adjust the intervention instruction is critical, because time counts: the clock is ticking for that student. There are a limited number of school days during the first several years of a child's life in which he needs to learn to read. By charting progress and comparing interim movements in a student's scores, it is possible to estimate whether the current rate of progress is likely to result in the student reaching benchmark by year-end.

When a student's scores on progress monitoring show that he is failing to make progress, or is making progress at a rate that is inadequate to close the gap, then the teacher can change the intervention instruction in a number of ways:

1. Increase the time allowed for intervention

2. Decrease the size of the group so that each child receives more feedback

3. Change the materials or strategies used

4. Move the student to a different group that more effectively targets the skills the student needs

Generally teachers see progress within about six to nine weeks of when a student starts in an intervention group of three or fewer students for 30 minutes daily. Sometimes lack of progress is most evident when two students in a group are making gains and the scores of the third student are level, even though he or she has been receiving exactly the same instruction. By examining intervention logs that contain records of what instructional practices were followed for this group, teachers and coaches can make decisions about what to change for the student who is not making adequate progress. This is where those record-keeping practices really pay off for children.

These intervention groups are flexible. They are not the reading groups of the past when a student stayed in the "blue birds" group for the entire year. Flexible means that students are regrouped (or considered for regrouping) at least every nine weeks, based on the data and teacher observation. If you use DIBELS progress monitoring every three weeks, then you will have three sets of data at the nine-week point. Progress monitoring data makes these regrouping decisions far easier. Two teachers reflect on their experiences in using DIBELS:

> *I have moved one student out of intervention because she has 'taken off' and no longer needs the extra help. The two students I continue working with are improving.*
>
> First grade teacher

> *DIBELS has been a valuable tool for me to find who needs immediate attention for intervention. The progress monitoring is equally valuable for me to see at a glance who has improved or reached benchmark, and who needs more intense instruction that hasn't progressed at a steady rate.*
>
> Kindergarten teacher

DIBELS as an Outcome Measure

DIBELS data can be consolidated for the school or district to be reviewed with several types of questions in mind. At the school level, the data helps inform administrators about the level of resources that need to be devoted to intervention instruction. It is possible to comment on how well the preschools and community are preparing students for kindergarten based on the fall kindergarten benchmark scores. For the students who enter kindergarten with benchmark level skills, are the core curriculum and instruction enabling them to continue at or above benchmark by the middle and end of the year? For the students who enter kindergarten at risk, how effective is the core and intervention instruction at catching them up to benchmark? It is also possible to compare one school's data with that of other schools in their own district as available, or with the other schools in the University of Oregon database (Good et al. 2003, 236).

One use of the data that is inappropriate is to decide to retain a student based on his DIBELS scores. Retention generally does not solve a reading problem. For too long there has been a misperception that retaining a struggling reader will give him the "gift of time." The better alternative is to use the data to intervene aggressively, and to keep changing the intensity of the instruction until it is right and the student is on track in reaching those critical reading milestones. For more information on retention, see the position statement published by the National Association of School Psychologists (www.nasp.org).

What Does DIBELS Measure?

DIBELS uses seven *indicators* to measure five early reading skills. The indicators are similar to *subtests* in other assessment instruments. The seven indicators measure the following skills:

- Initial Sound Fluency (ISF)—ability to recognize and produce initial sounds in words

- Letter Naming Fluency (LNF)—ability to recognize and name a random mixture of uppercase and lowercase letters on a page, including several fonts

- Phoneme Segmentation Fluency (PSF)—ability to segment a spoken word of two to five phonemes into the individual sounds

- Nonsense Word Fluency (NWF)—ability to read two-letter and three-letter nonsense words, primarily consonant-vowel-consonant patterns

- Oral Reading Fluency (ORF)—fluency and accuracy in reading grade-level passages aloud, as measured by words read correctly per minute

- Retell Fluency (RTF)—ability to retell information from a passage just read, as a measure of comprehension

- Word Use Fluency (WUF)—measures vocabulary by a tally of the number of words spoken in accurate utterances or definitions in response to target words

Although there are seven indicators, at any given time for any individual, only three to five are administered. Administering the maximum number of five indicators only occurs twice: in the winter and spring of first grade. At nine of the twelve administration times, only three indicators are given. Table 2.1 shows when each indicator is delivered.

Initially, DIBELS included more measures, but fortunately the research team was sensitive to feedback from teachers. The more skills assessed in an early literacy screening instrument, the longer it takes to administer with each student. Teachers said that the instrument had to be short to be practical to implement in schools. Over time and with much work, the researchers were able to tell which measures were important and which could be eliminated without jeopardizing the ability to predict accurately who was on track and who was at risk.

After the initial development period, DIBELS included five indicators for many years. With the National Reading Panel's articulation of the five essential components of reading instruction and the Reading First Program's focus

Table 2.1

Administration of Indicators by Grade Level and Time of Year

	Kindergarten			1st Grade			2nd Grade			3rd Grade		
	Beg	Mid	End	Beg	Mid	End	Beg	Mid	End	Beg	Mid	End
Letter Naming Fluency (LNF)	X	X	X	X								
Initial Sound Fluency (ISF)	X	X										
Phoneme Segmentation Fluency (PSF)		X	X	X	X	X						
Nonsense Word Fluency (NWF)			X	X	X	X	X					
Oral Reading Fluency (ORF)					X	X	X	X	X	X	X	X
Retell Fluency (RTF)					X	X	X	X	X	X	X	X
Word Use Fluency (WUF)	X	X	X	X	X	X	X	X	X	X	X	X

on assessment in all five of these areas, the research team from the University of Oregon designed a measure of comprehension and vocabulary to measure the final two components. These two new measures are called Retell Fluency (an indicator of comprehension.) and Word Use Fluency (an indicator of vocabulary). There is also a Spanish version of DIBELS, an extension for grades four through six, and a version for preschool students.

What DIBELS Doesn't Include

As mentioned above, DIBELS is not intended to be an exhaustive measure of all skills involved in acquiring early literacy abilities—just the ones that are the most highly predictive of later passage reading ability. If you examine different early literacy assessment instruments, you will notice that some instruments contain measures of skills not included in DIBELS. Examples include:

- Concept of word

- Print and book awareness

- Reading lists of real words, as opposed to nonsense words

- Assessing for letter sounds using lists of letters

- Spelling inventory

Why aren't these skills measured in DIBELS? The DIBELS research team determined that these other indicators were either unnecessary for the purpose of predicting which students will have difficulty or measured substantially the same skills as the existing measures. For example, concept of word and book and print awareness, while interesting and potentially necessary for reading, are not as powerful in their predictive ability as the skills measured by DIBELS.

Reading single words out of context accurately and rapidly is decidedly important in learning to read and is an excellent predictor after mid-first grade, but the problem with using real words in an assessment instrument is that it is impossible to know whether students can use the alphabetic principle to decode new words or whether they have simply memorized the words that appear on any given list.

DIBELS assesses the ability to read nonsense words in isolation and real words in passages. Those who are concerned that reading should be assessed only with "authentic" tasks sometime question the use of nonsense words to measure decoding skills. The purpose of assessing with nonsense words, however, is to see how well the student can apply sound-symbol correspondences when he comes upon a word he doesn't recognize by sight. Instead of including a subtest in which the assessor shows students letters and asks for the sounds, DIBELS assesses sound-symbol association within the nonsense word format, along with the student's ability to apply these letter-sound correspondences to blend words.

Spelling inventories provide rich information, yet they are time-consuming to score. They can still be administered to selected students as needed, rather than for all students in the initial benchmark screening.

The composition of a screening instrument, as well as the weighting of measured reading skills, determines how well the instrument predicts reading outcomes. For example, if concept of word, book and print awareness, or rhyming skill are heavily weighted in a student's total score and phoneme segmentation is barely weighted at all, the measure may not be as powerful in identifying at-risk students. Therefore, the selection of the assessment instrument your district or school uses is one of the most critical decisions affecting the ultimate success of your early identification and intervention initiative.

How Are the Seven DIBELS Indicators Linked to the Five Essential Components?

The seven DIBELS indicators are closely tied to the five essential components of reading articulated in the National Reading Panel Report (National Reading Panel 2000). Although there are two measures of phonemic awareness, and letter naming does not relate as clearly to the components, the relationship is quite straightforward for the others, as shown in Table 2.2.

Table 2.2

DIBELS Indicators Are Tied to the Five Essential Components

DIBELS Indicators	Five Essential Components
Initial Sound Fluency (ISF)	Phonemic Awareness
Phoneme Segmentation Fluency (PSF)	
Letter Naming Fluency (LNF)	(Tied to Alphabetic Principle)
Nonsense Word Fluency (NWF)	Phonics
Oral Reading Fluency (ORF)	Fluency in Passage Reading
Retell Fluency (RTF)	Comprehension
Word Use Fluency (WUF)	Vocabulary

Importance of Different Skills at Different Grade Levels

The ultimate goal of reading instruction is to teach students to comprehend what they read. Comprehension depends on accurate and fluent decoding, as well as understanding the words and concepts that are included in the reading passages. In fact, many studies have shown that oral reading fluency measures are valid at measuring not only fluency, but at predicting a student's overall reading comprehension as well. One study found that the reliability of an oral reading fluency measure in predicting comprehension was .91 (Davidson & Towner 2001). In this same study, only 2% of first grade students not identified as at risk with an oral reading fluency measure were later found to be poor readers on a grade two end-of-year general test.

Yet research has also shown that waiting until a student can read an oral reading fluency passage, generally during the second half of first grade, is not early enough to intervene. Throughout kindergarten and early first grade, we need to measure the precursor skills to successfully reading connected text. Although fluent reading of connected text is the best indicator of reading abilities, a kindergarten student would not be expected to read connected text fluently, if at all. However, a kindergarten student would be expected to identify letters by name, to identify sounds in words, and match some letters and sounds. Therefore, those are the skills that DIBELS assesses in kindergarten and at the beginning of first grade.

By the middle of the year, a first grader would be expected to read connected text, but not nearly as fluently or accurately as a second grader; even an excellent first grade reader is still mastering basic skills. For that reason, DIBELS measures not only connected text reading in first grade, but also phonemic awareness (PSF) and phonics (NWF). At the beginning of second grade, DIBELS measures phonics (NWF) in addition to connected text reading because some beginning second graders are still struggling with the concept of matching sounds and letters.

By focusing on the skills that we teach and expect students to master at various stages during kindergarten through third grade, DIBELS gives teachers the information they need to design intervention for the basic skills immediately when it is recognized that a student is missing those skills. As Dr. Roland Good says, "These are remarkably powerful one-minute measures."[2]

Are the Seven Indicators Linked to Each Other?

Five of the indicators link to skills that are typically acquired in a progression of reading development. In fact, the research team refers to these as "stepping stones" from one important early reading skill to the next, through the developmental progression. This "stepping stone" concept of reading development is helpful to teachers, as expressed by two teachers below:

> *The DIBELS assessment data really helps tell exactly what stage they have reached. I have students who have not been able to learn the letters and others who can read nonsense words.*
>
> **Kindergarten teacher**

> *When you know those steps, you're looking for them. It all clicked when I was testing, too. I would think: "OK, with this student, we need to go back to this skill." I could see it with each individual child as I was doing the testing.*
>
> **First grade teacher**

---

[2] Comment during the Implementation Team Training workshop sponsored by Sopris West in Boulder, Colorado, May 5–6, 2003.

Reading books fluently with comprehension is the ultimate goal, a feat that is not accomplished until second, third, or a later grade for some children. Yet if schools wait until third grade to see if the student reads well, critical time has been lost when early intervention may well have averted the reading difficulty. Because of the importance of intervening early, it is imperative to look for indications of risk long before the child is beginning to read text. Even waiting until the middle of first grade, when children are expected to begin reading simple text, to explore the possibility of difficulties and begin intervention is too late. The solution is to look in kindergarten and at the beginning of first grade for pre-reading skills that link to the ultimate skill of reading passages. DIBELS uses the early developing skills of letter naming, phoneme identification, and phoneme segmentation to predict how likely it is that the later skills that ultimately lead to proficient reading will also develop.

The University of Oregon researchers publish benchmark levels for all indicators in order to help educators determine which children are likely to be at risk for reading difficulty unless effective instruction is provided. (Good, Wallin, Simmons, Kame'enui, & Kaminski 2002). For example, the benchmark level for oral reading of a passage at the end of first grade is 40 words read correctly per minute. Below 20 is considered "at risk," and between 20 and 40 is labeled "some risk."

Table 2.3 lists the benchmark goals in DIBELS for fluently and accurately reading grade-level passages.

Table 2.3		
DIBELS Benchmark Goals for Oral Reading Fluency	**Grade Level**	**Words Read Correctly in Grade Level Passages**
	First	40 words correct per minute (1st grade passage)
	Second	90 words correct per minute (2nd grade passage)
	Third	110 words correct per minute (3rd grade passage)

A student who reads an absolute minimum of 40 words correct per minute (w.p.m.) at the end of first grade is more likely to read on grade level in second and third grade than a student who doesn't make this important goal. What earlier indications predict whether a student will read 40 w.p.m. at the end of first grade? The strongest predictor in DIBELS of whether a student will read 40 w.p.m. at the end of first grade is his adeptness at decoding nonsense words in the middle of first grade. If a student in the middle of the first grade reaches the established level of reading 50 letter graphemes correct per minute blended as words, where the vowels represent the short sound in nonsense words, the probability that he will read passages at benchmark level at the end of first grade is extremely high. Similarly, if a student reaches the benchmark goal of 35 on Phoneme Segmentation Fluency (PSF) by the winter of kindergarten, he has a high probability that he will also make the next benchmark, which is for Nonsense Word Fluency (NWF), by the winter of first grade. As you can see, reaching benchmark on any one step along the progression increases the chance that the student will stay on benchmark and continue along until he reads well at the end of third grade. Table 2.4 provides a chart summarizing the probabilities that once a student achieves intermediary goals at several different times, what the odds are that he will reach the ORF goal by the end of first grade.

Table 2.4

Reaching Intermediary Goals Improves Odds of Attaining ORF Goal at the End of First Grade

Indicator*	Intermediary Goal**	Percent of Children Who Reach This Goal Also Reach ORF Goal
ISF	25 i.s.p.m. by middle of K	87% of children reach ORF goal
PSF	35 p.s.p.m. by end of K	80% of children reach ORF goal
NWF	50 g.p.m. by middle of 1st	91% of children reach ORF goal

Source: Good, Kaminski, Smith, Simmons, Kame'enui, & Wallin, 2003.

* ISF—Initial Sound Fluency
  PSF—Phoneme Segmentation Fluency
  NWF—Nonsense Word Fluency

** i.s.p.m.—initial sounds per minute
   p.s.p.m.—phoneme segments per minute
   g.p.m.—graphemes per minute

The student must achieve all the goals, and achieve them on time, to be on track for successful reading. It is not sufficient to meet only one early literacy goal; a student must meet each of these goals to stay on track and be a successful reader. DIBELS not only provides information about the minimum benchmark a student must achieve, but also the range of scores that should be considered at-risk. Table 2.5 shows these levels, as well.

Table 2.5

Benchmark and At-Risk Scores for Each Indicator

Grade	Time of Year	Measure	Goal	At-Risk
K	Winter	ISF	25 i.s.p.m.	<10
K	Spring	PSF	35 p.p.m.	<10
1st	Winter	NWF	50 g.p.m.	<30
1st	Spring	ORF	40 w.p.m.	<20
2nd	Spring	ORF	90 w.p.m.	<50
2nd	Spring	ORF	110 w.p.m.	<70

How Was DIBELS Created?

DIBELS has been available for over 15 years, although it was used primarily in Oregon for much of this time. The research on DIBELS began around 1985. For many years its use was local and limited, as researchers gathered data and refined the instrument. Recently, however, the assessment requirements of Reading First have caused exponential growth in the use of the instrument. Some of the early interest in this assessment in Oregon may have been driven by the desire to help assure that more students would pass the reading section of the third grade high-stakes state test. The third grade Oral Reading Fluency (ORF) in DIBELS is highly correlated with the Oregon State Assessment Test in reading (.73) . Similar results have been found with other states, including Colorado and Illinois.

Dr. Roland Good and Dr. Ruth Kaminski led the design of DIBELS, with many other colleagues contributing. Sources of funding for the research and development of the instrument included the Early Childhood Research Institute on Measuring Growth and Development, the Institute for the Development of Educational Achievement, and the University of Oregon, College of Education.

Additional Information About DIBELS

The Importance of Fluency

For reading success it is important that a child can perform certain skills automatically and without conscious thought, so she can devote total attention to making meaning. Therefore we need to know not just whether a child knows letters, sounds, and letter-sound associations, but also whether she can process this information quickly and without a great deal of conscious analysis.

DIBELS relies upon the speed with which a student can perform a task accurately to predict whether the student is at risk for reading failure or on track for reading success.

All of the DIBELS measures are fluency measures, and the student's responses are timed to measure the student's ability to rapidly process information while performing a task. Although teachers are accustomed to thinking of fluency as a term associated with reading connected text, in DIBELS, the term fluency is used to indicate whether a student can perform a task associated with early reading quickly enough for it to be automatic and useful in skilled reading.

Predictive Test

DIBELS is different from standardized, norm-referenced tests such as the Woodcock-Johnson Tests that yield percentile ranks and standard scores. Although the designers of DIBELS have gathered a very large set of data from 10-40,000 children (depending upon grade level) (Good, Wallin, Simmons, Kame'enui, & Kaminski 2002), the purpose is to establish predictive benchmarks or indicators of later reading success. Benchmarks are scores typically achieved at critical milestones by children who are at grade level, and below-benchmark scores are those typically achieved by children reading below grade level. "Grade level" is estimated to be equivalent to about the fortieth percentile. Once the assessment is given to a child in your school, you will immediately know if your student is at risk by comparing his score to the published benchmark table. You will need to use other types of tests, however, to compare the child to a national normative sample.

Standardized Administration

There are many benefits of using DIBELS, including the immediate feedback of comparing a student's scores to the published benchmarks. On the other hand, the assessment requires standardized administration in order to yield reliable and valid results: it must be given the same way every time in order for the results to be valid. It is an administrative challenge to ensure that all teachers and aides who will be administering DIBELS have been properly trained and are consistently and accurately using the standardized directions and scoring procedures. In order to assure that DIBELS is administered and scored correctly, someone in your school should be an expert in scoring and administration, and this "DIBELS expert" should oversee the fidelity of the assessment process. Some teachers are not accustomed to administering this type of test one-on-one and find it very difficult not to give students a little extra coaching or time. Deviation from the directions, scoring, or timing prescribed may risk the validity of the data as an accurate predictor of which children are at risk.

Administration Is Timed and Must Be "Cold"

All of the measures are one-minute measures that are intended to be administered "cold." This means that the child is not to practice reading the passage or answering the task using the DIBELS pictures, words, or passages before the screening takes place. The reason practice is not permitted is that the assessment is intended to see if children have the skills to perform the tasks without having seen the materials before. All students have the same disadvantage, and the benchmarks have been created using data from children who are seeing the materials for the first time.

Children are timed, directions and practice items are given in a standardized way, and corrective feedback is given in a prescribed manner. The purpose of the corrective feedback is to teach the procedure, not to teach the skill. If the child doesn't seem to understand the directions, you can teach the child at a later time how to do the task, using materials other than DIBELS, and then reassess.

For all measures but Initial Sound Fluency (ISF), the stopwatch is turned on and used to observe when the minute has passed and the child can stop. For ISF, the child is shown pictures and asked questions about the beginning sounds in words. The stopwatch is used to accumulate the student's response time for the 16 questions, and this time is used to calculate the number correct per minute.

DIBELS Can Inform Instruction but Is Not Diagnostic

DIBELS was not designed to be a diagnostic assessment instrument, nor does the Reading First Assessment Committee validate it as a diagnostic instrument. The score on a DIBELS indicator, when compared to grade-level benchmark scores, simply tells if the child is on track or requires intervention. The score alone will not make the reason for the deficit clear, but many teachers feel that DIBELS student scoring booklets provide additional information about where to begin intervention. Teachers are finding that by carefully analyzing the errors in a student's scoring booklet, they can find patterns in the errors, which give them specific information they can use to begin intervention instruction immediately.

For example, a kindergarten child who is above benchmark in letter naming probably does not need any additional help in that area. If he is behind in knowing the initial sounds in words, his score will indicate lack of a critical early emerging skill in phonemic awareness. The teacher looks at the ISF page of the scoring booklet and may discover the source of the problem. For example, the teacher can identify whether the student is having more difficulty expressing sounds or identifying sounds, or whether the difficulty is a combination of both. Because DIBELS is also a fluency measure, it may be that the kindergarten student knows the sounds but is slow at identifying and producing them.

The teacher can use the information she gleans from the student's ISF booklet to begin the intervention instruction. For example, if the student has a score of 16 out of a possible 16 but was very slow, the teacher knows to begin intervention by working on fluency, and no time is wasted on teaching the student to recognize or produce sounds—something the student already knows.

There is a great deal of confusion about whether analyzing the scoring booklet for error patterns is using it diagnostically. It is not. Teachers analyze student writing samples and make decisions about what students may not know based on listening to them read aloud. Every day we use student work to make decisions about what a child seems to understand and where he might need clarification or additional instruction. Analyzing a DIBELS scoring booklet is no different.

Informal vs. Formal Diagnostic Data

The type of information derived from analyzing a DIBELS student booklet is informal and not equivalent to the thorough exploration of a student's background, history, knowledge, and abilities that is included in a formal diagnostic evaluation. The purposes are completely different.

The purpose of a formal diagnostic evaluation is to determine the underlying processing issues that cause a student to struggle in learning. The types of instruments used to make these determinations are extensive and require a highly trained and skilled evaluator, usually someone with training in psychological testing, to administer an extensive battery of tests and to observe with a careful and experienced eye how a child performs on each test.

The DIBELS assessment is far too brief to be able to tell why a child is struggling with learning. Its purpose is to see if the child can perform a quick task and then to compare his scores to those of other children who were studied to see their ultimate success at reading. The approach to analyzing the student error patterns recommended in this book would not be appropriate for diagnosing whether a child has dyslexia or a related learning disability. Yet once a child is identified for intervention instruction, teachers need to make judgments about where to begin intervention and which students to place together in a group. Based on a careful analysis of the student's error patterns, teachers can make some observations about:

- Which letters the child recognizes and names easily (LNF)

- Whether he is stable on beginning, ending and medial sounds (PSF)

- How well he is able to attack words using sound-symbol correspondences with an unknown word (NWF)

- How fluently he is pulling all the skills together in reading a passage (ORF)

The data also tell you which skills are established, which helps you group students with similar deficits and identify what type of intervention instruction to try initially with each group. Any decisions made based on analyzing the student booklets must be confirmed once the interventionist begins to work with the students. An effective intervention instructor can tell quite quickly if a student has mastered a skill or needs instruction at a more basic level. Since the intervention groups are typically between three and five students, the small size of the group enables the instructor to observe which students are responding to questions with correct or incorrect answers.

In addition to the intervention instructor's observations, frequent progress monitoring serves as a feedback loop about whether students are grouped appropriately and if the instruction is helping the student make progress. If the progress monitoring assessments show that the student is not responding to intervention, first the teacher may try changing the intervention by increasing time, moving the child to a different group, lowering the group size, or changing the type of instruction given. If that still doesn't work, the teacher can decide whether to continue intervention or recommend the child for more extensive testing to diagnose the problem, including exploring the possibility of a learning disability. For a list of diagnostic instruments, see the Reading First Assessment Committee's list, which appears on the Web site of the University of Oregon (http://idea.uoregon.edu/assessment/index.html).

What Research Has Validated the Effectiveness of DIBELS?

There is an expansive body of research that has informed the design, development, and revisions of DIBELS over more than 15 years. The best way to learn about this research base is to go to the DIBELS Web site (http://dibels.uoregon.edu) and from the main menu go to the section called "technical reports." There are many articles that provide research on topics about DIBELS. Some of the information in the technical reports has been summarized in the Appendix of this book.

Benefits of Using DIBELS

DIBELS is most effective when there is a sense of urgency about improving reading in a school, and screening is embedded in a setting where early identification leads to intervention instruction to prevent reading problems. One of the most important benefits of adopting DIBELS in a school is that it focuses teachers on very important practices in early reading. Some additional benefits include focusing teachers' and administrators' attention on:

- The importance of early identification and intervention

- The benefits of using data to inform instruction

- The importance of implementing small group instruction to meet the needs of struggling readers

- The necessity for the teaching team to monitor the effectiveness of the core reading program in instructing all students

- The vital nature of the five essential components of reading instruction

- The key stages of skills development in early reading development, from phonemic awareness, the alphabetic principle, phonics, vocabulary and oral language, the fluent and accurate reading of connected text, and comprehension

- The philosophy of establishing goals for all students reaching grade level, and then being held accountable for constant improvement toward this goal

One kindergarten teacher wrote about accountability in her journal.

I look at student booklets at least monthly, trying to analyze who to work with on an intervention basis. I've also tried to put class scores on spreadsheets to see scores, as I feel very accountable now that I have these valuable DIBELS resources and information to implement.

Kindergarten teacher

Sometimes there are questions about whether using the DIBELS encourages teachers to teach only what is assessed by DIBELS. Clearly, teachers do need to teach a broader range of skills than just the skills measured by DIBELS. For example, students who show deficiency in Letter Naming Fluency should work not only on letter matching, formation, and naming, but on alphabetizing skills if those are also lacking. If students show a deficit in Phoneme Segmentation Fluency, teachers must ensure that students can both blend and segment phonemes in words, even though DIBELS measures only segmenting. If students show a deficit in Nonsense Word Fluency, teachers need to ensure that students can read both real and nonsense words and they must include instruction for accurate and fluent reading of both real and nonsense words in their intervention groups. They also need to teach many phonic patterns beyond the ones that are assessed in NWF. Some reading of connected text should also be included, and in some cases students will need help with spelling, a skill not measured by DIBELS.

It must also be kept in mind that small group intervention instruction is always in addition to the core, comprehensive reading program instruction. Instruction during intervention time does focus only on one or two skills at a time. Because of this, it is essential that students are still present for the instruction in the remaining five essential components of reading instruction during the core reading program time. For example, while a kindergarten student is receiving extra help in phonemic awareness in the intervention group, it is critical that he also participate in instruction on reading comprehension during a read-aloud story. Although DIBELS does not measure some skills that are essential to fluent reading, it does measure the most important early reading skills that have been shown to be necessary for students to read at grade level by the end of third grade. The reading skills that are not measured, such as verbal reasoning, prediction, inference, etc., tend to be higher level skills that are covered in the core reading curriculum. Spelling and writing skills are important adjuncts to reading comprehension but are not assessed in screening.

DIBELS' intent is to sample only the critical early reading skills that predict successful reading, including comprehension, by the end of third grade. DIBELS does not attempt to access all the skills that constitute a complete reading program. That is why a core, comprehensive reading program is an essential tool for the regular classroom, and why teachers need a strong professional development experience to keep the "big picture" in mind.

Chapter 3

Process for Grouping Students

> *DIBELS is making a huge impact. Our intervention groups are working, especially with our lowest students. In Title I for kindergarten, we choose which students get help from the DIBELS screening. By using DIBELS, we know who the at-risk students are and in what area they are at risk. We know how to group kids who have similar deficits, how to intervene, and how to improve the deficiencies. Small group work is essential.*
>
> Title I director

Overview

One of the benefits of using the DIBELS measures is that the data informs decisions about which students can logically be placed in an instructional group together. While grouping decisions should be based on a portfolio of information, DIBELS results can be one of these pieces of information because they provide data that help pinpoint specific skill deficits.

The intent of small group intervention instruction for students below benchmark is to focus on one or two key skill areas for students whose instructional needs are similar. DIBELS data are helpful for placing students in intervention groups because many of the indicators assess the student's abilities in precursor or underlying skills in reading, including phonemic awareness and the alphabetic principle. Once it is clear what skills the student lacks, the teacher can provide the student with focused instruction delivered in a small group.

Small groups of three to five students are more effective than whole class instruction for these students because the instructor can provide each student with immediate corrective feedback on any error, along with follow-up explanations and guided practice, until the student learns the skill. This type of instruction is simply not possible when working with an entire class of 20 to 30 children. It is impossible to overstate the importance of fully utilizing all instructional time to improve skills of students at risk, especially those valuable minutes when the student is receiving instruction in a small group. This is one of the reasons that groups need to be formed in an analytical rather than incidental manner, resulting in tight, cohesive groups.

Educators today are hearing a great deal about "data-driven instruction." My preferred term is to view the DIBELS data as **informing** instruction rather than driving instruction; the teacher is driving the instruction based on careful observations and analysis of data about the student's response to instruction. The data can help teachers decide which skills are lacking, where to begin instruction, and whether the student's skills are improving with instruction. The goal of carefully grouping students based on similar deficits is motivated by the desire to have a tight link between the student's deficient skills and the instruction given to the group.

This chapter describes different approaches for using the DIBELS data to help inform decisions about which students to group together. Keep in mind that the DIBELS data is only one piece of data used in making these grouping decisions. Other sources of data are the teacher's observations of the student's errors, additional informal assessments, student writing samples, and student text reading levels. No matter which approach a school uses for grouping, the goal is for each student in an intervention group to receive the maximum benefit from this critical instruction.

Factors to Consider When Forming Groups

Homogenous Groups Are a Necessity

Some teachers prefer to plan groups that are heterogeneous and may be uncomfortable with homogeneous grouping. This is understandable since in the past homogeneous grouping has been denigrated, especially if it led to "tracking." In spite of concerns about tracking, it is imperative that students are homogeneously grouped by their skill deficits for intervention instruction. Remember that intervention time is generally half an hour and rarely longer than one hour. Hopefully, all educators can agree that it is not appropriate to group students homogeneously for the entire day, or even the entire language arts block. However, during this short portion of the school day, the teacher must explicitly teach specific missing skills and not rely on students to learn from other students who cannot be expected to fully understand the instructional needs of at-risk students. Many students who are at risk failed to learn skills necessary for reading during the whole classroom instruction already provided or by observing their peers who answered ahead of them.

At-risk students need a smaller group where their attention can be focused and they can receive extra wait time before answering, if needed. Receiving immediate and appropriate feedback on errors is another important characteristic of intervention group instruction. Additionally, students will be provided as many repetitions of a strategy, or variations in explanations, as needed until they master the skill being taught. Only by placing students together who need the same type of instruction can teachers maximize instructional time for everyone in this group.

During intervention time it is critical that the teacher carefully selects approaches that teach students while providing numerous opportunities for repeated practice, feedback, and help with errors. When all students in a group have the same skill deficit, the teacher can select instructional strategies that are targeted on one or two key skills. The more alike the students in the group are in terms of skills they lack, the more likely that each student in the group is benefiting from the activities and strategies introduced and practiced during group time. A student who is proficient in a skill should not be in a group that is practicing that skill. Probably the best testimonial for homogeneous intervention groups is from this teacher who, through her participation in the Early Intervention Project (EIP) during the 2002-03 year, changed her views on grouping.

The idea of ability grouping used to have a negative connotation. The lower achievers had to be with higher achievers to have the modeling. For the intervention groups, I'm ability-grouping rather than keeping some "lows" and some "highs" together. I still intermix students with differing abilities for other subject areas, but during our DIBELS center time, the kids are grouped according to ability and it's been fantastic. My benchmark group is doing so much more than I would have been able to do with them, had they been put in with others at a lower reading level. They're reading books and writing sentences. I'm excited. They're excited and are not held back by instruction below their level. My little low group of three is a challenge. It is difficult to keep them all on task and focused; however, they would be drowning and getting even less if grouped in a larger group with students that were at a higher level. Because of DIBELS, I'm able to group my students appropriately so all can reach their potential. It really is great to individualize this way.

Kindergarten teacher

The kindergarten teacher in the quote above teaches at the school that is described in Chapter 1 and is called Lilly School in this book. Although she uses the term "ability grouping" in her quote, the groups recommended in this book are homogeneous skill groups that are flexible because students are moved out of a group once they have mastered a skill. Two first grade teachers from different schools in the Early Intervention Program described in Chapter 1 wrote the following comments in their journals:

> *They work harder (with fewer distractions) in the intervention groups. Some of these children have difficulty attending in the large group.*
>
> First grade teacher

> *While being grouped with students who have similar needs, students experience more success and attack words more confidently.*
>
> First grade teacher

Grouping Students Is Not Always Straightforward

> *I am learning to be more careful. I tend to go with a 'gut' reaction based on my observation and assessment of the student in a classroom setting. Now I'm learning to look for error patterns and group similar students for intervention.*
>
> First grade teacher

Teachers often find that the task of grouping students into small groups for intervention instruction is challenging and somewhat less straightforward than they expect. This is because forming groups requires balancing data from several DIBELS indicators at the same time, as well as using other information the teacher knows about the student. Let's focus first on how to use the DIBELS data for grouping decisions. We will discuss how to use other sources of information at the end of this chapter.

If grouping decisions were simple, groups could be formed using scores on only one DIBELS measure. This process would be simple because teachers could construct a list of all the students who are below benchmark on a single indicator, decide how many groups to form, and then divide the students up.

For example, if six students in a class were below benchmark in Phoneme Segmentation Fluency (PSF) and the teacher decided to have two groups of three students, then the students with the lowest PSF scores might be grouped together and the ones closer to benchmark might be placed in the second group.

There are two problems with this simple approach to grouping. First, sometimes a student's scores on another indicator influences your view about the student's overall needs. Grouping on the basis of a single indicator fails to acknowledge the link between many early literacy skills. For example, grouping students only on their Nonsense Word Fluency (NWF) scores is not as informative as also considering their scores on the other indicators, including PSF. Students who are at or above benchmark in phoneme segmentation skills may make quicker progress from instruction in letter-sound correspondences than students whose PSF scores are below benchmark, an indicator that they may not be able to manipulate phonemes in words heard orally.

The second problem with the simple view of grouping based on a single indicator is the assumption about how instruction will be delivered. If students are grouped based on only one indicator, what happens if a student is showing deficiencies in several areas? Would the student with deficits in multiple skill areas work in several groups to meet all his instructional needs? The difficulty in scheduling and the loss of time in transition between groups makes this approach problematic. Additionally, this approach may not recognize that instruction in these skills is often blended. For example, take the case of a student who is just below benchmark in PSF and quite a bit below in NWF. The teacher may start by using manipulative objects to represent sounds and teach the student how to segment all the sounds in the words. If the student demonstrates a sense of sounds in words, the instructor can then add letters so that the emphasis changes to working on the alphabetic principle. Research shows that adding letters once the student has an adequate level of phonemic awareness can actually aid in developing phonemic awareness. For these reasons, it is worth the extra time and effort to assign groups based on the whole picture of the student's needs rather than having students rotate to multiple groups.

What makes the decision for grouping students challenging is that often there is interplay between indicators, and several indicators must be studied at the same time before a group can be formed. When students' scores are similar for one indicator but different for another, deciding how to place them is not obvious. When this is the case, it helps to remember that students most often need to be grouped according to the score that is lowest on the continuum of reading skills (see Table 3.1).

Table 3.1

"Stepping Stones" in DIBELS

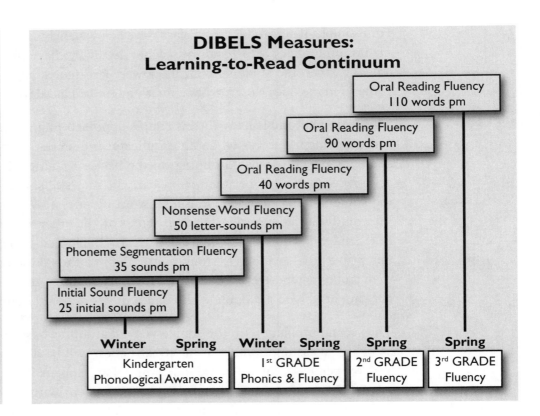

DIBELS Measures: Learning-to-Read Continuum

Oral Reading Fluency
110 words pm

Oral Reading Fluency
90 words pm

Oral Reading Fluency
40 words pm

Nonsense Word Fluency
50 letter-sounds pm

Phoneme Segmentation Fluency
35 sounds pm

Initial Sound Fluency
25 initial sounds pm

Winter	Spring	Winter	Spring	Spring	Spring
Kindergarten Phonological Awareness		1st GRADE Phonics & Fluency		2nd GRADE Fluency	3rd GRADE Fluency

Let's look at an example of the interplay between indicators using scores for just three students in the middle of first grade.

Table 3.2

DIBELS Scores at Middle of First Grade

	PSF	NWF	ORF	Status
Benchmark	35	50	20	
Student				
Juan	20	12	10	Intensive Support
Kelly	34	10	12	Intensive Support
Roberto	8	10	8	Intensive Support

Table 3.2 shows that Juan, Kelly, and Roberto all are below benchmark in Phoneme Segmentation Fluency, Nonsense Word Fluency, and Oral Reading Fluency and that their NWF fluency scores are similar. Their ORF scores are low, however the focus of instruction must be on both phoneme segmentation and the alphabetic principle to improve their ability to accurately and rapidly read words before focusing on building fluency in reading passages.

Even though Kelly and Roberto both have the same NWF scores, Kelly's PSF score indicates that she may have a higher level of phonemic awareness than Roberto. In fact, Kelly is just barely below benchmark in PSF, with a score of 34 versus benchmark of 35. After the teacher confirms that Kelly's score is valid through another assessment or observation of her ability to push counters for sounds in words (for example, Move-It and Say-It, Chapter 9), her intervention instruction is best started at the phonics level, learning to match letters and sounds in words. In spite of the fact that Kelly has reached benchmark in PSF by the middle of first grade, there is a sense of urgency because she didn't reach the benchmark of 35 at the end of kindergarten. Look back to her beginning-of-the-year first grade PSF score to discover if she was close to 35 at that time. A delay in reaching the established level of a DIBELS indicator is a red flag that the student is at risk. It is easy to be lulled into celebration that the student finally reached the benchmark goal, when actually by reaching the goal several months later than the recommended time, the student may not be making adequate progress in the next skill. In this example Kelly should have been focusing on connecting sounds and letters with print during the first half of first grade, and her low NWF score (10 vs. 50) signals a lack of progress in that area.

If Roberto's PSF score is an accurate indication of his low level of phonemic awareness, then he may benefit from more instruction in how to manipulate all the sounds in words. The teacher can validate that Roberto's low PSF score is an accurate representation of his low skill in this area by using other informal measures of this skill. One informal way to assess a student's PSF skill is to ask him to demonstrate his awareness of sounds in words by moving counters such as the Move-it-and-Say-It (see activity in Chapter 9). If he struggles in moving counters for simple three-sound words, then Roberto would need some further instruction in phoneme segmentation, whereas Kelly does not appear to need this and is ready to move on to applying sounds and letters in words.

Juan's PSF score (20) is in the middle between Roberto (8) and Kelly (34). He is not as low as Roberto, but is still well below benchmark. Ideally the teacher will be able to group him with other students whose deficits are similar. If not, one approach would be to start his instruction with Roberto and then move him to a group working on phonics as soon as his progress monitoring scores show that he has mastered phoneme segmentation. Sometimes it is beneficial to increase the pool of students so the students can be more tightly grouped. Some schools form groups across two classrooms, or even the entire grade, when the teachers can arrange for students from different classrooms to receive intervention at the same time.

There is one last comment that is important concerning instructional focus. With first-grade students who are well below benchmark in both PSF and NWF at mid-year, there is no time to waste. The focus must be on teaching the alphabetic principle. Although most students whose phoneme segmentation scores are below benchmark benefit from additional instruction in this area, they also need to be making progress in letter-sound connections. Instruction on phonemic awareness must be accelerated and rapidly build to letter sounds because these mid-first grade students have two goals to accomplish if they are going to get back on track. Some teachers prefer to focus on phonemic awareness until it reaches benchmark. Yet a case can be made that when a student is this far behind, it may be necessary to forego trying to master one skill before beginning instruction on the next one, especially since instruction in the alphabetic principle may actually reinforce further development of phonemic awareness. Some schools place the lowest performing students—those who are substantially behind in multiple skill areas—in a group with an experienced teacher using a published program. An important characteristic of an appropriate program for these lowest performing students is that the teacher uses a set of lesson plans that include instructions on how to teach phonemic awareness, phonics, and letter knowledge in an explicit and sequential manner.

Group Sizes

One of the factors that contributes to accelerating progress for below-benchmark students is determining an appropriate group size for instruction. The lowest performing students need to be in the smallest groups so they get the most corrective feedback and maximum time to practice the skill. Try groups of three for the lowest students, and change to two if needed for the students who aren't making enough progress. Groups of five may be effective for the highest of the intervention students. Groups with more than five students tend to be less effective because the instructor cannot see and respond to each error. These suggested group sizes are ideal; in some schools there are so many students needing intervention instruction that resource limitations lead to larger group sizes. Additionally, if 80% of the students in a class have scores in the intensive range, the type of instruction provided to the whole class will mirror some of the explicit and systematic characteristics of intervention instruction.

Approaches for Grouping Students

Grouping Process Using the DIBELS System Instructional Recommendations

For schools using either the University of Oregon's DIBELS Data Management System or the Wireless m:class reports, some information is provided that can be used in forming intervention groups. In the University of Oregon's Class Report, the far right column provides an "Instructional Recommendation." There are three levels: benchmark, strategic, and intensive. Benchmark is the label used for students that are making adequate progress on the indicators and have the characteristics of the children in the research pool who continued to develop skills and read well later. The DIBELS system recommends that the other two levels, strategic and intensive, receive additional instruction because their current indicators are enough below the benchmark level that there is a higher probability that they will not reach the next critical literacy milestone.

In the reports provided by Wireless Generation as of the date of publication of this book, the Class Summary report is structured a little differently than the University of Oregon's report. Instead of listing all the students in descending order by one indicator, the report divides students into three sections by the level of instructional recommendation. The first section of the report lists all the students who are recommended for intensive instruction, with the strategic and benchmark sections following. Wireless Generation's m:class reports use the same formulas to evaluate the student's scores and determine an instructional recommendation as the University of Oregon's DIBELS data management system. These recommended instructional levels are actually a weighted average of the student's performance on most of the indicators measured for that time period. Although more than one indicator may be included, they are not weighted equally; some are viewed as more important than others (see the *DIBELS Administration and Scoring Guide* for an explanation of the rules for the instructional recommendations). Please note that as of the publication date of this book, the student's score on the Word Use Fluency (WUF) or Retell Fluency (RTF) was not included in the calculation of the instructional recommendation.

For teachers whose schools or districts use either the University of Oregon's or the Wireless Generation's data management system, students in the same category of instructional recommendation can be grouped together. If there are more than three or four students at each level, then the teacher has to decide how many groups to form and which students should be placed together. The teacher will then have to determine what basis to use in deciding who should be grouped with whom. Should a single indicator be used for grouping students together, or should there be some consideration of the student's scores on several indicators? The discussion below may help in thinking through these questions.

When a school or district doesn't use either the University of Oregon or the Wireless Generation data management systems, then teachers need to determine which students need intervention and which should be considered at benchmark. Students above benchmark on all indicators measured at that assessment period can be considered at benchmark and not needing any small-group intervention instruction at this time. Similarly, students scoring below benchmark in all areas would be highlighted for consideration for extra help. The issue is when a student is above benchmark in some indicators and below in others. Some schools may advocate that any student below in any one indicator be considered for inclusion in a small group. Even with these broad guidelines, teachers still face decisions about how to balance the data from various DIBELS indicators. When the child's scores are mixed and resources are limited, it can be difficult to figure out which students need help the most.

Nine-Step Process for Grouping Students

For teachers who do not have access to either the University of Oregon or Wireless Generation's data management system and therefore don't have instructional recommendations for their students, there is a need for another approach. The approach that is outlined below is an iterative process in which groups are formed, checked to find if the best fit has been made, adjusted, and checked again. At first the benchmark students are set aside, but at the end they are evaluated for possible inclusion in an intervention group. Data on benchmark students are also examined to discover if any students with high scores need to be provided with enrichment because their scores indicate they are ready for higher level work. After setting aside the benchmark students, all intervention students are listed in rank order by one of the DIBELS indicators. First a group is formed among the lowest students, then a group among the highest intervention students, and finally the ones in the middle are added to the two groups or additional groups are formed. For a graphic overview of the process, see Table 3.3.

Table 3.3

Overview of Nine-Step Process for Grouping Students

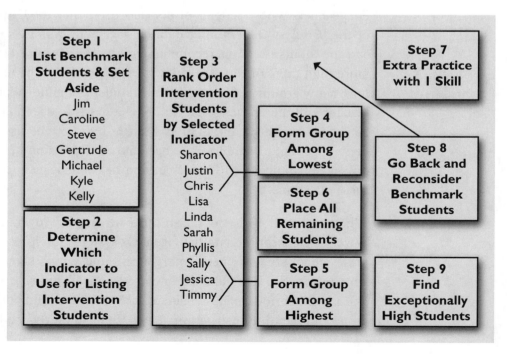

The nine-step process outlined in this book is only one way to group students. It is designed to help teachers who are beginning to use DIBELS data have an efficient way to form groups for targeted instruction. If you have been working with DIBELS data and use an approach that differs from the nine-step process, continue using your approach if it has been successful. An approach is successful when the students in groups are making improvements and closing the gap, as measured by using the DIBELS progress monitoring.

Grouping an Artificially Created Class—Miss Hanson's Class

Preparing to Group Students

Step 1: Identify the Benchmark Students and Set Them Aside

Step 2: Determine Which Indicator to Use for Sorting Intervention Students

Step 3: Rank Order Intervention Students by Selected Indicator

Grouping Students

Step 4: Form a Group Among the Lowest Students

Step 5: Form a Group Among the Highest Students

Step 6: Place Remaining Intervention Students in a Group

Refining Groups

Step 7: Look for Students Who Need Practice With an Excluded Skill

Step 8: Look for any Benchmark Students Who May Have Been Missed

Step 9: Find any Exceptionally High Students

Each step of the process is explained in more detail below, and the steps are illustrated with students from Miss Hanson's class sample shown in Table 3.4. The names are in alphabetical order so that it is easier to find students on the report.

Step 1: Identify the benchmark students and set them aside. First, establish which students are at benchmark, list them and their scores, and set them aside for now (we will revisit them later). This way we have fewer students to study at the same time and our focus is initially directed to the students requiring intervention instruction. If using the DIBELS data management system, look at the far right column of the classroom report to select the students listed as "benchmark" under the column titled "Instructional Recommendations." If your school does not use the DIBELS data management

Table 3.4

Miss Hanson's Class at the Beginning of First Grade

Student	Letter Naming Fluency		Phoneme Segmentation Fluency		Nonsense Word Fluency		Instructional Recommendation
	Score	Status	Score	Status	Score	Status	
Alli	21	At risk	2	Deficit	0	At risk	Intensive support
Brittney	9	At risk	3	Deficit	2	At risk	Intensive support
Courtney	16	At risk	2	Deficit	3	At risk	Intensive support
Devon	27	At risk	8	Deficit	5	At risk	Intensive support
Evelyn	27	At risk	9	Deficit	7	At risk	Intensive support
Fred	28	At risk	8	Deficit	9	At risk	Intensive support
Greg	29	Some risk	27	Emerging	18	Some risk	Strategic support
Harry	32	Some risk	32	Emerging	19	Some risk	Strategic support
Ingrid	33	Some risk	28	Emerging	21	Some risk	Strategic support
Joe	35	Some risk	34	Emerging	21	Some risk	Strategic support
Kelsey	34	Some risk	33	Emerging	22	Some risk	Strategic support
Lizzie	47	Low risk	36	Established	25	Low risk	Benchmark
Mary	45	Low risk	44	Established	27	Low risk	Benchmark
Natalie	58	Low risk	33	Established	28	Low risk	Benchmark
Oscar	42	Low risk	36	Established	31	Low risk	Benchmark
Penny	55	Low risk	69	Established	38	Low risk	Benchmark
Quinn	57	Low risk	53	Established	40	Low risk	Benchmark
Ralph	61	Low risk	46	Established	55	Low risk	Benchmark

system, consider a student as benchmark if she is at or above benchmark for each of the skills measured.

The students listed as benchmark in Miss Hanson's class are:

Table 3.5

Miss Hanson's Class—List of Benchmark Students

Student	LNF Score	PSF Score	NWF Score	Instructional Recommendation
Lizzie	47	36	25	Benchmark
Mary	45	44	27	Benchmark
Natalie	58	33	28	Benchmark
Oscar	42	36	31	Benchmark
Penny	55	69	38	Benchmark
Quinn	57	53	40	Benchmark
Ralph	61	46	55	Benchmark

Step 2: Determine which indicator to use for sorting intervention students. After setting aside the benchmark students, you are ready to consider all the students identified as needing intervention. To begin to look for three to five students whose needs are similar, it is helpful to list the intervention students in rank order from most to least in need of help. Even though students are going to be grouped by considering several indicators at the same time, the rank ordering by one indicator is an efficient mechanism to identify a few students who have some similar needs and may be a potential group.

It is necessary to select one of the indicators to use for the rank ordering.

In this book, intervention groups are formed primarily to improve accuracy and fluency in reading words because this is where the majority of early reading difficulties in kindergarten through third grade reside. (If problems in comprehension persist after accuracy and fluency are obtained, different intervention strategies will be employed.) In general, ISF, PSF, NWF, and ORF relate most directly to accurate and fluent word reading. Although letter naming (LNF) is a highly predictive indicator in determining which students are at risk, most researchers agree that teaching sounds is more important than teaching letters; therefore, letter naming is not included as an indicator for rank ordering students for grouping. WUF indicates the student's facility with vocabulary, and RTF indicates the student's ability to comprehend. Therefore, ISF, PSF, NWF or ORF are the recommended indicators selected to use for the first ranking of students, although which one is preferred changes across time.

Letter naming is an intriguing skill, and one that merits further discussion. In spite of the fact that this skill is a powerful predictor of which students will struggle in learning to read, the relationship of letter naming to reading is less clear. The research is not certain about whether difficulty in letter naming causes difficulty in reading, or is related to other things that cause difficulty. Some researchers have hypothesized that a low letter naming score could actually measure low speed in cognitive processing or deficiencies in rapid automatic naming. Another possibility that has been suggested is that fluency with letter names may actually be an indirect measure of parental involvement (Good, Kaminski, Smith, Simmons, Kame'enui, & Wallin 2003).

Tables 3.6 and 3.7 provide recommendations for the specific indicator to use for ranking students initially.

In general, use the measures of phonemic awareness in kindergarten (ISF & PSF), the measure of alphabetic principle in early and mid-first grade (NWF),

Table 3.6

Suggested DIBELS Indicator for Listing Intervention Students

Grade	Time of Year	Indicator to Use for Ranking	Comment
K	Beginning	ISF	
K	Middle	ISF	ISF is to reach established level of 25 by this time.
K	End	PSF	PSF is to reach established level of 35. ISF is no longer assessed.
1	Beginning	PSF / NWF	NWF is preferred, yet examine PSF closely as well.
1	Middle	NWF	NWF is to reach established level of 50 by this time. Examine PSF also.
1	End	NWF	Although the established level of ORF is 40, NWF is more revealing.
2	Beginning	NWF	Use NWF for struggling readers. Also consider ORF carefully.
2	Middle	ORF	
2	End	ORF	
3	Beginning	ORF	
3	Middle	ORF	
3	End	ORF	

Table 3.7

Recommended Indicators for Rank Order Sort

		LNF	ISF	PSF	NWF	ORF
K	Beginning	↙	(↙)			
	Middle	↙	(↙)	↙	↙	
	Ending	↙		(↙)	↙	
1st	Beginning	↙		↙	(↙)	
	Middle			↙	(↙)	↙
	Ending				↙	(↙)
2nd	Beginning				↙	(↙)
	Middle					(↙)
	Ending					(↙)
3rd	Beginning					(↙)
	Middle					(↙)
	Ending					(↙)

and the measure of fluency in passage reading (ORF) from the end of first grade onward. The recommended indicator for rank ordering at the beginning and middle of kindergarten is ISF and, for the end of kindergarten, PSF. Use either PSF or NWF at the beginning of first grade. In a school where many students are scoring well below benchmark, it may be best to use PSF for the first grade rank ordering. In a more average school, many students will have reached the benchmark of 35 in PSF by the end of kindergarten, in which case ranking by NWF is preferable. Since we will make grouping decisions on the basis of both scores, it really doesn't matter which one is used to construct the rank ordered list.

The recommended indicator for rank ordering at the middle of first grade is NWF, and from the end of first grade through second and third grade, it's ORF. However, even with students beyond the middle of first grade, when NWF is no longer required for benchmark screening, NWF can be administered to students who are below benchmark, and the data can help in making grouping decisions. In addition to the preference for the phonemic awareness and alphabetic principle measures during kindergarten and first grade, another factor that influences the selection of which measure to use for grouping is the instructional goal along the DIBELS stepping stones to literacy.

Step 3: Rank order intervention students by selected indicator. After selecting an indicator for rank ordering students, list the students beginning with the lowest score for the selected indicator, and ending with the intervention student with the highest score for the selected indicator. Be sure to construct your table to include scores for the other indicators. For example, for the beginning of first grade, the table will list students by rank order of NWF and include a column for PSF scores and LNF scores. Even though LNF isn't considered a key determinant for ranking, it does provide information that can be used in grouping students. Not only does it give information about the overall level of risk of the student, but may also be considered when determining whether the group may benefit from strategic instruction in letter knowledge.

Let's work through this process with Miss Hanson's first grade class. Table 3.8 shows intervention students ranked by Nonsense Word Fluency (NWF) scores, and it lists only the indicator raw scores, with NWF in the first column, PSF in the second column, and LNF in the third column. This "barebones" table, which excludes the percentiles and status for each indicator, makes grouping easier for many teachers. Indicator raw scores are more beneficial than percentiles because they can be compared to the benchmark scores. It is important to note that although we are using the actual score for rank ordering the students, differences of three to four points would be below the threshold of accuracy on DIBELS. Differences of 10-15 points are more meaningful, according to the DIBELS research team.

Table 3.8	STUDENT	NWF	PSF	LNF
Miss Hanson's First Grade Class— Beginning of the Year		Score	Score	Score
	Alli	0	2	21
	Brittney	2	3	9
Students Requiring Intervention	Courtney	3	2	16
	Devon	5	8	27
	Evelyn	7	9	27
	Fred	9	8	28
	Greg	18	27	29
	Harry	19	32	32
	Ingrid	21	28	33
	Joe	21	34	35
	Kelsey	22	33	34

Step 4: Form a group among the lowest students. Now that the students are identified in rank order, look at the lowest students, based on NWF, to begin forming groups. Why group the students with the lowest scores first? The process could just as well have started with the highest intervention students first. However, it is more intuitively appealing to focus our attention initially on the students who need the most help.

Miss Hanson's class will continue to serve as our example. Look at the student with the lowest score on the list and select one other student whose scores are also low. For the first pass, groups will be based solely on NWF and PSF scores; later the LNF scores will be considered. The four lowest students are examined (see Table 3.9).

Table 3.9			
Lowest Students in Miss Hanson's Class			

STUDENT	NWF Score	PSF Score	LNF Score
Alli	0	2	21
Brittney	2	3	9
Courtney	3	2	16
Devon	5	8	27

There are three steps to forming groups among the lowest students in Miss Hanson's class.

1. *Find students with similar NWF and PSF scores.*
   Alli and Brittney have very low scores on both NWF and PSF for this assessment period of the fall of first grade. Because Alli and Brittney's PSF scores are so far below the benchmark of 35, the instructional focus for this group must include phonemic awareness as well as letter-sound correspondences during the first semester of first-grade. We'll call this Group 1.

2. *Look for a third student who fits into Group 1.*
   Courtney's low NWF and PSF scores make her a good candidate to add to Group 1. What about Devon? Since our lowest group will only have three students, Devon will be added to another group later. All three students in this group may benefit from intervention instruction focused initially on phonemic awareness. Because none of these three children have reached anywhere near benchmark in phoneme segmentation, this is where instruction would begin. There is no point in beginning to teach letter-sound correspondence and working on skills that would lead to higher NWF scores until the students develop a greater proficiency in

orally recognizing the separate sounds in words. Since it is the beginning of first grade and their PSF was supposed to be at the established level of 35 at the end of kindergarten, instruction in phonemic awareness must be provided. The teacher will need to accelerate the students' progress in phonemic awareness and move on to letter-sound instruction as soon as possible so that they can accomplish two goals between September and January of first grade. This group needs to reach 35 in PSF <u>and</u> 50 in NWF within this four-month period to get them on track. It is clear that these students need very substantial and effective instruction in both phonemic awareness and the alphabetic principle during the first semester of first grade.

A word of caution is appropriate at this point about using these DIBELS scores in this manner. Because differences in DIBELS scores of only three to four points are not meaningful, the six lowest students in Miss Hanson's class may not be significantly different in their PSF and NWF scores to view these numbers as distinctly different. These lowest six students could also initially be grouped more haphazardly followed by close monitoring of their response to instruction with DIBELS progress monitoring measures. Frequent progress monitoring enables verification of a single measure through repeated assessment. A pattern of similar scores on repeated assessments on different days under different conditions allows a greater confidence in estimates of a student's skills than is possible with a single measure on one day. In the case of the lowest six students in Miss Hanson's class, where the scores are all clustered within a narrow range from one administration only, the student's progress with intervention instruction is a more important subgrouping strategy than small differences in their initial skills.

3. *Look at LNF scores to determine if some of the intervention time should be devoted to improving the speed of letter naming.*
   Since Alli, Brittney, and Courtney's LNF scores are at some risk in letter naming (between 9 and 21 versus established level of 37), they could benefit from practice in letter naming. So some attention will be paid in this group to letter naming fluency instruction. Because the most important skills for reading are phonemic awareness and phonics, more time will be initially devoted to phonemic awareness, which is the lowest skill on the reading skills continuum for these students. However, teachers can also strategically instruct in letter naming to facilitate spelling instruction later.

Step 5: Form a group among the highest intervention students. Why group the highest students now rather than continue moving to the next lowest students? The needs of the top and bottom groups are typically quite distinct from one another and form an obvious contrast. Students in the highest group are often at, or nearly at, benchmark in one or more indicators, yet lacking on the more advanced skill measured. Because of the contrast, there will be a cohesive group at the bottom and a cohesive group at the top. This makes it easier to group from each end first, and then place all the middle students as a final step for dealing with intervention students. It can be more obvious where to place the students whose scores fall in the middle of the rank order list after the obvious high and low groups have been identified.

Since this is the highest of the intervention students, look for three to five students to group together. Table 3.10 shows that Miss Hanson's class is quite typical in that the scores of the highest and lowest groups are quite distinct. The lowest group is deficient in both NWF and PSF. The highest group is deficient only in NWF, and very near benchmark in PSF.

Table 3.10

Miss Hanson's Class— Highest Students Requiring Intervention

STUDENT	NWF	PSF	LNF
	Score	Score	Score
Greg	18	27	29
Harry	19	32	32
Ingrid	21	28	33
Joe	21	34	35
Kelsey	22	33	34

Identify the students with the highest NWF scores and similar PSF scores. In Miss Hanson's class, the five highest intervention students all have similar scores in NWF, ranging from 18 to 22. Their PSF scores, which range from 27 to 33, while not quite yet at Benchmark, are considered "emerging" in the DIBELS categorizations. This group might need some brief initial work in phoneme segmentation, but it would be easy to forecast that this skill will develop fairly quickly and reach benchmark of 35 within a short period of time. This group will be able to move on to associating letters and sounds fairly quickly. If resources are not an issue, then these students can be placed in groups of three rather than five. However, if staffing is more limited, then this is the group to have five students provided that progress is confirmed throughout the fall, thereby ensuring that the lowest students are placed in the smallest groups.

Step 6: Place remaining intervention students in a group. Having formed a group of lowest and highest intervention students, the focus now turns to the remaining students in the middle. The most difficult part of grouping the students in the middle is deciding how many groups to form. Because these decisions are affected by the staffing available to provide intervention, it is not straightforward.

Let's look at the three students in Miss Hanson's class who have not yet been placed in a group (see Table 3.11).

Table 3.11

Miss Hanson's Class— Tentative Groups

STUDENT	NWF	PSF	LNF
	Score	Score	Score
Lowest Group			
Alli	0	2	21
Brittney	2	3	9
Courtney	3	2	16
Students Not Yet Placed in Groups			
Devon	5	8	27
Evelyn	7	9	27
Fred	9	8	28
Highest Group			
Greg	18	27	29
Harry	19	32	32
Ingrid	21	28	33
Joe	21	34	35
Kelsey	22	33	34

Do Devon, Evelyn, and Fred make a good group? Actually, given that this class was artificially constructed, they make an ideal group. But why? They are a great group not just because their NWF scores are so close, but because their PSF scores are also similar. Because these students' NWF scores are only in the single digits and need to be 50 by the middle of the year, they have a ways to go to reach benchmark. There isn't much difference between this middle group and the lowest group in terms of intervention needed in phonemic awareness. The intervention instruction may start back with activities and strategies to develop their awareness of the sounds in words orally before adding the letters for sound-symbol relationships. However it will need to be aggressive in order to add instruction in letter-sounds within a short time because they also will need to reach the established levels in both PSF and NWF during this first semester in order to increase the probability that they will read 40 words per minute by the end of first grade. In kindergarten it may be possible to go step-by-step from instruction in phonemic awareness to the alphabetic principle, but in early first grade there must be an urgent instructional focus on both. Although their letter naming is a bit stronger than the lowest group, all three students are still below benchmark in LNF, and some limited time on developing letter knowledge would also be beneficial.

The director of Title I at an Indiana school described her groups as follows:

> *With the help of the kindergarten teachers, we used the DIBELS scores and put the students into ability groups in our Title I classroom. We have one group of readers, and two or three groups writing consonant-vowel-consonant words with dry-mark boards. The students take these C-V-C words and use them with sight words to write sentences. The students who need letter-sound skills are grouped so that many intervention materials are presented to them. We really feel the students are receiving what they need.*
>
> Title I director

Step 7: Look for students who need practice with an excluded skill.
When we determined which indicators were important to consider in grouping students, a few were excluded. Earlier we stated that LNF, WUF, and RTF would not be considered in determining the groups. Although grouping on LNF is not recommended, it is a skill to reexamine.

Sounds and letter sound correspondences are clearly more important skills to teach than letter naming, but can we really ignore letter knowledge? Letter naming knowledge may be important in serving as an anchor for children as they connect sounds with letters. Fluency in letter recognition may help students so that they simply don't have to spend any attention thinking about which letter they are looking at. Many teachers prefer that students have fluency in letter naming, and so they often choose to offer some instruction in letter naming knowledge for students who lack it. One solution is to form a group to work specifically on letter recognition and naming. This group would meet in addition to the sound-based groups. Experience indicates that this group can be composed of students who generally are in other groups for their regular intervention and who get some extra help with letter naming during another time of the day. The LNF group might be larger than the regular intervention group because the feedback and practice in letter naming does not require quite the same level of attention and listening between the instructor and student as work with sounds.

Vocabulary intervention might be quite different. Usually children whose WUF scores are low have very low oral language skill or are English Language

Learners who may have strong vocabularies in their first language. Intervention that includes work in oral language can either be provided separately, or if enough students have low oral language and are part of a group, it can be included in the intervention group. However, this group will generally need more intervention time to cover all these skills. Since many young children cannot attend for more than 30 minutes at a time, often this group meets a second time during the day for additional work.

Work on comprehension for students with low RTF scores typically follows development of accurate and rapid word recognition. Since most kindergarten through third grade students who struggle in comprehension actually have difficulties at a lower level, that is, in accurate and automatic word recognition, the majority of the intervention groups spend time developing these skills through instruction in phonemic awareness and phonics. Once all the underlying skills are developed for word attack, students may need help in building fluency. Only once fluency is achieved is it possible to assess if the student is having a problem related solely to comprehension. For students struggling to comprehend, there are special techniques to model what engaged and active construction of meaning looks like, including the process of creating pictures or mental images as the words are read.

Step 8: Look for any benchmark students who may have been missed. Since the DIBELS data management system determines the instructional recommendation on the classroom reports by a weighted average of the underlying skills, it is wise to go back and revisit the benchmark students. Your district or school may make different judgments about who needs help. For example, your district or school may decide that any student who is below benchmark in any one indicator ought to be provided extra help. Since Miss Hanson's class was artificially constructed so that a student recommended for intensive intervention was deficit or at risk in all areas assessed, this would not be a necessary step with this class list.

Step 9: Find any exceptionally high students. One additional reason to revisit the benchmark list is to look for any students whose scores are exceptionally high. We are so accustomed to using DIBELS to identify the at-risk students that sometimes we forget to look for students at the other end of the exceptionality profile—those who are way above benchmark for their age. Look back at the benchmark students again and identify any students whose scores place them above the 80th or 90th percentile. Depending upon your district's practices, these DIBELS scores could provide additional data to merit providing a student with enrichment instruction.

In Miss Hanson's class there are no students who fall within this category. The highest student, Ralph, is only somewhat above benchmark and not exceedingly high in any area. Penny is the most advanced in any skill area with a PSF score of 69.

Grouping When the Groups Aren't Perfect—Miss Smith's Class

Miss Hanson's class was artificially constructed to illustrate the nine-step process for grouping students without worrying about challenges presented by students whose scores make them more challenging to group. Often a student will have a score in one indicator that is at a different instructional level than the score of another indicator. For example, if Alli's score of 0 on NWF falls in the Intensive Instruction area, it is less tidy if her score on PSF is in the Emerging or Established level instead of Deficit. This exact alignment across all skills is unrealistic and never happens quite this perfectly.

Having completed a nine-step process for grouping a tidy Miss Hanson's class, our next step is to examine a more realistic class where a student's scores are all across the board in terms of instructional implications. For this section, Miss Smith's class will provide an example of a more realistic class. This example is from a real class in a school in Indiana in 2002-2003; the names of the students and teacher have been changed to protect their privacy. Students and their scores are listed in Table 3.12 in the order they appeared on the classroom report for the DIBELS data management system in the fall of 2002.

Step 1: Identify the benchmark students and set them aside. Construct a chart of Miss Smith's benchmark students and their scores (Table 3.13).

Step 2: Determine which indicator to use for sorting intervention students. For our analysis of Miss Smith's class, we will use NWF to sort the intervention students. PSF is the other indicator that we could use. If you use the University of Oregon's DIBELS data management system, there is an assumed indicator for rank ordering students. You can discover the indicator used at a given point in time by seeing which indicator lists the students in ascending order. For the middle of first grade, it is NWF.

Step 3: Rank order intervention students by selected indicator. In Table 3.14, the intervention students are placed in order of their NWF scores.

Step 4: Form a group among the lowest students. For this step, prepare a chart of the lowest four or five students needing intervention listed by NWF in the first column, followed by PSF and LNF (see Table 3.15).

Table 3.12

**Miss Smith's
Class at the
Beginning of
First Grade**

Student	Letter Naming Fluency		Phoneme Segmentation Fluency		Nonsense Word Fluency		Instructional Recommendation
	Score	Status	Score	Status	Score	Status	
Abbie	16	At risk	16	Emerging	0	At risk	Intensive
Brian	25	Some risk	16	Emerging	0	At risk	Strategic
Carla	25	Some risk	5	Deficit	2	At risk	Intensive
Daniel	31	Some risk	27	Emerging	3	At risk	Strategic
Elaine	47	Low risk	37	Established	3	At risk	Strategic
Franklin	45	Low risk	52	Established	5	At risk	Strategic
Gwen	37	Low risk	62	Established	5	At risk	Strategic
Hillary	47	Low risk	4	Deficit	8	At risk	Strategic
Iris	41	Low risk	12	Emerging	11	At risk	Strategic
Jackie	46	Low risk	57	Established	14	Some risk	Benchmark
Ken	63	Low risk	0	Deficit	17	Some risk	Strategic
Lloyd	53	Low risk	14	Emerging	17	Some risk	Benchmark
Madelyn	45	Low risk	44	Established	25	Low risk	Benchmark
Nathan	58	Low risk	33	Emerging	27	Low risk	Benchmark
Oliver	28	Some risk	36	Established	31	Low risk	Benchmark
Pat	55	Low risk	69	Established	38	Low risk	Benchmark
Quentin	57	Low risk	53	Established	40	Low risk	Benchmark
Richard	88	Low risk	46	Established	72	Low risk	Benchmark

There are three steps to forming groups among the lowest students in Miss Smith's class:

1. *Find students with similar NWF and PSF scores.*
   Abbie and Brian both have scores of 0 on NWF and 16 on PSF, so this is a perfect fit for an intervention group. (It's unusual that two students

Table 3.13

Miss Smith's Class— Benchmark Students

Student	LNF Score	PSF Score	NWF Score	Instructional Recommendation
Franklin	45	52	5	Benchmark
Jackie	46	57	14	Benchmark
Madelyn	45	44	25	Benchmark
Nathan	58	33	27	Benchmark
Oliver	28	36	31	Benchmark
Pat	55	69	38	Benchmark
Quentin	57	53	40	Benchmark
Richard	88	46	72	Benchmark

Table 3.14

Miss Smith's First Grade Class— Beginning of the Year

Students Requiring Intervention

STUDENT	NWF Score	PSF Score	LNF Score
Abbie	0	16	16
Brian	0	16	25
Carla	2	5	25
Daniel	3	27	31
Elaine	3	37	47
Gwen	5	62	37
Hillary	8	4	47
Iris	11	12	41
Ken	17	0	63
Lloyd	17	14	53

Table 3.15

Miss Smith's First Grade Class— Beginning of the Year

Lowest Several Students Requiring Intervention

STUDENT	NWF Score	PSF Score	LNF Score
Abbie	0	16	16
Brian	0	16	25
Carla	2	5	25
Daniel	3	27	31
Elaine	3	37	47

would have the same NWF and PSF scores. Most often they will be close, but not exactly the same.) Because Abbie and Brian have PSF scores are so far below the benchmark of 35, the instructional focus for this group will include instruction in phonemic awareness and letter-sound correspondences. We'll call this Group 1.

2. *Look for a third student who fits into Group 1.*
Daniel's high PSF score of 27 makes him less of a fit. A better fit for Daniel would be a group of students whose scores for PSF are in the mid 20s to mid 30s. Since the established level of PSF is 35, these students would be close to benchmark and would be expected to need less help with phonemic awareness than Brian and Abbie.

Carla's extremely low score of 5 on PSF makes her potentially the weakest student in terms of phonemic awareness. She can be placed in the lowest group with Abbie and Brian because they all can benefit from intervention instruction that includes a focus on phonemic awareness as well as the alphabetic principle.

3. *Look at LNF scores to determine if some of the intervention time should be devoted to improving the speed of letter naming.*
Examine the Letter Naming Fluency scores for all three students. Since all three students are below the established score of 37-40 in LNF for the beginning of first grade, they could benefit from practice in letter recognition. The instructor may strategically teach letter recognition skills in this group. In spite of recommending some minor attention to letter naming fluency, the most important skills for reading are phonemic awareness and phonics because it is the middle of first grade and they are deficient in both areas.

Step 5: Form a group among the highest intervention students. Look for three to five students to place together (Table 3.16).

Identify the students with the highest NWF scores and similar PSF scores. In Miss Smith's class, the intervention students whose scores are the highest in NWF are Iris, Ken and Lloyd, with scores ranging from 11 to 17. Iris and Lloyd also have PSF scores (12 and 14) that are fairly close. Therefore, we know that Iris and Lloyd can logically be grouped together. Which student would be an appropriate student to add to these two?

Ken's NWF score of 17 makes him a logical candidate, yet his score on the PSF indicator is curious. When we look at Ken's PSF score of 0, a logical question to ask is: "How could that be?" This is a good example of an inconsistency in a student's data, and possibly an error. Ken's scores would mean that he was

Table 3.16

Miss Smith's Class— Highest Students Requiring Intervention

STUDENT	NWF	PSF	LNF
	Score	Score	Score
Gwen	5	62	37
Hillary	8	4	47
Iris	11	12	41
Ken	17	0	63
Lloyd	17	14	53

able to read 17 letter-sound correspondences correctly in nonsense words, yet could not respond orally with *any* sounds in words in the PSF task. This is unlikely to occur because most students who can decode nonsense words in print have at least a minimal level of phonemic segmentation skill.

So how could this inconsistency in Ken's scores happen? One possible explanation is that Ken did not understand the PSF task, and therefore didn't follow the instructions. This is a place where it would be very helpful to go to the student scoring booklet and look at how Ken got the score of 0 in PSF. The most likely scenario is that the discontinue rule was reached. Otherwise he would have had a score of at least one, and continued for the full minute. Did he discontinue because he simply repeated all the words back? How would we know if this is what he did? The first five words would each be circled, and then the examiner would have discontinued administering the PSF indicator because he failed to get any phoneme correct in the first five words.

Now what do we do about Ken's PSF score of 0? When a student's scores are inconsistent, the perfect solution is to administer a progress monitoring assessment to determine if he knows how to segment the sounds. It is possible to spend a few moments practicing the skill, of course without using any words from the DIBELS tests, before administering the progress monitoring version to make sure he understands the task. Considering more than one assessment of a DIBELS indicator is critical because a pattern is more likely to give an accurate impression of the student's performance than any one single score. Let's assume that Ken will perform better than 0 on PSF when administered a progress monitoring version. Using that assumption, we will group Lloyd, Ken, and Iris together. What type of intervention instruction do these students need? They have some level of PSF skill yet need some additional work in this area. They are making connections between sounds and letters, as demonstrated on their NWF scores. So their intervention can include some time on phonemic awareness, hopefully at the segmentation level, and also on letter-sound correspondences.

Step 6: Place all remaining intervention students in a group. Let's start by examining the two groups formed so far, along with the students that haven't been grouped yet (see Table 3.17).

Table 3.17

Miss Smith's Class— Students Not Yet Placed in Groups

STUDENT	NWF	PSF	LNF
	Score	**Score**	**Score**
Lowest Group			
Abbie	0	16	16
Brian	0	16	25
Carla	2	5	25
Students Not Yet Placed in Groups			
Daniel	3	27	31
Elaine	3	37	47
Gwen	5	62	37
Hillary	8	4	47
Highest Group			
Iris	11	12	41
Ken	17	0	63
Lloyd	17	14	53

Because of their similar level on PSF, Daniel and Elaine can be grouped together. Hillary is another student who hasn't been grouped, yet her very low PSF score of 4 doesn't make her a good fit with this group.

Hillary is an interesting student to study. If the grouping decision is made strictly on the NWF score, she would most likely not be grouped appropriately. Her NWF score of 8, although stronger than Daniel and Gwen's scores of 3 and 5 respectively, has to be given lower priority in the grouping decision. Her PSF score of 4 indicates that, even though she may be beginning to make some letter-sound correspondences as indicated by her NWF score of 8, her intervention needs to include some instruction in phoneme segmentation. One possible group for her is the lowest group. Clearly she has a PSF score that is nearly equal to Carla. Yet look at Hillary's LNF score. If she is placed in the lowest group and that group received some instruction in letter naming, then this is not a good placement for her. Therefore she is better placed in the group with Iris, Ken, and Lloyd. This group's intervention instruction will include phonemic segmentation, which Hillary clearly needs. None of the students in this group needs help in letter naming, which is also the case for Hillary. So the best place for her is in this group.

Table 3.17 shows that Miss Smith's class is quite typical in that the scores of the highest and lowest groups are quite distinct. The lowest group is typically deficient in both NWF and PSF. The highest group is usually deficient only in NWF, but at or above benchmark in PSF.

Now that we have formed the groups, let's reexamine which is the "highest," "lowest," and "middle." We might conclude one order based on NWF. Yet, looking at both the PSF and NWF, it can be argued that the highest group is actually Daniel, Elaine, and Gwen because they have developed quite a bit more extensive phonemic segmentation skills. Therefore, their intervention will be quite short in phonemic segmentation and concentrate primarily on associating letters and sounds.

We might conclude that although the students are still combined in the same groups as above, we may want to "relabel" the groups more appropriately, as shown in Table 3.18.

Table 3.18

Miss Smith's First Grade Class—Final Groups

STUDENT	NWF	PSF	LNF
	Score	Score	Score
Lowest Group			
Abbie	0	16	16
Brian	0	16	25
Carla	2	5	25
Middle Group			
Hillary	8	4	47
Iris	11	12	41
Ken	17	14	53
Highest Group			
Daniel	3	27	31
Elaine	3	37	47
Gwen	5	62	37

Step 7: Look for students who need practice with an excluded skill.

The groups were formed to focus on phonemic and alphabetic principle skills. However, there are a couple of students who might benefit from a little extra work in letter naming. A solution to this problem that some teachers like is to form a special letter naming group that meets at a different time than the other groups.

Because Daniel and Iris are in groups that will not be working on letter naming, they each can be considered for this extra practice in letters. Their scores are 31 and 41 respectively.

Step 8: Look for any benchmark students who may have been missed.

In Miss Smith's class we can see that Franklin is considered a benchmark student. Yet his NWF at 5 is still weak, even though his PSF is strong at 52. A prudent decision would be to add Franklin to the highest intervention group for a while. The extra help for a few weeks in blending words would not hurt, and would ensure that he continues to make adequate progress before the next benchmark.

Additionally Oliver, another benchmark student, might benefit from a little help with letter naming since his LNF score at 28 is considerably below the benchmark of 40. He can be added to the letter naming group with Daniel and Iris.

Step 9: Find any exceptionally high students.

In Miss Smith's class there are three students whose scores are exceptionally high. Pat, Quentin, and Richard are all extremely strong and would benefit from some enrichment work using above grade-level materials.

Defining the Instructional Focus of Each Group

After all the groups have been formed, write an instructional focus for each group. An example is provided in Table 3.19.

Other Sources of Information

Throughout this chapter we have voiced cautions about making decisions based on limited data. There are several ways to overcome the risks of making decisions on too limited of data. First, when making grouping decisions we recommend that teachers look at all other data along with the student's scores on the DIBELS indicators. Some schools use multiple assessment instruments, and then data from several sources can be compared with the DIBELS data. For example, if the school administers the Peabody Picture Vocabulary Test (PPVT), the student's achievement on the PPVT can be compared to his score on the WUF indicator of the DIBELS.

Table 3.19

Miss
Hanson's
Class

Recommended
Instructional
Focus of
Intervention
Groups

STUDENT	NWF	PSF	LNF
	Score	Score	Score
Lowest Group—intensive work on alphabet principle, phonemic awareness, and letter naming			
Abbie	0	16	16
Brian	0	16	25
Carla	2	5	25
Middle Group—start with phonemic awareness moving to phoneme segmentation—then sound-symbol—no letter naming work			
Hillary	8	4	47
Iris	11	12	41
Ken	17	0	63
Lloyd	17	14	53
Highest Group—start with phonemic segmentation—then quickly move to sound-symbol			
Daniel	3	27	31
Elaine	3	37	47
Gwen	5	62	

Other times teachers will conduct their own informal assessments of skills. A few months ago while meeting with one teacher to form her groups, we compared the information from the DIBELS with data she had collected through her own informal assessments of the number of letter names and sounds that the students answered correctly when shown a flash card with a letter on it. We noted that her informal evaluation of these skills was untimed and there was no benchmark to serve as a guide of acceptable levels. However, the teacher's informal data were still useful in confirming the impressions from DIBELS indicators when placing each student in a group.

During the first week of instruction for new groups, the teacher should informally confirm the student's level of skills by observing how each student responds to an instructional activity. For example, if a kindergarten student who scores low in ISF is placed in an intervention group, the teacher still needs to confirm that the appropriate place to begin instruction is in isolating initial phonemes in words. Sometimes when a student scores low in ISF, he doesn't understand the concept of how to segment sound units in words and needs to go back to segmenting words in sentences, then syllables, then onset-rimes, and finally to segmenting the initial sound from the rest of the sounds in the word. Therefore, response to instruction is essential in confirming placement in groups.

After considering other assessment data, the teacher's informal evaluations, and observation of the child's response to instruction, repeated and regular progress monitoring assessments in DIBELS is the most powerful way to confirm groupings. Keep in mind that DIBELS is a one-minute measurement at a specific point in time. Each time a teacher gets a similar score through repeatedly administering an alternate form of the DIBELS measure by using a progress monitoring form, the certainty about the data increases. Therefore it is best to make all decisions about students based on patterns of data rather than a single score.

Summary on Placing Students in Groups

This nine-step process for grouping students may seem complicated the first time you try it, but most teachers become comfortable with it quickly. Just remember that whatever decisions you make on groups is temporary. This generally gives teachers a sense of relief that any incorrect placement decisions can be corrected when students are regrouped. After you begin using the progress monitoring, students will be moved between groups anyway. Some students will make considerable progress within about six to nine weeks of working in the intervention groups. The scores of others will not respond much at all, and these students will need to receive more intense intervention.

Here's a testimonial from a kindergarten teacher in a school that implemented intervention groups based on DIBELS.

My lowest group has 2 children that scored 0 on NWF and PSF, and very low (6 & 5) on ISF, and 0 on LNF. It doesn't take much analyzing to know that we must go back to just "listening" to sounds. I try to just get them to focus on sounds that are the same and different. They don't "get" rhyming yet, so I've just gone back to having them hear basic sounds of objects to see if they can tell me "same" or "different." They still struggle with that. Before DIBELS I wouldn't have known to do that. My highest group is focusing on reading and writing. It's fantastic to see my kindergarten students having that specialized/individualized time geared to their abilities. I've never been able to do that before. They have all reached benchmark in all areas, so the aide has them writing sentences she dictates, journaling, reading books to her one-on-one. It's awesome!

Kindergarten teacher

Chapter 4

Analyzing a DIBELS Student Booklet

When I have a concern about a child being behind, I make sure to analyze the booklet of that student to see where he's having problems and if it reflects in everything or specific areas. Otherwise, I mostly look at the scores.

Indiana teacher

Introduction and Purpose for Analyzing Error Patterns

When teachers first begin using the DIBELS assessment, they quickly learn to compare a student's scores on each indicator to the benchmark. This comparison is important because the scores tell the teacher whether the student is on track in that skill area and is therefore predicted to read well later. However, DIBELS scoring booklets offer much more than just the numerical scores. An analysis of the student's responses in the DIBELS booklet can enhance the information revealed in the scores alone about what instruction is needed and how to design and tailor instruction to meet the needs of the individual student.

In order to design intervention instruction that is as focused as possible, teachers need to analyze the DIBELS scoring booklets. When teachers analyze the error patterns marked in the booklets, they can learn much about what a student does and does not know. In fact, teachers should be encouraged to write all over their DIBELS booklets and note what the student said in making errors, if at all possible, after the student has completed the assessment (so it doesn't interfere with the required scoring procedures). The time spent analyzing the errors and designing focused lessons is valuable because teachers cannot afford to waste an inordinate amount of time reteaching a skill the student has mastered or, worse yet, missing a skill that is critical. Analyzing the pages of the students' booklets gives invaluable insights about exactly what concepts and skills the student needs. These error patterns inform intervention decisions, but are not as thorough as the type of testing required for diagnostic purposes.

The process for analyzing a DIBELS student booklet outlined in this chapter helps teachers learn as much as possible about students. As you work with your own students' booklets, you may develop your own process, including new questions to ask and additional observations to make. The process in this chapter will help you get started with your detailed analysis of error patterns so that you can use information from DIBELS to inform your decisions about data-driven intervention instruction.

Steps for Analyzing a DIBELS Student Booklet

The process below includes four steps:

> Step 1: Analyze the Whole Picture

> Step 2: Note Areas of Concern or Questions

> Step 3: Study Error Patterns on Each of the Booklet Pages

> Step 4: Summarize Observations for Intervention Lesson Plan

Each step is outlined in detail below.

Step 1: Analyze the Whole Picture

The first step is to study the summary chart of scores on the outside cover (or on the inside page if you are using the Sopris West 2003 materials). The purpose of this step is to get an overall sense of how well the student is doing before diving into the details to look for any concerns or questions. While still looking at the scores on the summary chart, you can compare the student's scores to interim benchmark levels. You can identify areas of weakness, areas of strength, and note questions and areas of concern to explore while looking at all the scoring pages of the booklet.

Step 2: Note Areas of Concern or Questions

While looking at the summary chart of the indicator scores, you should think about any areas where the data is inconsistent. Inconsistencies occur when a higher-level skill develops before an underlying one, or related skills are not equally strong or weak. Several examples of inconsistencies include:

- PSF above benchmark, ISF low. Normally, the ability to segment and identify initial sounds develops before a student can segment all the sounds in a word.

- High NWF, low PSF and LNF. Generally, students with a high NWF will have already developed a strong fluency with phoneme segmentation and letter naming.

- High ORF, low NWF. Typically students with ORF scores above benchmark are proficient in applying sound/letter correspondences (alphabetic principle) in reading nonsense CVC words.

- High WUF, strong PSF, low scores on the fourth question of each set in ISF. The fourth question on the ISF indicator requires the student to say the sound instead of pointing to, or naming, the picture. It is related to the ability to express the sounds as well as to know them receptively.

- High RTF, low WUF. A student with a high RTF often is more expressive or verbal, and would have a high WUF score.

By identifying these inconsistencies first, it is possible to look for explanations while studying the scoring pages for all the indicators.

Step 3: Study Error Patterns on Each of the Booklet Pages

DIBELS has helped me to be more specific with error patterns, such as leaving off ending sounds, vowel sounds, and hearing sounds but not knowing they come together.

First grade teacher

This step takes more time, but is worth every moment. After gaining an overall sense of the student's skills from comparing his indicator scores to benchmark levels and generating questions, the analysis turns to the details. Study each page of the scoring booklet and look at the mistakes the child made. Start by looking at the child's accuracy and fluency rates on the individual indicator. Then look at the child's mistakes and try to identify any error patterns. What part is the child consistently getting right? What is he consistently getting wrong? From this, some conclusions can be reached about where he needs help, and what area should be addressed first.

Step 4: Summarize Observations for Intervention Lesson Plan

Teachers often like to use some kind of a chart to summarize observations from their analysis. Table 4.1 shows a sample chart with a place to write comments, noting observations on each indicator and the implications for instruction.

Table 4.1

Worksheet for Analyzing a Student Booklet (Kindergarten)

Kindergarten		
DIBELS Indicator	**Observations**	**Instructional Implications**
Initial Sound Fluency **ISF**		
Letter Naming Fluency **LNF**		
Phoneme Segmentation Fluency **PSF**		
Nonsense Word Fluency **NWF**		
Word Use Fluency **WUF**		

This chart for kindergarten, plus one for first and second grades, is provided at the end of this chapter.

One of the conclusions you may reach is that a student's performance on DIBELS seems inconsistent or difficult to interpret. Assessment results with young children may be unreliable. When in doubt, reassess to check the reliability of the results. Remember that you can have more confidence in a pattern of performance than in a single score.

How to Use Data From Word Use Fluency and Retell Fluency

Teachers often ask how to use data from the two new measures. As of the date this book went to press, the norms on these two new measures had not yet been released. By the time you read this, the norms may be available.

The Word Use Fluency (WUF) gives information about the student's overall language and vocabulary level. When this score is very low it is a "red flag." The score can also provide another data point to help explain why children may be scoring low in other indicators. For example, a student who has difficulty expressing the sound on the fourth question of ISF and has a low WUF score may not be secure enough with the sounds to recall them on cue. The fourth ISF question on each page asks what sound a target picture begins with. The student can only get this correct if he can say the sound, not just point to the picture. Recalling and pronouncing the sound is a more advanced skill than recognizing the sound in a picture. Students with vocabulary deficits, as confirmed with the WUF measure, need to be in intensive language intervention groups, preferably using systematic programs such as SRA's *Language for Learning* or Steck-Vaughn's *Elements of Reading: Vocabulary.*

The purpose of the Retell Fluency (RTF) measure is to identify students who can decode proficiently, but who do not comprehend what they read. Many teachers are more familiar with other approaches to assess comprehension, including asking specific questions. Although the retell approach may be harder to score than some other measures, it gives the student the opportunity to retell what he recalls, and avoids the common problem of multiple choice questions in which the student may guess at the right answer without truly processing what he read. During this retell, the students who are proficient decoders and are not comprehending are easy to identify because when you ask them to tell you about what they just read, they look at you blankly and say something like, "I don't know." The number of poor comprehenders who can decode accurately and fluently ("word callers") is far fewer than those whose comprehension is eroded by inaccurate or dysfluent decoding.

Example of Analyzing a Kindergarten Student Booklet

In order to describe an approach for analyzing a student booklet, we'll start with kindergarten and use example student booklets to describe the approach. Sometimes we will look at two booklets together in order to highlight different error patterns. For kindergarten we will analyze the booklets of Keisha and Garrison (see Tables 4.2 and 4.3).

Table 4.2

Keisha and Garrison's Student Booklets Kindergarten —Mid-year

	Keisha		Garrison		Benchmark	
	Fall	**Winter**	**Fall**	**Winter**	**Fall**	**Winter**
ISF	4	12	2	23	8	25
LNF	14	24	27	51	8*	27*
PSF		8		8		18
NWF		5		6		18
WUF	8	13	35	45	n/a	n/a

Note: LNF scores of 8 & 27 are risk indicators and not instructional benchmarks.

Table 4.3

Summary
Table
for Two
Kindergarten
Students

Two Kindergarten Students

Keisha

Dynamic Indicators of
Basic Literacy Skills™ 6th Ed.
University of Oregon

Kindergarten Benchmark Assessment

Name: _____ Teacher: _____

School: _____ District: _____

	Benchmark 1 Beginning/ Fall	Benchmark 2 Middle/ Winter	Benchmark 3 End/ Spring
Date	9-16-02	1-9-03	
Initial Sound Fluency	4	12	
Letter Naming Fluency	14	24	
Phoneme Segmentation Fluency		8	
Nonsense Word Fluency		5	
Word Use Fluency (Optional)	(Optional) 8	(Optional) 13	(Optional)

Garrison

Dynamic Indicators of
Basic Early Literacy Skills™ 6th Ed.
University of Oregon

Kindergarten Benchmark Assessment

Name: _____ Teacher: _____

School: _____ District: _____

	Benchmark 1 Beginning/ Fall	Benchmark 2 Middle/ Winter	Benchmark 3 End/ Spring
Date	9-16-02	1-9-03	
Initial Sound Fluency	2	23	
Letter Naming Fluency	27	51	
Phoneme Segmentation Fluency		8	
Nonsense Word Fluency		6	
Word Use Fluency (Optional)	(Optional) 35	(Optional) 45	(Optional)

Keisha and Garrison are both imaginary kindergarten students. These scores are from the middle of the year benchmark screening. In the winter of kindergarten, DIBELS consists of three indicators that were also used in the fall (ISF, LNF, and WUF) and two new ones (PSF and NWF).

Step 1: Analyze the Whole Picture

Keisha and Garrison each have about the same score on PSF, yet on the ISF there is a completely different picture. Their NWF score is also low and about the same, which is no surprise given that their PSF is so low. The expected benchmark for ISF in mid-kindergarten is 25. Keisha's fall benchmark score was 4 and her winter score is 12. Garrison started below Keisha at 2 but has made significant gains and is now at 23, just below benchmark.

Step 2: Note Areas of Concern or Questions

Keisha's lack of progress in ISF distinguishes her results from her classmate. As we look further we can observe several other indications that cause concern about Keisha. In letter naming, Garrison also made more progress during the first half of the year. Keisha's very low WUF score of 13 raises questions about her oral language and vocabulary. However, low scores are common at this point in kindergarten because some students have a very difficult time following the instructions in the Word Use Fluency measure. We should always be careful not to overinterpret a low score until we have reassessed a student or received independent evidence that the skill is not developing normally.

Keisha's scores on each indicator compared to benchmark levels place her in the following categories:

- ISF-12—Deficit

- LNF-24—Some risk (LNF is a risk indicator and not an instructional benchmark)

- PSF-8—Some risk

- NWF-5—Some risk

- WUF-13—Compare to local norms

In DIBELS the terms "at risk, some risk, and low risk" are used before the skill should be established. At that time, and for each period thereafter, the terms change to "deficit, emerging, and established." Keisha is in the deficit range in ISF, and is at "some risk" in all other areas. There are no major inconsistencies in her scores.

Step 3: Study Error Patterns on Each of the Booklet Pages

Once we have noted Keisha's low sound knowledge and meager level of letter recognition, the next step is to open the booklet and begin to look at each page. The first page is the Initial Sound Fluency page (see Table 4.4).

Initial Sound Fluency (ISF)

- **How accurate is the student with initial sounds?**
  Keisha is very accurate because she got all 16 questions correct.

- **How fluent is the student with initial sounds?**
  Keisha took 80 seconds of response time to complete this task. Although she was very accurate, she was too slow. The ISF score is extremely sensitive to the response time. This is demonstrated by

Table 4.4

Initial Sound Fluency—Two Kindergarten Students

Keisha

Benchmark K–1 DIBELS Initial Sound Fluency		
This is tomato, cub, plate, jail (point to pictures).		
1. Which picture begins with /j/?	0	①
2. Which picture begins with /t/?	0	①
3. Which picture begins with /k/?	0	①
4. What sound does "plate" begin with?	0	①
This is bump, insect, refrigerator, skate (point to pictures).		
5. Which picture begins with /sk/?	0	①
6. Which picture begins with /r/?	0	①
7. Which picture begins with /b/?	0	①
8. What sound does "insect" begin with?	0	①
This is rooster, mule, fly, soldier (point to pictures).		
9. Which picture begins with /r/?	0	①
10. Which picture begins with /fl/?	0	①
11. Which picture begins with /s/?	0	①
12. What sound does "mule" begin with?	0	①
This is pliers, doctor, quilt, beetle (point to pictures).		
13. Which picture begins with /b/?	0	①
14. Which picture begins with /pl/?	0	①
15. Which picture begins with /d/?	0	①
16. What sound does "quilt" begin with?	0	①

Times: __80__ Seconds   Total Correct: __16__

$$\frac{60 \times Total\ Correct}{Seconds} = \text{12 Correct Initial Sounds per Minute}$$

Garrison

Benchmark K–1 DIBELS Initial Sound Fluency		
This is tomato, cub, plate, jail (point to pictures).		
1. Which picture begins with /j/?	0	①
2. Which picture begins with /t/?	0	①
3. Which picture begins with /k/?	0	①
4. What sound does "plate" begin with?	⓪	1
This is bump, insect, refrigerator, skate (point to pictures).		
5. Which picture begins with /sk/?	0	①
6. Which picture begins with /r/?	0	①
7. Which picture begins with /b/?	0	①
8. What sound does "insect" begin with?	⓪	1
This is rooster, mule, fly, soldier (point to pictures).		
9. Which picture begins with /r/?	0	①
10. Which picture begins with /fl/?	0	①
11. Which picture begins with /s/?	0	①
12. What sound does "mule" begin with?	⓪	1
This is pliers, doctor, quilt, beetle (point to pictures).		
13. Which picture begins with /b/?	0	①
14. Which picture begins with /pl/?	0	①
15. Which picture begins with /d/?	0	①
16. What sound does "quilt" begin with?	⓪	1

Times: __31__ Seconds   Total Correct: __12__

$$\frac{60 \times Total\ Correct}{Seconds} = \text{23 Correct Initial Sounds per Minute}$$

comparing Garrison's score with Keisha's. Her ISF total score was 12 with 16 answers correct, whereas he got only 12 out of 16 correct, yet his total score was 23 because he only took 31 seconds.

- **Is the student more able to identify initial sounds when he can point to the answers rather than supply the sound?**
  Keisha was able to correctly answer both forms of the questions. Look at the patterns of Garrison's errors. He answered the first three questions in a set correctly, but consistently missed the fourth one each time. Recall of sounds is more difficult than recognizing them in spoken words; Garrison needs more practice isolating and producing beginning phonemes.

- **Look for any other unusual error patterns.**

  Sometimes a child, typically one who doesn't know the answers, will point to the pictures in the order in which the practice was given. For example, the practice goes from left to right on the top row, and then left to right on the bottom row. Keisha followed the directions well and there were no unusual patterns.

Letter Naming Fluency (LNF)

The second indicator for the kindergarten benchmark is LNF (see Table 4.5).

Keisha—Letter Naming Fluency (LNF)

c	c	N	u	o	M	u	h	S	i
n	b	e	N	F	f	o	a	K	k
g	p	k	p	a	H	C	e	G	D
b	w	F]	i	h	O	x	j	l	K
x	t	Y	q	L	d	f	T	g	v
T	V	Q	o	w	P	J	t	B	X
Z	v	U	P	R	l	V	C	l	W
R	J	m	O	z	D	G	y	U	Y
Z	y	A	m	X	z	H	S	M	E
q	n	j	s	W	r	d	s	B	l
r	A	E	L	c	c	N	u	Q	M

Total: __24__ /110

- **How accurate is the student's letter naming skill?**

  Keisha got 24 correct out of the 33 letters that she attempted to name. This results in an accuracy rate of 73% (24/33 times 100).

- **How fluent is the student in naming letters?**

  Keisha named only 33 letters in a minute, a relatively slow time. Even if she had gotten them all right, her score would have been only 33. In order to score above the risk indicator level of 40 letters correct per minute she will need to be faster, as well as more accurate.

- **Are more of the letters the student missed at the end of the alphabet?**

  Keisha's errors were relatively evenly divided between the first and second half of the alphabet. When a student misses more at the end of the alphabet, the teacher may be teaching a letter per week in alphabetical order, and instruction simply has not yet reached the letters toward the end of the alphabet.

- **Did the student miss more lowercase letters than uppercase letters?**
  Of the 9 letters that Keisha missed, all but the capital letter *Q* were lowercase letters. In fact, she missed the lowercase *k* when it appeared directly after the upper case K. She particularly seems to have trouble with the letters that hang below the mid-line, such as *g*, and *p*.

- **Does the student get any letters correct one time and incorrect another time?**
  Keisha was inconsistent in her letter naming. She named lowercase *u* correctly once and incorrectly right after that. Keisha also got the lowercase *b* incorrect on the second line, but named it correctly on the fourth line.

- **Does the child correctly name the letters in her own name?**
  All of the letters in Keisha's name appeared in this assessment, and she got nearly all of these correct. She missed only the lowercase *h*. Interestingly, she got the uppercase *K* correct and missed the lowercase *k* next to it.

- **Did the student skip more than 1 line, or not read across the row left to right?**
  Keisha did not skip any rows while completing the letter naming task in DIBELS. While it is not uncommon for a student to lose their place and skip one row, losing track of place or sequence multiple times may signal a problem with left to right tracking.

Keisha appears to know her letters, but not fluently enough. One of the important differences between DIBELS and many other early literacy screening instruments is that in DIBELS the indicators are timed. Timing is critical because there is no other way to determine if a student recognizes the letters automatically. Children who automatically recognize and can name the letters have an advantage once they begin phonics instruction because they don't have to devote any attention to thinking about letter identity. The student can then dedicate all her attention to associating the sound with the letter symbol. Students can go unnoticed as candidates for extra help in letter naming unless fluency counts. It is important to compare the fall and winter benchmark pages to see what improvements a student has made from the instruction she received.

Phoneme Segmentation Fluency (PSF)

PSF, the third indicator for the kindergarten benchmark, is next (see Table 4.6). Does the student know how to segment or does she simply repeat the whole word back? A score of 0 may indicate that the examiner discontinued

Table 4.6

Keisha—
Phoneme
Segmentation
Fluency
Scoring Page

Keisha—Phoneme Segmentation Fluency (PSF)						Probe 5
star	/s/ /t/ /ar/		give	/g/ /i~/ /v~/		3 /6
yet	/y/ /e~/ /t~/		hid	/h/ /i~/ /d~/		2 /6
sled	/s/ /l/ /e~/ /d/		walk	(/w/ /o/ /k/)		2 /7
you	/y/ /oo~/		hook	(/h/ /uu/ /k/)		1 /5
she	/sh/ /ea/		swing	/s/ /w/ /i/ /ng/		__ /6
coal	/k/ /oa/ /l/		oak	/oa/ /k/		__ /5
						Total 8

screening because the student did not get any correct in the first five words. If the student repeated the entire word back and was discontinued, the first five words would each be circled and the score of 0 would be recorded. If the student attempted to segment but was unsuccessful on all items, there would be slash marks through each of the sounds for the first five words and a score of 0 correct out of approximately 15 sounds in the first five words.

After confirming that the student understands how to segment, you should look to see if the student segments all the speech sounds in the word or not. Partial segmentation is indicated when there are lines under some of the sounds, yet some segments are combined or forgotten. Sometimes students don't segment consonant blends (e.g. *st*, *pr*, *cl*, and *br*), or they segment by onset and the rime (e.g., *s-at*, or *br-ush*) without going to the phoneme level. The results can then be analyzed to note whether the student demonstrated proficiency in initial sounds, ending sounds, and middle vowels.

- **Does the student know how to segment phonemes?**
  Keisha appears to know how to segment because there are lines under the phonemes. The circles around the last two words indicate that she repeated these words, but she may not have felt confident so she went back to an earlier level of skill.

- **How many times does the student partially segment rather than completely segment the word?**
  The only sounds that Keisha partially segmented are the consonant blends. Since many teachers teach the blends as units, it is not uncommon to see this error. While blends are taught as a unit for spelling, teachers much teach them as separate sounds for phonemic awareness.

With direct, systematic instruction, most students quickly learn how to segment consonant blends into the two sounds.

- **How accurate is the student in segmenting phonemes?**
  Keisha's accuracy is an issue because she got only 8 correct out of the 24 phonemes she attempted. That is an accuracy rate of only 37%.

- **How fluent is the student in segmenting phonemes?**
  Keisha is not fluent enough because she attempted only 24 phoneme segments in a minute. Even if she were 100% accurate with a score of 24, she would fall short of the benchmark of 35. Fluent students can generally attempt more than 12 words in a minute.

- **How accurate is the student's knowledge of initial sounds?**
  Keisha demonstrates a strong awareness of the initial sound in words. She got nearly all the initial sounds correct in the words she was given.

- **How accurate is the student's knowledge of ending sounds?**
  Keisha is not quite as strong with ending sounds as initial sounds.

- **How accurate is the student's knowledge of vowels?**
  Keisha appears to have very limited knowledge of middle vowels. She was presented with words containing the short *i* sound, /ĭ/, twice, and missed the phoneme both times.

Word Use Fluency (WUF)

The fourth indicator for the kindergarten benchmark is WUF (see Table 4.7).

Table 4.7

Keisha—Word Use Fluency Scoring Page

	Keisha—Word Use Fluency (WUF)		
felt	⓪ 1 2 3 4 5 6 7 8 9 10 11 12 13 14 15	__ C Ⓘ
fence	0 1 2 3 ④ 5 6 7 8 9 10 11 12 13 14 15	4 Ⓒ I
which	⓪ 1 2 3 4 5 6 7 8 9 10 11 12 13 14 15	__ C Ⓘ
coach	0 1 2 ③ 4 5 6 7 8 9 10 11 12 13 14 15	3 Ⓒ I
front	0 1 2 ③ 4 5 6 7 8 9 10 11 12 13 14 15	3 Ⓒ I
nobody	⓪ 1 2 3 4 5 6 7 8 9 10 11 12 13 14 15	__ C Ⓘ
meant	⓪ 1 2 3 4 5 6 7 8 9 10 11 12 13 14 15	__ C Ⓘ
path	⓪ 1 2 3 4 5 6 7 8 9 10 11 12 13 14 15	__ C Ⓘ
woman	0 1 2 ③ 4 5 6 7 8 9 10 11 12 13 14 15	3 Ⓒ I
answered	⓪ 1 2 3 4 5 6 7 8 9 10 11 12 13 14 15	__ C Ⓘ
		Total 13

- **How many utterances are correct versus incorrect?**
  Keisha got only four correct out of ten words attempted, for an accuracy rate of 40%.

- **Was the student equally responsive to abstract and concrete words?**
  Keisha responded more to concrete words (*fence, coach, front,* and *woman*) than to abstract words (*which, nobody, meant, felt, path,* and *answered*).

- **Did the student take much time to respond?**
  Keisha exhausted the five seconds on many of the words and was unable to give a response at all. It's unclear whether she didn't know what the words meant, or whether she was formulating her sentences so slowly that she ran out of time.

- **Did the student's total points on this indicator come primarily from short or long responses?**
  Keisha gave only very short responses to the four words she did know. She gave three-word responses and one four-word response.

- **How much variability was there in the length of responses?**
  There was almost no variability in her responses as they were all very short utterances.

Step 4: Summarize Observations for Intervention Lesson Plan

Based on the DIBELS data, where would Keisha's intervention begin? Keisha is below benchmark on ISF and her PSF is also weak. Since Keisha was accurate but not fluent on the ISF task, intervention will need to begin with more rapid and automatic identification and pronunciation of the initial phoneme in a target word. Since she got all 16 ISF questions correct it is likely that she will not need to go back to a lower level of phonological awareness, such as breaking sentences into words, breaking words into syllables and onset-rime units before she practices phonemic awareness. She also needs practice with serial letter naming.

One quick way to validate the results of the DIBELS assessment is to begin working on activities emphasizing these skills. Informal observation of her response to instruction should corroborate the assessment findings. By observing her errors on repeated progress monitoring assessments of the ISF and PSF indicators, the teacher can continue to observe the pattern of responses and confirm her original impressions about appropriate intervention instruction.

Example of Analyzing a First Grade Student Booklet

The process of analyzing a DIBELS student booklet for a first grade student is very similar to that of a kindergartner. We will use first grade sample scoring booklets that include fall and winter scores for the benchmark screening as examples. By the middle of first grade, the student is supposed to have reached the established level in several skills:

- ISF of 25 initial sounds per minute (i.s.p.m.) by the middle of kindergarten

- LNF of 40 letter names per minute (l.n.p.m.) by the end of kindergarten

- PSF of 35 phoneme segments per minute (p.s.p.m.) by the end of kindergarten

- NWF of 50 graphemes per minute (g.p.m.) by the middle of first grade

This is the first benchmark assessment period in which ORF and RTF are administered. The winter interim benchmark for ORF is 20. The recommendation from the University of Oregon during this period before the norms are available is that any students whose RTF score is at least 25% of their ORF score can be considered at benchmark.

We will explore the first grade results for two imaginary students, Enrique and Emily, to model an approach to booklet analysis. Both students are at about the same level in ORF and RTF, but there is a great difference between the other subskills for these students. For most students, ORF is just emerging in the middle of first grade. ORF is more useful in identifying the benchmark for established readers than it is for the struggling readers who are usually below 20 on this measure. Students can score between 10 and 20 because they have memorized some sight words. For them, the other indicators are more informative in determining where to start intervention. Typically NWF and PSF give better information than ORF for deciding how to group students, as discussed in Chapter 3. It's not that we will throw out the ORF information, but rather that the other indicators may be more revealing at the middle of first grade.

Step 1: Analyze the Whole Picture

Emily and Enrique both got about the same score in ORF and RTF (see Table 4.8). Both their ORF scores are below the interim benchmark of 20. Are these students at about the same level in early reading because their ORF scores are so close? In order to answer that question we need to look at their scores on the other indicators. On PSF, Emily's score of 24 is considerably below

Table 4.8

Emily and
Enrique's
Student
Booklets

First Grade
—Mid-year

Two First Grade Students

Emily
Dynamic Indicators of
Basic Literacy Skills™ 6th Ed.
University of Oregon

First Grade Benchmark Assessment

Name: _____ Teacher: _____

School: _____ District: _____

	Benchmark 1 Beginning/ Fall	Benchmark 2 Middle/ Winter	Benchmark 3 End/ Spring
Date	9-16-02	1-9-03	
Letter Naming Fluency	32		
Phoneme Segmentation Fluency	10	24	
Nonsense Word Fluency	7	10	
DIBELS Oral Reading Fluency		(middle score) 13	(middle score)
Retell Fluency (Optional)		(middle score) 9	(middle score)
Word Use Fluency (Optional)	(Optional) 8	(Optional) 15	(Optional)

Enrique
Dynamic Indicators of
Basic Early Literacy Skills™ 6th Ed.
University of Oregon

First Grade Benchmark Assessment

Name: _____ Teacher: _____

School: _____ District: _____

	Benchmark 1 Beginning/ Fall	Benchmark 2 Middle/ Winter	Benchmark 3 End/ Spring
Date	9-16-02	1-9-03	
Letter Naming Fluency	45		
Phoneme Segmentation Fluency	21	39	
Nonsense Word Fluency	16	48	
DIBELS Oral Reading Fluency		(middle score) 15	(middle score)
Retell Fluency (Optional)		(middle score) 10	(middle score)
Word Use Fluency (Optional)	(Optional) 34	(Optional) 57	(Optional)

	Emily		Enrique		Benchmark	
	Fall	**Winter**	**Fall**	**Winter**	**Fall**	**Winter**
LNF	32	–	45	–	37	
PSF	10	24	21	39	35	35
NWF	7	10	16	48	24	50
ORF	–	13	–	15	–	20
RTF	–	9	–	10	–	n/a
WUF	9	15	34	57	n/a	n/a

the benchmark of 35, whereas Enrique's score of 39 is above it. Emily's fall LNF score was 32. Since LNF is not included at the winter benchmark for first grade, this score is not available to us. It might be helpful to know if she improved during the last few months and is above 40; letter naming fluency can be administered by using one of the three kindergarten benchmark assessments for LNF.

After looking at all the scores, we should be more concerned about Emily than Enrique in spite of their almost equivalent ORF scores. Emily's scoring booklet will help us determine where to start her intervention. Here are Emily's levels of risk compared to interim benchmarks:

- PSF-24—Emerging
- NWF-10—Deficit
- ORF-13—Some risk
- RTF-9—Was more than 25% of ORF
- WUF-15—Compare to local norms

Step 2: Note Areas of Concern or Questions

Despite scoring similarly to Emily in ORF, Enrique is more likely to reach the ORF benchmark of 40. His phonemic awareness is better developed and his knowledge of sound-letter combinations is superior, as measured by NWF.

Emily's letter naming score was below benchmark in the fall. She is considerably below where she needs to be in phonemic awareness, having missed the benchmark of 35 p.s.p.m. in both the fall and the winter. The low level of NWF may well be caused by a lack of fluency in both letter naming and sounds. Additionally, her low level of WUF is a red flag.

Step 3: Study Error Patterns on Each of the Booklet Pages

Phoneme Segmentation Fluency (PSF)

- **Does the student know how to segment phonemes?**
  Emily has no circled words on her scoring booklet (see Table 4.9), which means that she never repeated the entire word back to the examiner. She appears to understand the task and demonstrated that she knows how to segment words into sounds.

Table 4.9

**Emily—
Phoneme
Segmentation
Fluency
Scoring Page**

Emily—Phoneme Segmentation Fluency (PSF)							Probe 5
star	/s/ /t/ /ar/		give	/g/ /i/ /v/			4 /6
yet	/y/ /e/ /t/		hid	/h/ /i/ /d/			5 /6
sled	/s/ /l/ /e/ /d/		walk	/w/ /o/ /k/			4 /7
you	/y/ /oo/		hook	/h/ /uu/ /k/			4 /5
she	/sh/ /ea/		swing	/s/ /w/ /i/ /ng/			4 /6
coal	/k/ /oa/ /l/		oak	/oa/ /k/			3 /5
safe	/s/ /ai/ /f/		bones	/b/ /oa/ /n/ /z/			___ /7
							Total 24

- **How many times does the student partially segment rather than completely segment the word?**
  Emily partially segmented rather than completely segmented the words with the blends *st* and *sl* (*star* and *sled*).

- **How accurate is the student in segmenting phonemes?**
  Emily's accuracy is an issue since she got only 24 correct out of the 35, an accuracy rate of 66%.

- **How fluent is the student in segmenting phonemes?**
  Emily is not very fluent because she attempted only 35 phoneme segments in a minute. With a target of 35 phonemes in a minute, she would have to have 100% accuracy to reach the benchmark.

- **How accurate is the student's knowledge of initial sounds?**
  Emily demonstrates a strong awareness of the initial sound in words. She got nearly all initial sounds correct in the words she was given.

- **How accurate is the student's knowledge of ending sounds?**
  Emily is also fairly strong in final sounds, with all correct except two of the more difficult sounds, *ng* and *v*.

- **How accurate is the student's knowledge of vowels?**
  Emily's knowledge of short vowel sounds is not well established. Emily correctly isolated the short *i* three times in the words *give*, *hid*, and *swing*. She made errors on both short *e* words. She missed the short *u* and short *o* once each.

Nonsense Word Fluency (NWF)

NWF is the next indicator for the kindergarten benchmark (see Table 4.10).

Table 4.10

**Emily—
Nonsense
Word
Fluency
Scoring Page**

Emily—Nonsense Word Fluency (NWF)					
k̸ı̸k	w̸ø̸x̸	s̸ı̸g	f̸ø̸x̸	y̸ı̸s	6 /15
k̸ø̸x̸	f̸ø̸k̸	ø̸x̸	z̸ı̸ø̸	z̸ø̸x̸	4 /14
l a n	n u l	z e m	o g	n o m	__ /14
y u f	p o s	v o k	v i v	f e g	__ /15
b u b	d i j	s i j	v u s	t o s	__ /15
					Total 10

- **Does the student read sound-by-sound or by whole word?**
  Emily read all the attempted words sound-by-sound. Students who can complete the nonsense word fluency task by pronouncing the whole word, as indicated with a solid line under the whole word, are at a more advanced level in letter-sound correspondence than those who read sound-by-sound. Students reading the whole word are most likely so automatic in associating a sound with each letter symbol that they can recognize letter-sound sequences automatically and then say a whole word. Some students will give the word both ways, indicated by individual lines under each letter and then another line under the entire word. While this will take more time and negatively impact the student's score, most students who can do this will reach benchmark. This pattern suggests that the student has developed an effective strategy of sounding out unknown words and is obtaining a reasonable pronunciation, followed by not yet abandoning the intermediate step of going sound-by-sound before blending. An instructional goal for this type of student is to teach him to fade away from the scaffolding of the extra intermediate step. If you believe that the student doesn't need to use the sound-by-sound strategy and has simply misunderstood the instructions, say "or" with emphasis when giving the instructions on his next progress monitoring assessment.

- **How accurate is the student's knowledge of sound-letter correspondence?**
  Emily is still struggling at the accuracy level. She got only ten correct out of the 29 she attempted, an accuracy rate of 34%.

- **How fluent is the student in reading nonsense words?**
  Emily is not very fluent. She attempted 29 letter-sound correspondences, which is only 58% of the 50 letter-sounds-per-minute benchmark.

- **How accurate is the student's knowledge of initial letters?**
  Emily is very accurate in reading the initial sounds. She got all but two initial sounds correct, and the two that she missed are some of the more difficult and less common letters, *y* and *a*. If we look back at the PSF scoring page, it is possible to see that she did accurately segment the sound of *y* in the PSF task, but doesn't appear to know the letter *y*. Looking back at the fall LNF scoring sheet, she did not name the letter *y* at that time either.

- **How accurate is the student's knowledge of final letters?**
  Emily missed nearly all of the final letters in the nonsense word chart. Interestingly, she got some letters right when they were in the initial position of a word, yet missed them when they appeared in the final position, as we can see with the letter *z*. Since she missed nearly all of the vowels, it is possible that once she missed the medial vowel she became flustered and didn't concentrate on the final letter.

- **How accurate is the student's knowledge of middle vowels?**
  Emily missed all the vowels in this screening. It's interesting to note that she did know short *i* in the PSF task, so she may be able to hear and repeat the sounds when spoken to her. Clearly she is having difficulty recalling and pronouncing the sounds of the short vowels during reading, as measured in the NWF assessment.

Oral Reading Fluency (ORF)

- **How accurate is the student's reading of words in passages?**
  Emily read only 13 words correctly out of 20 words attempted in this passage (see Table 4.11), for an accuracy rate of 65%. On the other two passages she read, her accuracy was 56% and 42%, which is very low.

- **How fluent is the student's reading of words in passages?**
  Because Emily attempted to read only 20 words during the minute of assessment, her fluency is quite low. She attempted only 22 and 25 in the other two passages. If the passage where she attempted 25 was not the one recorded on the outside chart, then she had an even lower accuracy rate for this passage. The minimum number of words she should have attempted is 20 if the examiner was prompting every three seconds, so this is a very dysfluent rate.

- **How well did the student read nonphonetic sight words?**
  In looking at all three passages that Emily read, the list of common words that are not phonetically regular that she read includes: *and*, *the*, and *said*. She appears to be making good progress in memorizing some of these common words.

- **How well did the student read phonetically regular words?**

  Emily successfully decoded a number of one syllable phonetically regular words, including *wind*. It is also encouraging to note that she successfully read the word *winter* in the first passage, which is a two-syllable word. It is impossible to know whether she knows this word by sight, but if she sounded it out, then she is showing her skills in sounding out words that have more than one syllable.

- **Did the student remember a word provided and successfully read it the second time it occurs in the passage?**

  The examiner presented the word *blew* to Emily and she read it correctly when it was repeated two words later. Yet she did not read *rained* correctly after it was provided and it appeared again.

Table 4.11

Emily— Oral Reading Fluency Scoring Page

Emily—Oral Reading Fluency (ORF) and Retell Fluency (RTF)	
Spring is Coming	
It has been so cold this winter.	7
The wind blew and blew. It rained	14
and rained. The days have been gray	21
and dark. I had to wear mittens and a	30
hat to school every day. It even	37
snowed twice.	39
Retell: 9	Total: 13

0 1 2 3 4 5 6 7 8 (9) 10 11 12 13 14 15 16 17 18 19 20 21

Retell Fluency (RTF)

- **What percent of ORF is the student's RTF score?**

  Emily's RTF was 9 and her ORF was 13 (see Table 4.11). This is 69%. Although this does meet the 25% guideline, with such a low ORF score, it is difficult to draw much from this information.

Word Use Fluency (WUF)

WUF is the last indicator for the kindergarten benchmark (see Table 4.12).

- **How many utterances are correct versus incorrect?**

  Emily had two correct and three incorrect, which is a fairly low rate of accuracy of 40%.

Table 4.12

Emily—Word Use Fluency (WUF)		
real	0 1 2 ③ 4 5 6 7 8 9 10 11 12 13 14 15	_0_ c Ⓘ
horse	0 1 2 3 ④ 5 6 7 8 9 10 11 12 13 14 15	_4_ Ⓒ I
funny	0 1 2 3 ④ 5 6 7 8 9 10 11 12 13 14 15	_0_ c Ⓘ
doing	0 1 2 ③ 4 5 6 7 8 9 10 11 12 13 14 15	_0_ c Ⓘ
face	0 1 2 3 4 5 6 ⑦ 8 9 10 11 12 13 14 15	_7_ Ⓒ I
dry	0 1 2 3 ④ 5 6 7 8 9 10 11 12 13 14 15	_0_ c Ⓘ
cow	0 1 2 3 ④ 5 6 7 8 9 10 11 12 13 14 15	_4_ Ⓒ I
		Total 15

- **Was the student equally responsive to abstract and concrete words?**

  Emily was more accurate in her responses to the concrete words presented to her (*horse* and *face*). All of the words she missed (*real*, *funny*, and *doing*) were abstract.

- **Did the student take much time to respond?**

  Emily attempted seven words, which means that she most likely took several seconds to think plus several seconds to respond.

- **Did the student's total points on this indicator come primarily from short or long responses?**

  Emily's total score of 11 was all cumulated from short responses of two to five words on the three words she got correct. Even on the four words she got incorrect, her responses were very short.

- **How much variability was there in the length of responses?**

  Emily's length of utterance was not particularly variable. Many times a student will give a much longer response for one or two words while most of their utterances for other words will be shorter and similar in length. This is more typical than the pattern we saw with Emily.

Step 4: Summarize Observations for Intervention Lesson Plan

It would be a good idea to give Emily an LNF assessment to see if she has reached benchmark of 40. She needs systematic and explicit instruction in phonics, with some attention to further developing her phonemic awareness as well. Emily may benefit from instruction using a systematic and sequential phonics program delivered in a small group where she gets lots of time to practice each skill along the way. Explicit corrective feedback for her errors, with time for additional rounds of practice applying each phonics concept, is merited to get her reading 40 words per minute by year-end. A quick informal assessment to make sure that she can isolate and identify sounds in the initial, final, and medial position would be prudent. In the context of an intensive focus on teaching phonics, her phonemic awareness skills should also be stressed and linked to the phonics instruction. The immediate goal is for Emily to rapidly achieve the PSF and NWF goals, and also progress monitor ORF to make sure that she is applying the phonics concepts within text passage reading. Emily's low WUF also suggests that her overall language development is problematic, and that she needs daily practice in all areas—listening comprehension, vocabulary, and verbal expression.

Revisiting Intervention Groups

In Chapter 3 a process was outlined for grouping students based on scores for each indicator. It is essential to revisit the groups with an eye toward the individual error patterns that each student in a group is making. Two students may earn the same score on a subtest but their overall profile may suggest different instructional needs. As a final step before beginning to create lesson plans, open the test booklets of all three students in the group to the same page. Their error patterns may indicate whether they are appropriately grouped for instruction.

The questions suggested throughout this chapter are provided in Table 4.13 at the end of this chapter. Many teachers use this list of questions while analyzing student booklets.

Table 4.13

Questions for Analyzing Student Errors

Letter Naming Fluency
• How accurate is the student's letter naming skill?
• How fluent is the student in naming letters?
• Are more of the letters the student missed at the end of the alphabet?
• Did the student miss more lowercase letters than uppercase letters?
• Does the student get any letters correct one time and incorrect another time?
• Does the child correctly name the letters in their own name?
• Did the student skip more than one line, or not read across the row left to right?
Initial Sound Fluency
• How accurate is the student with initial sounds?
• How fluent is the student with initial sounds?
• Is the student more able to identify initial sounds when he can point to the answers rather than supply the sound?
• Look for any other unusual error patterns.
Phoneme Segmentation Fluency
• Does the student know how to segment phonemes?
• How many times does the student partially segment rather than completely segment the word?
• How accurate is the student in segmenting phonemes?
• How fluent is the student in segmenting phonemes?
• How accurate is the student's knowledge of initial sounds?
• How accurate is the student's knowledge of ending sounds?
• How accurate is the student's knowledge of vowels?
Nonsense Word Fluency
• Does the student provide sound-by-sound or whole word?
• How accurate is the student's knowledge of sound-letter correspondence?
• How fluent is the student in reading nonsense words?
• How accurate is the student's knowledge of initial letters?
• How accurate is the student's knowledge of final letters?
• How accurate is the student's knowledge of middle vowels?

Table 4.13

continued

Oral Reading Fluency
• How accurate is the student's reading of words in passages?
• How fluent is the student's reading of words in passages?
• How well did the student read nonphonetic sight words?
• How well did the student read phonetically regular words?
• Did the student remember a word provided and successfully read it the second time it occurs in the passage?
Retell Fluency
• What percent of ORF is the student's RTF score?
Word Use Fluency
• How many utterances are correct versus incorrect?
• Was the student equally responsive to abstract and concrete words?
• Did the student take much time to respond?
• Did the student's total points on this indicator come primarily from short or long responses?
• How much variability was there in the length of responses?

Table 4.14

Worksheet for Analyzing a Student Booklet

Kindergarten		
DIBELS Indicator	**Observations**	**Instructional Implications**
Initial Sound Fluency **ISF**		
Letter Naming Fluency **LNF**		
Phoneme Segmentation Fluency **PSF**		
Nonsense Word Fluency **NWF**		
Word Use Fluency **WUF**		
First Grade		
DIBELS Indicator	**Observations**	**Instructional Implications**
Letter Naming Fluency **LNF**		
Phoneme Segmentation Fluency **PSF**		
Nonsense Word Fluency **NWF**		
Oral Reading Fluency & Retell Fluency **ORF & RTF**		
Word Use Fluency **WUF**		
Second and Third Grade		
DIBELS Indicator	**Observations**	**Instructional Implications**
Oral Reading Fluency & Retell Fluency **ORF & RTF**		
Word Use Fluency **WUF**		
Nonsense Word Fluency **NWF** (If available)		
Other Indicators (If available)		

Chapter 5

Linking the Instruction to Student Need

After watching a student being tested, I was able to find out exactly why he was struggling with segmenting. When the tester said "mop," he heard only the /p/ and began a word with /p/. I never noticed that during classroom instruction. Concerns about a particular student continue to be supported by DIBELS results. I can see where exactly he is breaking down, which is helpful.

Kindergarten teacher

A critical step in planning data-informed intervention is to carefully select activities for intervention instruction that address the specific skill the student lacks. The closer the link between student needs and instruction, the more effective the intervention will be. Teachers must analyze instructional strategies and activities to identify exactly which skill each one teaches. Even if a school has purchased an intervention curriculum that provides lesson plans, teachers still need to know how to link skill deficits and activities to appreciate why they are teaching a particular lesson, and so they can constantly evaluate the effectiveness of a particular curriculum for their students. All the work invested in analyzing the student booklet to determine student needs may be for naught if this step is not done well.

The topic of this chapter is how to map appropriate instructional strategies to student needs. This information is the bridge between analyzing the DIBELS data in a student booklet and preparing a lesson plan. (Preparing lesson plans will be discussed in the next chapter.) Intervention instruction is most effective when teachers can take any activity or instructional strategy and clearly pinpoint which skill it is teaching. Both sides of the equation have to be equally strong. Without a strong perception about what an activity is teaching, all the in-depth analysis to appropriately group students and to see error patterns in the DIBELS student booklet may not result in maximum student improvements.

Intervention Instruction Is Intensive and Focused

Intervention instruction should be intensive and focused. Intensive, focused instruction allows the struggling reader to practice a limited set of skills while the instructor gives immediate corrective feedback to errors. Working in small groups not only enables students to respond to more questions than would be possible in a classroom setting, but also allows the teacher to tailor a follow-up question based on whether the student answered correctly or incorrectly. Teachers can explicitly teach a skill and then give the students a chance to immediately apply the skill. It is the targeted question-error-question loop that makes it different from whole-class instruction.

Intervention instruction is not intended to serve as the entire reading curriculum, but rather is intended to address a small number of essential skills at a time. Each lesson typically covers three to five activities, and most interventionists focus on a couple of skills within a narrow range. It is not advisable to cover all five components of reading instruction during an intervention group time, which typically is planned for one or two 30-minute sessions daily. A lesson may focus on one skill area, or it may span a couple of different skills, such as phonological awareness and letter-sound correspondences. For kindergarten students, the lesson may be primarily focused on phonological awareness with strategic instruction in letter knowledge for some groups that have deficiencies in both areas. For a first grade intervention group, a phonics lesson might include a phonemic awareness segment integrated into the lesson that is mainly focused on explicit instruction in letter-sound correspondence. For example, if the primary focus that day is on associating the /sh/ sound with the consonant digraph sh, most of the time would be spent practicing reading and writing words that include *sh*. However, the instructor may integrate a phonemic awareness routine such as thumbs up for words that contain the /sh/ sound in the initial or final position as a warm-up activity. But time is too short in one phonics lesson to spend too much time on other skills, such as a read-aloud to provide exposure to new vocabulary words. Vocabulary instruction should be part of the core instruction. Students who have very low vocabularies are typically in two groups a day—one just for vocabulary and the other to work on decoding. Attempting to thoroughly teach too many skills at a time can split the short intervention time too many ways, which risks diminishing its effectiveness. Different skills can be taught over time, but not all within the same lesson.

The focus of each group's instruction should be articulated, preferably at the top of the lesson plan. For example, assume that the DIBELS scores of a group of mid-year first graders showed that these students were at risk on PSF and NWF, and their ORF was also very weak. Even though these students have low ORF scores, the instruction would not initially focus on developing fluency at the passage level. Their low PSF and NWF scores indicate that the deficit is at a far lower developmental level than connected text in passages. In general, the intervention instruction would begin at the lowest deficient skill and move up. However, since these students are already in the middle of first grade, time is of the essence to get them back on-track. The teacher needs to accelerate their development of phonemic awareness and focus on mastering letter-sound correspondences. This group will work at mastering their ability to understand sounds in words and to apply letter-sound knowledge while decoding consonant-vowel-consonant words accurately before moving to reading sentences and passages for fluency.

For the first-grade intervention group described above, the initial intervention lesson would focus on phonemic awareness and early decoding of simple words. Very little time will be spent on other areas, such as vocabulary instruction. In fact, not all the students in this group may need help with vocabulary. The students in this group were placed together because of their common need for help in phonemic awareness and their low ability to read nonsense words. Sometimes an interventionist may be able to include some explicit vocabulary instruction during the course of dialogue while working on phonemic awareness. But most of the time, this is very difficult to do. The words that are initially used for learning how to segment and manipulate sounds will contain only three or four sounds, and therefore are very common words that are typically part of the student's oral vocabulary. If a student's vocabulary is especially low, then he needs to be placed in a group for oral language development, in addition to his intervention group for phonemic awareness and phonics. Low oral vocabulary is a major red flag, and if not addressed, can impair the student's fluency and comprehension even after his decoding skills are improving.

Intervention Instruction Should Not Replace the Core Reading Curriculum

Because intervention instruction suggested in this book focuses on only a couple of skills at a time, it is critical that students attend intervention group when it won't interfere with the language arts instruction time. Students must continue to receive decoding, vocabulary, fluency, comprehension, and writing instruction in the core program while intensively working on their weak skills in intervention group. Intervention instruction must be in addition to, rather than replace or supplant, the core reading instruction.

This suggestion that intervention instruction supplements, but does not replace, the core instruction is also emphasized in a publication by the Center for Reading and Language Arts at University of Texas called *Three-Tier Reading Model*. As expressed in this publication, "For some students, focused instruction within the regular classroom setting is not enough. To get back on track, these students require supplemental instruction in addition to the time allotted for core reading instruction" (University of Texas Center for Reading and Language Arts 2003).

The Three-Tier Reading Model

The University of Texas' Center for Reading and Language Arts (UTCRLA) advocates a "Three-Tier Model" for reading whereby there are alternative layers of instruction for children. The three "tiers" of reading instruction are described in their publication as:

- Tier I—the core reading instruction that all students receive, generally 90 to 120 minutes daily.

- Tier II—30 minutes of daily small group reading instruction that students who do not score at benchmark on the screening assessment receive. This instruction is *in addition to* the core reading instruction.

- Tier III—60 minutes of daily small group reading instruction that students who do not make adequate progress with Tier II instruction receive. The 60 minutes is delivered in two daily 30-minute intervention sessions and is *in addition to* the core reading instruction.

Table 5.1 has an overview of the model.

Table 5.1

Overview of the Three-Tier Model

Tier	Type of Instruction	Curriculum Materials	# Minutes of Daily Instruction	Frequency of Progress Monitoring Assessment
I	Classroom	Core Comprehensive	60-120	Not needed
II	Small group (3-5)	Supplemental	Core + 30	Bi-weekly
III	Small group (3)	Supplemental	Core + 60	Bi-weekly

Under the Three-Tier Model, any student who is not making adequate progress in achieving early literacy skills with the core program receives supplemental instruction to enhance the classroom instruction. Children whose skills don't progress after a reasonable time in the Tier II level of intervention receive more intense intervention. Only after a child doesn't make adequate progress with both Tier II and Tier III intervention is he referred for testing for reading disabilities. This model is depicted graphically as a triangle in Table 5.2.

Table 5.2

The Three-Tier Model

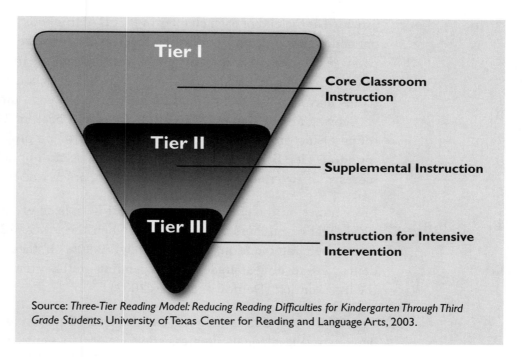

Source: *Three-Tier Reading Model: Reducing Reading Difficulties for Kindergarten Through Third Grade Students*, University of Texas Center for Reading and Language Arts, 2003.

The Three-Tier Model has been widely discussed and studied by states and districts as they implement the Reading First program. Increasingly, schools, whether they are receiving Reading First funding or not, are finding that the Three-Tier Model, or a variation of the model, is a helpful framework in conceptualizing how to improve students' reading scores. Some variations of this model include providing Tier II intervention instruction for 20 minutes daily, or placing students with at-risk DIBELS scores into Tier III after six to nine weeks of intervention without having them go through one or two entire cycles of Tier II instruction. The Three-Tier Model and some of the studies of the model are discussed in this section.

The effectiveness of a strong classroom-level comprehensive core reading program (CCRP) has been extensively researched, resulting in the finding that children become better readers with a CCRP. One summary of several research studies suggests that with a strong core curriculum program "only about 6% or less of children should be expected to experience reading problems requiring secondary intervention" (Denton & Mathes 2003).

Tier II is the first line of intervention in the UTCRLA model. Students who are below benchmark in DIBELS or another early literacy assessment are placed in a group of three to five students for 30 minutes of instruction provided by a teacher or aide in the classroom, or as a pull-out group. The UTCRLA model calls this tier "supplemental instruction" with a suggested duration of ten to twelve weeks. The materials used for this instruction should be specialized, research-based programs. (A list of recommended supplemental materials is provided at the end of each chapter in Part II of this book.) The UTCRLA recommends that progress monitoring for Tier II groups be administered every two weeks to see if the students are benefiting from the instruction. After ten to twelve weeks in Tier II, the student who achieves benchmark on DIBELS scores may stop intervention. Students who make good progress but are not yet scoring at benchmark on DIBELS are placed back in Tier II for another round of instruction. Students who show little or no progress with the first round of Tier II instruction, and students who do not achieve benchmark scores after two rounds of Tier II instruction, are moved to Tier III.

Five studies on the effectiveness of Tier II have been examined and summarized. The researchers concluded that when the lowest 12-18% of students were given intervention, approximately 70-90% of these intervention students were reading at grade level, depending on the intensity and duration of the intervention (Denton & Mathes 2003).

Tier III intervention is the most intense level. Children whose skills are not demonstrating adequate progress after one or two, ten to twelve week rounds of Tier II intervention are moved to Tier III. The UTCRLA calls this tier "Intensive Intervention." The UTCRLA recommends that Tier III students receive a total of one hour of small group intervention broken into two slots of 30 minutes each. They advise that the district must decide how Tier III and special education services are related. They also suggest that the materials can be the same as for Tier II, or they may be different, depending on the needs of the students in the group.

In this book, the term "intervention instruction" is used to designate both Tier II and Tier III instruction. Although the Three-Tier Model is a very effective framework to articulate that groups are flexible and intervention is provided at varying levels of intensity depending upon student need, in practice, the lines may blur more than this model suggests. Increasing levels of intensity can be accomplished in a gradual step-like fashion as the needs of the students in the group merit.

Increasing Intensity and Complexity of Intervention Over Time

Increasing Intensity of Instruction

What differentiates Tier III from Tier II instruction is that the intervention is more intensive. Greater intensity can be achieved in several ways:

- Reduce the size of the group to enable more corrective feedback

- Increase the time spent in intervention instruction

- Change the materials so they are more systematic, sequential, multisensory, or provide more repetitions

Instructional intensity is also adjusted by providing more examples, a wider range of examples, breaking a task into smaller steps, spending longer time on a task, and by asking the child to move along a continuum in type of response (see Table 5.3) (Good, Kame'enui, & Chard 2002).

Table 5.3

Ways to Adjust Instructional Intensity of Responses

Low Intensity	Medium Intensity	High Intensity
Yes/no response	Oral response	Oral independent response (no choices offered)
Point to correct answer	Multiple choice response	Written response

Complexity of Instruction Varies

An effective intervention instructor must be knowledgeable about how to change the complexity of the instruction. When an interventionist begins to design instruction, it may be necessary to think through how to adjust activities from simpler to more complex by formally documenting this logic in lesson plans. Eventually these shifts become so intuitive that the interventionist can make these adjustments on the spot during a lesson without formal pre-planning.

Intervention activities follow a progression from simple to more complex. For example, most students learn to isolate the initial sound in a word, then the final sound and lastly the middle sounds. The medial vowel sound is generally the most difficult for students to isolate. Therefore, the obvious order of instruction in teaching phoneme identification would be initial, ending, and medial sound.

Another way to increase complexity is by distinguishing between open and closed sorts. Generally a closed sort is easier than an open sort. For this reason it is best to use a closed sort when first teaching students a new feature of a word, such as how to focus on the initial sound. In word sorts, students discover patterns as they figure out how words are alike or different by examining words with and without the feature. If the interventionist is asking students to sort between two options, and all the words fit into one of the two categories, this is a closed sort. An open sort is more difficult because students have to decide if a word belongs in either of the two or whether it is another unspecified possibility.

Two examples of thoughtful progressions from easier to more complex intervention instruction follow.

Example 1: Teaching Sounds

- Activity: sound train and a set of picture cards—each train represents a sound. The student has a set of pictures and places the pictures on the train that have the same initial sound as the focus sound.
  - First level (easiest): all the pictures begin with the target sound and can be placed on the train. For example, the target sound is /h/ in the initial position and all the pictures begin with /h/. Examples could include *hill, hat, house.*
  - Second level (middle): closed sort with two initial sounds that are distinctly different—an /h/ train and an /m/ train. All the pictures fit on one train or the other.
  - Third level (hardest): open sort with three sounds that are close in articulation—an /n/, /m/, and /ng/ train (all three nasal sounds are similar). This is a sort based on ending sounds. Additionally, some pictures don't fit on any of the three trains. The pictures could include *ring, lamb,* and *sun,* which would be placed on the trains, and *knife, leaf,* and *mouse,* which would not be placed on a train.

Example 2: Teaching Reading and Writing Words With Short Vowel Sounds

- Activities to apply sound-letter correspondence in spelling and reading CVC words with short vowels.
  - First level (easiest): student picks a picture from a small set of choices and places it on a box in the middle of a word strip that already has the beginning and ending letters. For example, the student places the picture of a pan on the strip with p_n.
  - Second level: student picks a picture from a bag, places it on the middle box for the vowel, and then writes the beginning and ending consonant. For example, the strip has three empty boxes. The student places the picture of a pan in the middle box and then writes the letter *p* in the first box and the letter *n* in the last box.
  - Third level: student looks at a picture and spells CVC words in boxes (Elkonin box technique) using a moveable alphabet, such as magnetic letter tiles. The picture of the word helps the child remember what he is supposed to be writing, and the three boxes indicate the number of letters needed to spell the word. The student chooses the letters from a selection of five consonants and two vowels. For ex-

ample, the letters might be *m, t, b, f, p, a, o*. The pictures could be *bat, top,* and *fat*.

- ◆ Fourth level: student spells CVC words with a moveable alphabet. Student has to find the letters from a board with all the letters of the alphabet and spell a spoken CVC word without any lines to tell him how many letters are needed to spell the word and without a picture reference.

- ◆ Fifth level: student writes the words from dictation.

The Focus of the Intervention Changes Over Time

For any given intervention group, the focus of instruction will evolve as time passes. Once the students demonstrate mastery at a level, the focus moves to a more complex skill. For example, imagine that a kindergarten intervention group is formed just after the fall benchmark. Based on DIBELS scores, students in the group need to develop both letter naming and phonemic awareness skills. Within two weeks of administering the fall benchmark, the students are placed in a group and are receiving their first lesson.

Initially instruction will focus equally on phonemic awareness and letter naming. For phonemic awareness, the interventionist may begin work on initial sounds. Imagine that early on in her work with this group, the interventionist uses an activity that develops initial sound awareness using miniature objects in a box. She pulls two objects out of the box, a cat and a pan, and asks the students to emphasize the sound at the beginning of each word. She tells the group that all the objects in the box start with one of the two sounds—/k/ or /p/. Students take turns picking an object out of the box, saying the name of the object, the initial sound of the selected object, and then the initial sounds of the two piles. Then the child decides which pile the selected object belongs in, based on the initial sound.

The other focus of this group's intervention instruction initially will be letter naming. Although the group will start with about equal time on letter naming and phonemic awareness, over the course of a month the time on letter naming will likely diminish as students learn to identify and name letters more automatically. As students improve their letter naming skills, the interventionist can devote more instructional time to phonemic awareness.

Assume for a moment that, by the end of the first month of intervention, the group is making good progress with letter naming. With this progress, the interventionist decides to concentrate more on phonemic awareness and reduce the focus on letter naming. Now her lesson plans show that 25 minutes is spent on phonemic awareness and only 5 minutes on letter naming.

In addition to more time on phonemic awareness, the focus of the phonemic awareness activities has also shifted a bit. Over the course of the month the group has worked on activities to isolate and identify initial sounds, ending sounds, and middle sounds. They have demonstrated proficiency in identifying and saying not only sounds that are distinctly different, such as /sh/ and /v/, but also sounds that are close together in articulation, such as /f/ and /v/. Their work includes more time now on segmenting and blending sounds using manipulatives so they can push an object while saying each distinct sound in three and four phoneme words.

If we could check in on this group in another month, they would most likely be working on yet more advanced phonemic awareness skills. They might be ready to add, delete, and substitute sounds to make new words. All of this is done without letters because it is phonemic awareness, not phonics. The students are learning to distinguish the sounds in words without using letters. At this point, they work on letter naming only once a week. On Fridays, they work with an activity called the Alphabet Arc to make sure that they have retained their skill in naming and placing all the 26 letters on the appropriate place on the alphabet arc.

Decisions About When to Exit a Student or Refer for Testing

When Do Students Exit an Intervention Group?

A general guideline for when a student is ready to exit an intervention group is when his score on the skill that must be established reaches benchmark and stays there for at least two progress monitoring periods. Most schools administer progress monitoring every two or three weeks. It is important to consider where a student is in relation to the skills that are supposed to be established by the next DIBELS benchmark period, not just what was supposed to be established at the last benchmark assessment date. The expectations continue to grow across the year, as evidenced by increasing interim benchmark scores up to the time when the skill is to be established. If for example, a student is in intervention in the middle of first grade and is lacking in both PSF and NWF, he would not be exited until both his PSF and NWF scores reach their respective benchmarks, even though initially instruction would only be focused on phonemic awareness. However, a student in the beginning of first grade who reaches 35 on PSF by mid-October may be exited from the intervention group if his score on NWF exceeds 24 as long as he is on track to reach the established level of 50 by the winter benchmark. (This is shown on the progress monitoring chart by whether the student's scores are on or above the aim-line. Instead of using the aimline, some schools estimate a series of weekly or monthly target scores between two interim benchmark scores.)

When schools first begin implementing intervention groups, one of the most common occurrences is that the teachers are hesitant to move a student out of an intervention group. This reluctance is normal because it is hard to know whether the student will retain the gains he has made. Most of the time when we catch students up in kindergarten and first grade, as evidenced by benchmark scores on DIBELS, they will not need extensive intervention again. If teachers are reluctant to exit a student, they can be reminded that it is always possible to continue to monitor the progress of a student after he exits the intervention group. If scores fall below benchmark, the student can be placed back into an intervention group.

Diagnostic Assessment Is Recommended After Lack of Response to Intervention

Students who have completed at least one round of Tier III intervention and whose skills are still not improving are candidates for further diagnostic testing. These students are easiest to spot by graphing progress monitoring scores for a group on the same graph, and comparing the rates of progress of the students in a group. What you see in Table 5.4 is that two of the students in the group are making significant progress. Then there is the third student, whose slope of improvement is too flat, especially in contrast to his peers, who started at approximately the same level and received the same intervention instruction. Clearly, the intervention is working with two of the students, but the third student's scores are not responding to the instruction. In this case, the third student would be referred for more extensive diagnostic testing and possibly referral for special education.

Table 5.4

Progress Monitoring

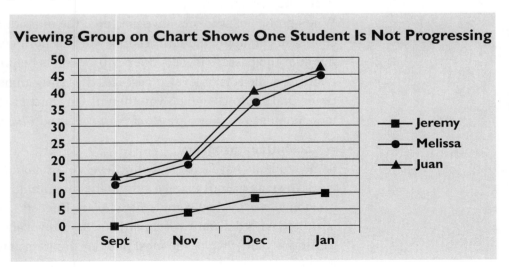

Planning Intervention Instruction

Purchasing or Designing an Intervention Curriculum

There are over 200 intervention curriculum programs available today. Only a few intervention programs have a broad focus; most are designed to develop only one skill, such as phonemic awareness or building fluency in reading text passages.

There are many good programs, and schools typically purchase a variety of programs so that they have materials for each of the five essential components. A school might select a program for each of the following areas:

- **A phonemic awareness and alphabetic principle program** for use with the lowest kindergarten and first grade students whose deficiencies are extensive and are in multiple areas. This type of program usually integrates instruction in phonological awareness, letter recognition, and the alphabetic principle in a well-designed set of lesson plans. These programs vary in cost and materials provided. Some of the most popular ones (from least to most costly) include *Road to the Code*, *Read Well,* and Scott Foresman *Early Reading Intervention.*

- **A systematic and sequential phonics intervention program.** Some first grade groups that are close to benchmark in phonemic awareness and letter recognition, but need extensive work in the alphabetic principle, may benefit from this type of program. The program provides the teacher with scripts to explicitly teach the sound and letter correspondence, lists of words to use for reading and writing, and decodable text for students to practice applying the concepts taught. Three programs that are very popular are *Phonics for Reading*, *Reading Mastery Plus*, and *Saxon Phonics and Spelling.*

- **A fluency program.** When groups of students have mastered the individual phonics concepts and can apply them in reading words accurately but are not fluent at the passage level, a fluency program is helpful. These programs provide sets of leveled passages that you can use for repeated, timed oral readings, which you then use to chart progress. Two of the most popular programs are *Read Naturally* and *Fluency First!*

- **A vocabulary program.** Some students have extremely low levels of oral language and need to work in small groups using a systematic program to introduce and use oral language. Typically students who are English Language Learners or others with deficient vocabularies work on vocabulary throughout the entire year. Two of the most popular programs are *Elements of Reading: Vocabulary* and *Language for Learning.*

There are many benefits of purchasing intervention programs, including:

- Provides a set of designed lesson plans that are systematic and sequential. It is difficult for teachers to prepare well-designed intervention lessons for each group. In some areas, such as phonics, it is complex to develop the sequence of instruction and write appropriate text that builds on the previously taught concepts.

- Includes scripts or sample instruction. Depending upon the teaching expertise of the intervention group instructor, scripts are critical. If instructional aides who have more limited training and experience teach the groups, lesson plans with scripts or sample instructions help provide scaffolding for this instruction.

- Validated with research. Pay attention to what use has been validated, especially the grade level and how it was delivered. Just because it is validated for one use doesn't necessarily mean that you can conclude how effective the program will be when implemented differently.

- Materials are provided. Programs that provide most or all the materials will save teachers time and make program implementation fidelity higher.

- Documentation is easier. When intervention groups are taught by Title I teachers or instructional aides, it is easier for the classroom teacher to understand what was taught if the instructor is following a program and writing in a log which lessons were covered each week.

Appropriate Use of Purchased Programs

Although there are many advantages of purchased intervention programs, it is critical to know how and when to use them. Ideally, the school will have a portfolio of programs to use, although not all intervention groups should be placed in a program. The best solution is that some of the groups are taught with published programs, and others are receiving teacher-designed intervention lessons in a specific area that is best addressed outside of a program. If teachers are using the DIBELS data to analyze student needs and place students in groups, it will be apparent that some groups have more pervasive needs than other groups. For the groups that have gaps in their knowledge, designing lessons that teach only what is missing is more effective for the students. Failure to use the data to inform instruction—placing all groups at the beginning of an intervention grogram and teaching every lesson—is inconsistent with the meaning of differentiated instruction.

One reason that some of the intervention programs are not right for every group is that they combine instruction in several skills and are not particularly flexible. One excellent intervention program commercially available that focuses on building early phonological awareness and phonics skills is Scott-Foresman's *Early Reading Intervention* program. This program was designed by researchers at the University of Oregon who are colleagues of the developers of DIBELS and was previously marketed by the reading center at the University of Oregon under the name of *Optimize*. Some advantages of using this program include that it is research-based, includes all the materials needed, and provides specific instructions that enable use by instructional aides. It is excellent for kindergarten students who are extremely low in both phonological and letter knowledge. Two disadvantages are that this program is expensive—over $1,000 per set—and it may be inflexible. It is designed to be taught by following the lessons in order from the first lesson through the ending lesson, although there is a placement test to assist in starting a group later in the sequence. This sequential series of lessons is especially helpful for students who are extremely deficient in the entire skill area of focus. However, it may not lend itself well when the instructor wishes to customize the lessons to exclude the skills the student already has mastered and to concentrate only on the missing skills.

Even the *Early Reading Intervention* program doesn't cover all the intervention needed for every student deficit at the kindergarten through third grade level; rather it is more focused on the kindergarten or first grade student who lacks phonemic awareness and early phonics. Most schools will need a set of different program materials to use for teaching phonemic awareness, phonics, fluency, vocabulary, and comprehension. At any time within a school, there is likely to be at least one group working on each of these skill areas; therefore, instructors need an assortment of program materials to use in instruction.

Many schools design their own intervention programs for phonological awareness through a combination of purchasing some materials and designing additional materials. There are many books that provide activities for developing phonological awareness and working with early CVC words for phonics. With these books, and some professional development, many teachers can do a good job of designing intervention in this area.

The area that is more challenging for developing your own intervention instruction is phonics. It is possible to design intervention lessons in phonics, but teachers need a deep knowledge to link the development of sound-letter correspondence with practice at the word and text level. The presentation of letter-sound correspondences must be systematic and the words and books children use for applying their letter-sound knowledge must be well correlated to the sequence. Therefore, most schools choose to use a structured program for intervention lessons focused on phonics. The money invested in purchasing a good program for phonics is well spent.

Deciding Where to Begin Intervention

Intervention starts at the lowest skill that is deficient and addresses this skill before moving up the continuum. Some examples include:

- Teaching a child to accurately and rapidly read individual words before working on building fluency in reading passages

- Making sure that the child demonstrates some proficiency with recognizing and expressing the initial sound in words before teaching the child to segment all the sounds in a word

- Verifying that the child can fluently and accurately recognize and name the letters as well as fluently and accurately segment the sounds in words before teaching the child to associate sounds with the letters

Generally, during the first lesson, the interventionist, whom we shall name "Joni" for this vignette, does a few routines that are designed to confirm the skills of the students in the group. For example, if all the kindergarten students in a group scored below 8 on LNF at the beginning of the year, the students probably need more work on letter naming. Joni can confirm this assumption quickly. She places a card with the letters A-E in front of one student, F-J in front of the second student, and K-O in front of the third student. Joni also gives each student five plastic letters, matching the ones on their cards. She asks each student to name each letter and place it on the card. As she watches the students, Joni makes a few notes and then shifts the cards and letters until each student has worked with all three cards. The last two cards are used to complete the alphabet. This entire routine takes about ten minutes. With this simple activity, Joni confirms whether the students are struggling with letter names.

Next Joni assesses the students' knowledge of phonological awareness. Because this group of kindergarten students all scored below 10 on ISF, she is concerned about whether any of the students are missing levels of phonological awareness that are even more elementary than identifying the initial sounds in words. First Joni asks all the students to stand and walk one step for each word in a sentence. Then Joni asks the students to clap syllables in their names, and other names they suggest. Next she asks the students to sit and match picture cards for words that rhyme. In the 15 minutes these activities take, she has observed that all three students appear to understand the concept of a word, how to segment syllables in words, and can identify the sounds in words that rhyme. Therefore, Joni has confirmed that this group is in fact ready to work on phonemic awareness, specifically at the level of initial sounds in words. (If the students are deficient in any of the lower skills, instruction would begin at that level.)

This short vignette is an example of the type of informal assessment that may be needed on the first day of an intervention group to confirm assumptions made from DIBELS screening scores and to further refine ideas for instructional activities.

Informal Assessment for Advanced Decoding Skills

The DIBELS provides sufficient information in the areas of phonemic awareness (ISF and PSF scores) and decoding of CVC words with short vowels (NWF scores). Yet, there are many advanced phonics skills that can cause a student who reaches benchmark in NWF to not achieve benchmark in ORF. Although the ORF score tells the teacher that the student is not reading as fluently as she should, it doesn't typically give enough information to determine where to begin her intervention instruction.

In order to learn more about where her difficulties in decoding are, it may be helpful to do further, more informal assessments. There are a variety of informal decoding assessments available. Most of them are designed to ask the student to read specific nonsense or read words so the teacher can analyze the student's skills in reading the following:

- Consonant digraphs and trigraphs

- Consonant blends

- Word endings (*ang*, *alk*, and *ing*)

- Long vowels

- Diphthongs and other vowels

- R-controlled vowels

- Multisyllabic words

Through analyzing error patterns on these words, it is possible to better pinpoint what to instruct.

Stepping Stone Skills Are Sequential

DIBELS has forced me to look at how my children learn. I firmly believe in the stair-step model of learning to read. I have been more conscious of where my students 'sit' on those stairs. DIBELS has been a kind of shot in the arm.

Indiana teacher

DIBELS indicators incorporate a progression that Roland Good sometimes refers to as the "stepping stones to early literacy." The order in the DIBELS indicators is listed below.

- ISF—25 initial sounds per minute by the middle of kindergarten

- PSF—35 phoneme segments per minute by the end of kindergarten

- NWF—50 graphemes per minute by the middle of first grade

- ORF—40 words per minute by the end of first grade, 90 by the end of second grade, and 110 by the end of third grade

Additionally, LNF is used as a risk indicator with an established level of 40 letters per minute by the end of kindergarten.

Table 5.5

DIBELS Benchmarks as Stepping Stones to Early Literacy

	ISF	LNF	PSF	NWF	ORF
Benchmark Time	K–Winter	K–Spring	K–Spring	1st–Spring	1st, 2nd, 3rd–Spring
Established Benchmark Level	25 i.s.p.m. (initial sounds per minute)	40 l.n.p.m. (letter names per minute)	35 p.s.p.m. (phoneme segments per minute)	50 g.p.m. (graphemes per minute)	40–110 w.p.m. (words per minute) 1st–40 2nd–90 3rd–110

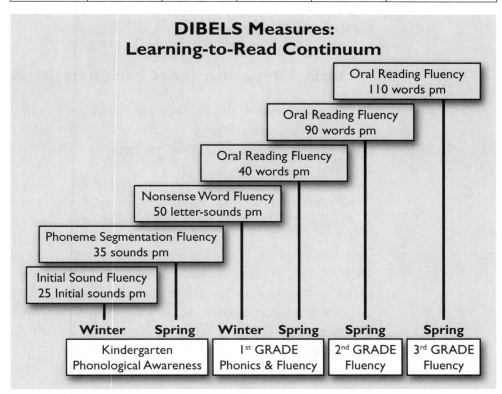

DIBELS Measures: Learning-to-Read Continuum

Oral Reading Fluency 110 words pm

Oral Reading Fluency 90 words pm

Oral Reading Fluency 40 words pm

Nonsense Word Fluency 50 letter-sounds pm

Phoneme Segmentation Fluency 35 sounds pm

Initial Sound Fluency 25 Initial sounds pm

Winter	Spring	Winter	Spring	Spring	Spring
Kindergarten Phonological Awareness		1st GRADE Phonics & Fluency		2nd GRADE Fluency	3rd GRADE Fluency

The stepping stone skills (see Table 5.5) in DIBELS are sequential and cumulative. (Some important literacy skills, such as vocabulary and comprehension, develop concurrently with decoding.) For most students who develop into good readers, the skills that are depicted in the DIBELS Stepping Stones develop sequentially. For example, a student who masters phonemic awareness and letter naming in kindergarten generally does well in early reading instruction and can decode unfamiliar words as well as read words that are in his sight vocabulary. Because of this sequential learning pattern, DIBELS data can be used to determine what is the lowest point of a student's deficit.

The DIBELS indicators follow a developmental progression from phonemic awareness and letter naming at the start to early phonics with the reading of CVC words (consonant-vowel-consonant) with short vowels, and then measuring fluency when reading grade level passages. There are a number of advanced decoding skills that must develop between the CVC words measured in the DIBELS NWF and being able to read grade-level passages fluently and accurately, as measured by ORF. Some of these advanced decoding skills include successfully decoding digraphs, consonant blends, long vowels, complex vowel spellings, multi-syllabic words, and prefixes and suffixes. Although measuring these advanced decoding concepts is not required for meeting the purpose of DIBELS, which is to predict which students are at benchmark, knowing which of these areas is causing difficulty for the below-benchmark students is necessary for planning where to begin intervention. As mentioned above, an informal assessment to measure advanced phonics skills can be helpful for some at-risk students.

DIBELS Benchmarks Are Minimums Rather Than Goals

In DIBELS, the benchmark levels are *minimum acceptable* levels rather than the goal. The goal is for most students to be above these benchmarks. In fact, other oral reading fluency levels are generally a bit higher than the DIBELS benchmarks.

Teachers may notice that DIBELS scores have two sets of labels for the three levels of scores given. The two sets of labels are shown in Table 5.6.

The labels under Established Benchmarks are used once the score for a DIBELS measure reaches its highest level. These scores can be used to measure any student's proficiency at any age with regard to that measure and will not change no matter how old the student. Interim benchmarks are provided to help see what level a student needs to achieve along the way to have a high likelihood of reaching the benchmark for the next Stepping Stone.

Established benchmarks for ISF and PSF are reached in kindergarten, whereas established benchmarks for NWF are not reached until first grade. There

Table 5.6

Terms to Describe Levels of Risk

Established Benchmarks	Interim Benchmarks
Established	Low Risk
Emerging	Some Risk
Deficit	At Risk

Terms for Risk Levels First Grade Benchmarks						
	Beginning of Year (Fall)		Middle of Year (Winter)		End of Year (Spring)	
	Performance	Status	Performance	Status	Performance	Status
Phoneme Segmentation Fluency	0–9	Deficit	0–9	Deficit	0–9	Deficit
	10–34	Emerging	10–34	Emerging	10–34	Emerging
	35+	Established	35+	Established	35+	Established
Nonsense Word Fluency	0–12	At Risk	0–29	Deficit	0–29	Deficit
	13–23	Some Risk	30–49	Emerging	30–49	Emerging
	24+	Low Risk	50+	Established	50+	Established
Oral Reading Fluency			0–7	At Risk	0–19	At Risk
			8–19	Some Risk	20–39	Some Risk
			20+	Low Risk	40+	Low Risk

Note: There is a point when students are expected to reach a benchmark goal for each skill. Before that time, interim benchmarks are provided to measure progress toward the goal. The terms "At Risk," "Some Risk" and "Low Risk" are used to indicate the student's likelihood of reaching the benchmark. Categories "Deficit," "Emerging," and "Established" are used to indicate whether the goal was met, and if the goal was not met, how far below the goal the student is.

are no established benchmarks for ORF because it is expected that a student's oral reading fluency rate will continue to increase beyond third grade, up to the approximately 200 words per minute level of adult readers. LNF also does not have an established rate because DIBELS found LNF to be a strong risk indicator, but is not viewed by the creators of DIBELS as a Stepping Stone or an instructional goal.

Can Paraprofessionals or Aides Provide Intervention Instruction?

Frequently there are questions about whether paraprofessionals can provide intervention instruction. This issue arises because educators often believe that the most capable teachers should be instructing the students with the greatest needs. While it is certainly the case that the most needy students deserve the best instructors possible, there are times when this may not be possible.

In a perfect world only fully certified teachers would provide intervention instruction. However, given the teacher shortages and budget shortfalls in education today, this isn't realistic in many schools. Especially in schools where over half the students are flagged for intervention, it is nearly impossible to meet every child's needs by only using highly certified and trained teachers. So then we face a critical question: Is it better to have smaller group sizes and provide more intervention instruction rather than less? The answer is a set of tradeoffs, and one tradeoff is that some intervention instruction is often provided by paraprofessionals. When this happens, a key issue is how to provide the training and supervision structure so that the work of the paraprofessionals is assured to be high-quality (see the training curriculum, *ParaReading*, by Deborah Glaser, Sopris West, 2005).

Experience shows that paraprofessionals or aides can be extremely effective in delivering small group intervention instruction. There are two critical conditions for success. First they must receive extensive training. One effective approach is for aides to attend the same professional development that the teachers receive, which also makes it more likely that teachers and aides will become a team with regard to intervention instruction. They need to work together, which requires that aides get some of the same training that teachers receive. The second condition is that the aides must be supervised extremely closely. In most schools this is accomplished through aides conferencing with teachers regularly to discuss lesson plans and the progress of students.

Small Groups Are Just as Effective as One-on-One Instruction

Research has shown that small groups can be just as effective as individual tutoring in this area. One research study where a similar treatment was provided for 11 weeks to struggling second grade readers in three different sizes of groups found that three students to one instructor is just as effective as one-on-one tutoring (Vaughn & Linan-Thompson 2003). Yet the group size can't be too large. This same study demonstrated that group sizes of 10:1 were less effective than 3:1 in improving some important skills. Some schools have to start their groups with four or five in a group. If resources are so tight that this has to happen, then the students who are most below benchmark should still be placed in small groups of three and the students who are closer to benchmark can be in groups of five students.

While groups of five are not optimal, by January about a third of the students who began intervention in September will have reached benchmark and can be exited from intervention. This, then, provides the opportunity to regroup so that the group size can be reduced to three if at all possible. As more children are exited out of intervention groups because they are achieving benchmark, the children whose progress monitoring scores show a decided lack of progress can be placed in groups of two, and finally even one-on-one, as the year progresses and the need is demonstrated for more intensive instruction.

How Many Times per Week Should the Groups Meet?

The ideal intervention time for a Tier II group is 30 minutes, five days a week. If a compromise must be made, it is better to provide regular instruction at least four times per week, even if for a shorter period of time, than to meet only twice a week for a longer time. Children need frequent, distributed practice, and meeting more often, even if for a shorter period of time, allows for more frequent practice. Students whose skills are the lowest typically need a minimum of 20 minutes at least four times a week. Less time with less frequency is unlikely to yield noticeable progress for the students who are most at risk according to DIBELS scores. Students who have only one skill that is emerging and others on target can benefit from a less frequent schedule. The only reason to even consider intervention shorter than 30 minutes and for fewer than five days a week is that some schools simply cannot accomplish 30 minutes, five days a week for all students who need intervention. However, these schools have been able to serve all below-benchmark students with 15 or 20 minutes of intervention three or four times a week and they have seen results when the instruction was appropriately focused and given by well-trained interventionists.

General Guidelines for Intervention Instruction

Several general guidelines for intervention instruction include:

- Start intervention at the lowest deficient skill.

- Make sure that the children reach automaticity or mastery at each level before increasing the complexity.

- Consider increasing complexity within an activity, as well as across activities.

- Use a scope and sequence with proven validity.

- Provide individualized practice as much as possible so students can't look on or copy each other's work and follow without thinking it through themselves.

- Move along the skills continuum as rapidly as possible.

Intervention in the DIBELS Skill Areas

Letter Naming Fluency (LNF) Skill

Children need to learn to name letters accurately and fluently. As with many other skills, accuracy generally precedes fluency. A helpful activity that can be used to help students become accurate and then fluent in naming the letters is called the Alphabet Arc (see Table 5.7) and is offered through the *Reading Readiness Manual* by the Neuhaus Education Center (2002). All the letters are arranged in an arc shape on an 11 × 17 paper. Children place plastic letters over the correct spot on the arc while simultaneously naming them.

Many children who enter kindergarten knowing very few letters cannot work with an arc that contains all 26 letters at the same time. In order to keep from overwhelming these children with too many letters at once, an effective way to begin is to ask these children to work with cards that have five letters per card and giving them only the five plastic letters that correspond with the letters shown on the cards. These cards can be called "Pre-Arc Cards." By mastering only five at a time before moving to the next five, children can progress in a manner that is comfortable for them.

After a student can name each letter while placing it on the appropriate place on the Pre-Arc card, it is possible to work with two cards and ten letters at a time. Once the student has practiced all five of the pre-arc cards, he is ready to work with all 26 letters and the entire arc. Kindergarten children in intervention groups generally work on this arc for a number of weeks before they can confidently name and place all the letters on the arc. Then the interventionist can shift from teaching accuracy to working on fluency through asking students to alphabetize the letters on the Arc in two minutes. Many interventionists have found that the students love to chart their own progress in moving from six to seven minutes down to two minutes after extended practice.

There are two versions of the Alphabet Arc—one has the 26 letters on the arc, and the other arc has only four letters to anchor each end and the top of the arc, with lines drawing in the rest of the shape of the arc. This second arc is more difficult than Arc I because it involves more skills. Students not only name the letters, but also learn the sequence from A to Z. Once a student can place the letters on this arc accurately with unlimited time, then establish a goal of completing it in two minutes. Time students to add the attention to fluency. A detailed description of the Alphabet Arcs is provided in Chapter 9.

Table 5.7	**Pre-Arc Cards**	**Alphabet Arc I**	**Alphabet Arc II**
Progression in Letter Naming	5 letters at a time	26 letters	26 letters
	Accuracy matching limited number of letters on a card and naming them	Accuracy naming letter while placing plastic letter on arc. Develop fluency after accuracy	Accuracy naming and placing all letters along arc line with only 4 letters on arc. Fluency after accuracy

Initial Sound Fluency (ISF) and Phoneme Segmentation Fluency (PSF)—Phonological Awareness Continuum

The learning process of phonemic awareness makes sense. If the lower process isn't mastered, it's not realistic to expect students to perform at a higher level. DIBELS has taught us to assess and know the proper sequence to teach kids how to read.

Indiana teacher

Phonological skills develop along a progression from easy to more complex. Some commonly accepted levels of phonological awareness are:

- Segmenting sentences into words

- Segmenting words into syllables

- Segmenting words into onset and rime, and identifying words that rhyme

- Phonemic awareness

Often children are exposed to rhyming at a very young age through reading nursery rhymes and other poems before they learn about syllables. Although rhyming words is more complex than syllable identification, children with phonological awareness difficulties are often identified at an early age because they do not understand the concept of rhyming words.

Phonemic awareness is the top level of phonological awareness, or the most complex. Yet within this top step, there are additional levels of complexity, as outlined in three levels from easiest to middle to hardest (see Table 5.8).

Below are examples of phonemic awareness activities that fall along a progression.

Table 5.8

Phonological Awareness Continuum

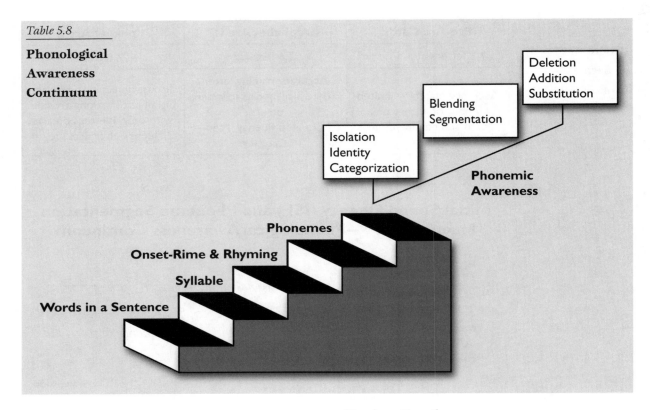

Easiest Level

- Phoneme identity and isolation—Find pictures that begin with a target sound. Then answer questions such as, What is the first sound in the word *man*? /m/

- Phoneme identity—What sound is the same in *kite, can,* and *king*? (/k/)

- Phoneme categorization—Which word doesn't belong? *Cat, car,* or *mop*? (*mop*, because it has a different beginning phoneme)

Middle Level

- Phoneme segmentation—What are the sounds in the word *dog?* (/d/ /ŏ/ /g/)

- Phoneme blending—Say the sounds /g/ /r/ /ă/ /b/. What is the word? (*grab*)

Hardest Level

- Phoneme addition—Say the word *eye*. Now say it again with /s/ at the beginning. (*sigh*)

- Phoneme deletion—Say the word *spark*. Now say it again without the /s/. (*park*)

- Phoneme substitution—Say the word *cat*. Now change the *c* to *h*. What's the new word? (*hat*)

These skills build upon each other. In order to identify which word doesn't belong in a set of three words, it is necessary to isolate the first sounds, and then determine which one isn't the same as the two other words. Phoneme segmentation requires isolation skills. In order to delete the initial sound in a word, first the student must isolate the initial sound from the other phonemes, delete the sound from the word and then blend the remaining sounds for a new word. The "granddaddy" phonemic awareness skill is phoneme substitution. Not only is it considered the most complex, but it also incorporates several other skills in the continuum. To substitute, a student must isolate one sound, delete it, add a different sound, and then blend the new initial sound with the remaining sounds to make a new word.

In DIBELS there are two measures of phonemic awareness. Initial Sound Fluency (ISF), which is administered in the fall and winter of kindergarten, measures phoneme isolation and identity. For the first three questions out of each set of four in ISF, the student is asked to point to or name the picture that begins with a target sound. This task requires the student to identify the first sound in order to tell which of the four pictures starts with the target sound. The fourth question asks the student to name the sound that begins a target picture. To do this, the student needs to identify the initial sound and also pronounce it. The two skills measured by ISF, phoneme isolation and phoneme identification, fall into the easiest level of phonemic awareness.

Phoneme Segmentation Fluency (PSF), which is administered from the middle of kindergarten through the end of first grade, measures the student's ability to segment sounds in words with two to five sounds. Segmenting is a skill from the middle level of our phonemic awareness progression, and it is more complex for four and five sound words than for two and three sound words.

There are many excellent phonemic awareness activity books that teachers love. Many of these books use a leveling system to categorize activities in order from simple to complex. Many times the level does not match the progression outlined above. One of my favorite activity books has a phonemic substitution activity within the Level 1 (easiest) level, when I would suggest that it should be at Level 5, or the hardest level. Often the skill listed as the target skill does not match the progression outlined in this book. The progression of phonemic awareness in this book follows the publication, *Put Reading First,* which is based on the National Reading Panel report (2000). It is imperative for teachers to consider the skill taught and the level of complexity in determining which activities are right for a group at a given point in time.

Nonsense Word Fluency (NWF)—The Alphabetic Principle and Phonics

There is also a progression of skills in the area of alphabetic principle, phonics, and word study. Children who have developed an adequate and sufficient level of phonemic awareness and letter naming knowledge are ready to associate letters with sounds. Most programs develop phonemic awareness and letter knowledge concurrently to a point, and then begin matching letters with sounds, which is the very beginning of phonics instruction.

Although it may be best to keep letter naming and phonemic awareness instruction separate to a point, research shows that it is advantageous to combine them as soon as possible because one skill may reinforce the other. For a large portion of our alphabet, the sound of the letter is similar to its name. A reciprocal relationship exists whereby learning the sounds helps with learning the letter names, and vice versa.

However, for the student who had difficulty with phonemic awareness, instruction must focus on sounds without letters until the student demonstrates mastery in identifying at least the initial, final, and middle sounds in three-sound words. These students have not learned phonemic awareness through the core curriculum, which may have introduced letter-sound relationships too early. It is especially true that phonemic awareness needs to be taught without letters to the student who can memorize words but cannot read unfamiliar words because he doesn't understand that letters represent sounds.

Students who are learning to associate sounds with letters often benefit from using cards that contain the letter and a picture for a keyword. Most core reading programs contain a set of letter-sound cards that can be tacked along a corkboard strip over the blackboard in a classroom. It is helpful for students in intervention groups to be able to see these cards, especially if the cards match what the student is accustomed to using with his core program. After students become fairly proficient in naming the letter when asked the sound, or the sound when shown the letter, it may be time to move to cards with only letters and no keyword pictures. The child who can name sounds for letters without pictures would be on his way to learning the alphabetic principle.

Phonics instruction is teaching letter-sound correspondences and the application of these correspondences to reading and writing. It is critical to be able to apply letter-sound correspondences right away within the context of reading words. This is why so many curricula teach a mixture of consonants and vowels, so that children can read words before completing the study of all 44 phonemes. Although the exact selection of letters varies, the pattern is remarkably similar between the sequence of teaching the phonemes in major core reading programs. The sequence typically starts with:

- Four to five consonants and one short vowel

- Another four to five consonants and a different short vowel

- A third set of three to five consonants and a third short vowel

This pattern continues until all the consonants and the short vowels have been taught. Typically some of the more complex phonics concepts are included toward the end of this progression. Digraphs are often taught at this point, as well as the common inflectional endings *s, es, ing*, and *ed*. Eventually, the *silent e* spelling for long vowels is taught. Some of the more complex concepts, such as consonant blends and vowel team spellings for the long vowels, come later in the sequence. Table 5.9 provides a sample sequence.

Table 5.9

Phonics A to Z: Sample Phonics Sequence

Shown in Sets of 10 Letters (read down vertical columns)

1st	2nd	3rd	4th	5th
m	g	r-controlled vowels (er, ir, ur)	ci	long u (ew, ue)
a	o	sh	long o (o, o_e)	/ou/ (ou, ow)
t	x	th	/z/ s	/ô/ (aw, au)
h	ar	ch	v	/oo/ (oo, ue, u_e, u, ew)
p	ck	tch	long u (u, u_e)	/oo/
n	u	k	long e (e, e-e, ea, ee)	kn
c	z	long a (a, a_e)	q	/oi/ (oi, oy)
d	l	j	long vowels plus r	wr
s	e	dge	long e (y, ie)	ph
i	ea	ge	long a (ai, ay)	
b	y	gi	long i (igh, y, ie)	
r	w	long i (i, i_e)	ng	
f	wh	ce	long o (oe, ow, oa)	

Source: Blevins, *Phonics A to Z* (1998), p. 90.

One critical component of teaching phonics is to begin using the learned letter-sound correspondences to read words as soon as possible. Often short *a* and short *i* are two of the first vowels taught. An enormous number of consonant-vowel-consonant (CVC) words can be read and spelled with ten consonants and two short vowels. This is fortunate because it is critical to ask students to read and write words as soon as possible to practice applying the letter-sound correspondences they are learning. Students can read and write sentences once they have gained proficiency with even a few simple words.

Once children have learned to read and write single-syllable CVC words, there are more complex phonics patterns to learn to be able to read more unusual words, including multisyllabic words. A technique for teaching students how to determine where to split the syllables, which uses syllable boards, is included in Chapter 10 of this book. Study continues with exploring root words and affixes. Word origin and morphology are two additional areas of study about the English language.

Nonphonetic high frequency sight words are generally taught at the same time as the teaching of the sound-letter correspondences. Instruction in these common words that are spelled irregularly, many of which come from the Anglo-Saxon language, typically begins in kindergarten. Most core reading curricula teach students to begin to recognize some of the most common irregularly spelled words in kindergarten, including *the*, *and*, *you*, and *said*.

Word Use Fluency (WUF)—Vocabulary and Oral Language

Word Use Fluency measures vocabulary and oral language skills. These skills are more general than some of the skills measured by other, more targeted DIBELS indicators, such as letter naming, phonemic awareness and phonics at the CVC level. In word use, oral language and vocabulary skills develop over a long time in many ways. Most students develop their oral language usage, including use and understanding of vocabulary, through their lifetime of experiences in the home, school, on family trips, with peers, etc. When a student's word use is low, there can be a multitude of diverse causes. Sometimes it is because the child has grown up in an environment where there is not much discourse, or in a home where they do not hear stories read aloud.

Intervention to build vocabulary and oral language skills occurs over a long time. The DIBELS indicators are not as likely to show the impact of the work on word usage as quickly. This is best understood by considering that if the words the student has learned since the last assessment period are not one of the fifteen or so words on that benchmark, then the score may not show the improvement the student made. What this measure is more sensitive to is whether a student has learned to give more elaborate responses to the words. For this reason, it may not be worthwhile to progress monitor every two or three weeks with the Word Use Fluency indicator. A less frequent schedule may be merited for students who are in intervention groups focused on improving word use fluency, possibly monthly.

Retell Fluency (RTF)—Comprehension

Retell Fluency predicts a student's ability to comprehend what is read by asking the student to retell what they read in the ORF passage. When providing intervention to students with low retell fluency scores, it is important to teach not only how to retell the facts from the story but also to teach more complex comprehension skills than a simple retell. Some interventions help students articulate a set of characteristics about what they just read, including:

- Stating the main idea

- Recounting the story in sequence of the events

- Describing the characters

- Developing a story web to summarize observations about the story

- Determining the main events of the story that led to the climax

Many teachers use graphic organizers to help students remember to think about these story characteristics as they read.

Other interventions are designed to model what comprehension looks like through think-aloud techniques. One of these techniques is called "Questioning the Author," by Isabel Beck and colleagues (Beck et al. 1997). It is an approach whereby the teacher models the types of queries that good readers ask while reading a passage for the first time.

Chapter 6

Designing Lesson Plans

DIBELS pinpoints specific problem areas instead of just saying "they have difficulty with reading skills." While comparing my students' scores over a period of time, I found one was not yet proficient with vowel sounds. He is now in an intervention group that is concentrating on the alphabetic principle. I have also relayed the information to the parents and given them possible activities to do at home along the same lines as the intervention group activities.

First grade teacher

To ensure that the assessment-instruction link is tight, it is critical to use lesson plans to guarantee that instruction is concentrated on the appropriate skill areas. These plans articulate the focus of the intervention group's instruction and ensure that the interventionist and the classroom teacher are communicating and planning which activities and strategies will meet the needs of the group. The focus of this chapter is how to develop data-informed lesson plans for teachers who are designing their own intervention program.

Overview of Lesson Planning

Why Interventionists Need Lesson Plans

There are several important reasons that developing lesson plans is encouraged and supported in this book. The process of developing lesson plans reminds teachers that instruction needs to be carefully planned to maximize its effectiveness. Except for all but the most highly experienced, intervention teachers acknowledge that it is extremely difficult to think of good activities on the spot.

Well-designed intervention includes attention to the specific sounds and words that are used in teaching. Additionally, lesson plans provide documentation of the instructional strategies that were employed with a particular group.

Key Characteristics of Lesson Plans

One of the most important things to include in a lesson plan is a place to write the instructional focus. Some other information to include is:

- List of activities

- Specific sounds or words to use for reading and spelling

- Allocation of time

A couple of sample lesson plans are included in this chapter.

Why Documentation Is Critical

Intervention teachers typically work with eight to twelve groups daily. It is easy to become confused about what you did with each group by the end of the day, let alone the end of the week. It is critical that there is a record of the type of intervention that was provided to each group. If a student is failing to respond to intervention instruction after a reasonable period of time, it is necessary to know what types of instruction he has received. This information helps in planning what other strategies to try next in order to increase the instructional intensity for this student. Ultimately these records will be used in making decisions about when it is time to refer a student for further diagnostic testing.

One of the most compelling types of data about a struggling student is progress monitoring charts showing that two other intervention peers who started at the same point have improved dramatically while the struggling reader has not. It is critical to know how much time was spent instructing in specific skill areas and which activities and strategies have been provided.

Sample Lesson Plans

Schools that choose not to purchase a program that provides a comprehensive intervention curriculum will need an approach for developing lesson plans. Many schools have achieved excellent results by developing their own approach for some of the instructional areas, although it is most difficult to create your own instruction in systematic phonics. If teachers are developing their own curriculum, then providing professional development and coaching is essential to assure good planning. One advantage of professional development and creation of lesson plans is that instruction is more customized to the needs of the individual group rather than merely following a set sequence of skills. Teachers who are designing intervention lessons need to be well trained to make informed decisions about which activities to incorporate. This process can lead teachers to buy-in because of their ownership for the program and its results.

In this chapter, sample intervention lesson plans are provided for students at different grade levels. A lesson plan format is also provided as an example to get teachers started in designing lessons, along with a weekly planning format. In my experience, teachers who are initiating intervention groups rigorously plan lessons carefully at the beginning. About a month or two after initiating the program, teachers will be able to ease off of the planning and begin to use a bi-weekly planning approach similar to the one provided in Chapter 7, "Progress Monitoring and Record Keeping."

Lesson Plans to Address a Phonemic Awareness Deficit

Kindergarten students who require intervention at the beginning of the year generally fall into one of two groups—those who are below benchmark in only ISF, and those below in both ISF and LNF. Planning interventions to address deficits in oral language and vocabulary will be handled separately.

For students whose ISF score is below benchmark, instruction in phonemic awareness is recommended. Even though the student's low ISF score indicates that he may need instruction in working with the initial sounds in words, this may not be the place to start his instruction. It is important to begin intervention at the lowest deficient skill on the developmental continuum and work up. A student who cannot isolate and identify initial sounds may not be proficient at other phonological awareness tasks, such as segmenting words into syllables or onset-rimes, or sentences into words.

DIBELS provides information about the student's ability to identify initial sounds in the ISF indicator. The PSF indicator measures phoneme segmentation skills. Yet DIBELS does not provide information about the student's phonological awareness at lower levels. The easiest way to determine what phonological awareness skills a student has is to conduct some informal evaluation during the first few days of intervention instruction. The interventionist can plan one or two activities at each level along the continuum and observe the student's skills. For example, in order to informally assess, the following activities can be planned.

- Segmenting sentences into words—Ask students to jump for each word in a sentence.

- Segmenting words into syllables—Ask students to clap once for each syllable in their names, or in a set of words spoken by the interventionist.

- Rhyming—Ask students to match pictures that rhyme.

- Phoneme Isolation—Students give a "thumbs up" sign if spoken words begin with a target sound.

- Phoneme Identity—Students tell which sound spoken words begin with.

- Phoneme Categorization—Students place picture cards under two columns, depending upon whether they begin with the sound /k/ or /m/.

This informal assessment gives information about where to begin intervention. Even if the student needs some help on one of the earlier skills in phonological awareness, it will probably not take long, leaving the majority of time for phonemic awareness.

The objective is to move as quickly as possible up the phonological awareness continuum to phonemic awareness. The most important skills are phoneme segmentation and blending. The interventionist can determine when it is time to move from working on isolating initial sounds to phoneme segmentation by analyzing progress monitoring scores for ISF. As the student gets closer to reaching the established level of 25 initial sounds per minute on ISF, the focus of intervention instruction can change to phoneme segmentation. PSF is supposed to reach the established level of 35 phoneme segments per minute (p.s.p.m.) by the end of kindergarten.

Imaginary Student Named "José"

Let's take an imaginary student we will call "José." José, a kindergartner, demonstrated very low scores on the DIBELS phonemic awareness measures. Let's suppose that it is late January just past the winter benchmark, and his recent assessment reveals a low PSF and low ISF score. With these scores, it is clear that he needs intervention in the area of phonological awareness. (This example also could apply to a first or second grader with a low PSF score whose student booklet reveals he does not consistently identify initial sounds correctly.)

The first step is to make sure, through a quick informal assessment, that he knows the lower levels of phonological awareness (word recognition, syllable recognition, rhyming, and blending onset-rimes). Once you have confirmed that he knows how to segment sentences into words, words into syllables, can segment the onset from the rime, and can recognize rhyming words, you know that he is ready for phonemic awareness instruction. Because José is below the benchmark score of 25 in ISF, it is obvious that he is struggling at the initial sound level. On the phonological awareness continuum he is most likely not ready for segmenting and blending phonemes orally if he cannot isolate and identify even the first sounds in words.

The scoring page for José's PSF winter benchmark confirms that he does not consistently segment any sounds in words. Many circled words on the scoring page confirm that he repeats the entire word back to the examiner. On a few words he attempts a beginning and ending sound, yet often these are incorrect. His scores show that accuracy is an even larger problem for him than his fluency with the task. After working with him to see that he understands the lower levels of phonological awareness, we have confirmed that José needs intervention at the initial sound level of words.

The following activities would be ideal for José to start his intervention instruction because they emphasize matching initial sounds, the easiest phonemic awareness activity for most children.

- Initial Sound Picture Card Sort (matching)—One picture serves as the column header. The interventionist hands the student a picture card and the student places the picture under the column with the word that starts with the same first sound.

- Initial Sound Train (matching)—A train has five cars attached. On the engine there is a spot to place a picture card to indicate which initial sound can ride on the train. The student chooses which pictures from a small set have the matching initial sound, then places each matching picture on a car of the train.

- Initial Sound Object Sort (matching)—The student picks a miniature object from a brown paper bag and decides which of two piles the object belongs with, depending on the initial sound.

It is helpful at the beginning to limit these matching activities to closed sorts, which means that all the objects or pictures fit with one of two sounds. The activities can be made more difficult by creating an open sort, where there is a "doesn't fit" pile or column to place the cards or objects for any sound other than the two that are designated.

Another progression from easier to harder is to consider which sounds are paired. It is easiest if the two sounds are very different. Examples of sounds that are different are stops (air flow stops) vs. continuants (you can keep saying it until you run out of breath). It is easier to tell the difference between

/m/ and /t/ (continuant and stop, respectively) than between /m/ and /n/ (two continuants). Not only is /m/ a continuant sound and /t/ is a stop sound, but /m/ and /n/ are both nasals (sounds made through the nose). Because both /m/ and /n/ are formed in a similar place in the mouth and they feel similar in their articulation, they are difficult for the student who is beginning to learn phonemic awareness to discriminate.

After José has mastered matching initial sounds, he is ready to learn to isolate and identify initial sounds. A good activity for identifying sounds is similar to the last question in each set of four for ISF. The student is shown a picture and asked to tell which sound is at the beginning of the word.

Once José can correctly isolate, identify, and articulate initial sounds, he is ready to begin learning to distinguish sounds in the final position in a word. All the same activities that are listed above for initial sounds can be changed to develop skills with the final sound. Some examples of activities to develop this skill include:

- Thumbs Up—Ask students to indicate if they hear a target sound in the final position of a word by giving a thumbs up sign

- Final Sound Picture Card Sort

- Final Sound Object Sort

- Final Sounds Dominos

After José has become proficient at identifying and articulating final sounds, it's time for him to learn to identify and articulate middle vowel sounds. Middle vowel sounds are generally the last of the three to develop because vowels are more easily confused than most consonants. The same activities can be used for the middle as for the initial and final sounds. Then to make things more complex, all three positions can be focused in one activity. For example, the thumbs up game can be made more complex by mixing the questions, as follows:

- Thumbs up if you hear the sound /s/ at the beginning of *Sam.* (yes)

- Thumbs up if you hear the /m/ sound at the end of *mop.* (no)

- Thumbs up if you hear the /e/ sound in the middle of *sip.* (no)

A summary of the intervention for José follows:

- Initial sound

- Final sound

- Middle sound

- Mixing all the positions

After mastering isolating, identifying, and categorizing the sounds, José is then ready to begin segmentation and blending using activities such as Move-It-and-Say-It. By moving one object for each sound in the word, he is clearly distinguishing all the sounds in the word, not just the sound in one position. Next, José will be ready for activities in which he has to add, delete, and substitute a sound and blend them together to say a different word. After that he will be ready to move to sound-letter correspondence.

A series of sample lesson plans for José's group are shown in Table 6.1. As you can see, these lessons represent days 1, 5, 9, 14, and 19 for this group. The tasks are increasingly more difficult as the group moves up the phonological awareness continuum.

Table 6.1

Lesson Plans for José

Phonological Awareness Lesson Plan			
Lesson Plan No.	I		
Date	January 12, 2004		
Group Members	José, Sam, & Yolanda		
Instructional Focus	Phonemic Awareness, starting at the initial sound level.		
Skill Area	Name of Activity	Number of Minutes	Activity Number
Initial Sound Matching	Initial Sound Picture Card Sort /m/ & /t/	10	9–19
	All Aboard!—Initial Sounds /p/ & /k/	10	9–14
	Sort Objects into Piles— Initial Sounds /d/ & /s/	10	9–20

Phonological Awareness Lesson Plan			
Lesson Plan No.	5		
Date	January 16, 2004		
Group Members	José, Sam, & Yolanda		
Instructional Focus	Phonemic Awareness—ending sound level		
Skill Area	Name of Activity	Number of Minutes	Activity Number
Ending Sound Matching	Thumbs Up—Ending sounds /m/, /t/, /p/, /k/, /d/, & /s/	10	9–17
	Sound Dominos— mixed sounds	10	9–18
	Sort Objects into Piles— Ending Sounds—/m/ & /k/	10	9–20

Table 6.1

continued

Phonological Awareness Lesson Plan

Lesson Plan No.	9		
Date	January 22, 2004		
Group Members	José, Sam, & Yolanda		
Instructional Focus	Phonemic Awareness—middle vowel sound level		
Skill Area	Name of Activity	Number of Minutes	Activity Number
Middle Vowel Sound Matching	Sound Picture Card Sort— Middle sounds—/ă/ & /ŏ/	10	9–19
	All Aboard!—Middle Sounds /ĭ/ & /ŭ/	10	9–14
	Thumbs Up!—Middle Sounds /ĕ/ & /ŏ/	10	9–17

Phonological Awareness Lesson Plan

Lesson Plan No.	14		
Date	January 29, 2004		
Group Members	José, Sam, & Yolanda		
Instructional Focus	Phonemic Awareness—segmentation and blending		
Skill Area	Name of Activity	Number of Minutes	Activity Number
Phonemic Segmentation & Blending	Review: Initial sound matching —mix beginning, ending, & middle Isolate That Sound	8	9–13
	Move-It-and-Say-It— CVC words	12	9–26
	Head, Waist, & Toes— 3 sound words	10	9–25

Phonological Awareness Lesson Plan

Lesson Plan No.	19		
Date	February 5, 2004		
Group Members	José, Sam, & Yolanda		
Instructional Focus	Phonemic Awareness—segmentation and blending		
Skill Area	Name of Activity	Number of Minutes	Activity Number
Phonemic Addition, Deletion & Substitution	Review: Phonemic Segmentation Move-It-and-Say-It—words with 5 sounds, including blends	7	9–26
	Take Away a Sound	15	9–29
	Make a New Word	8	9–30

Lesson Plans for Phonics Instruction

Let's explore how to create lesson plans for a first grade student whose deficit area is a bit further along the developmental progression. For a middle of the year first grade student who has reached proficiency with phoneme segmentation, as measured by PSF, but is low on NWF, the types of intervention activities he needs are completely different than those José needed. Let's call this first grader "Karen." First we need to make sure we know why Karen's NWF score is below benchmark. Look at her LNF score for the fall of first grade. If she had reached benchmark of 40 by the fall, most likely she is still proficient enough in letter naming. If she was below 40 in September, even though the LNF is not delivered after the first grade fall benchmark, use her fall administration and cover the lines she read in the fall and begin below those. Generally children who don't reach benchmark only read about four or fewer rows out of the ten provided, so there are more than enough rows to use for this purpose.

Let's assume that Karen's letter naming (LNF) was 50 by the fall and therefore is not likely to be contributing to her difficulty with NWF. We already know that her PSF is above benchmark of 35. Therefore the problem is either accuracy with the letter-sound correspondences, or fluency in applying them fast enough. If the difficulty is accuracy, then she needs help with letter-sound correspondences. There is no point in beginning to work on fluency until she is accurate.

In order to determine which letter-sound correspondences Karen knows, we can start by examining the NWF page of her scoring booklet. This may give us an idea of whether the issue is with consonants or short vowels. Let's assume that Karen knows all but the most uncommon consonants, but is not reading the vowels accurately. Then her intervention would begin with a brief identification of which consonants she needs help with, and a confirmation of whether she accurately knows any short vowels or will need instruction on all the vowels.

An informal way of assessing her letter-sound knowledge is to take a deck of plain letter cards without keyword pictures. Ask Karen to name the sound for each one as quickly as she can while you flip them over. Place any sound that she doesn't know in a separate pile. Then ask her to write the letter that spells the sound while you say the sounds of the 44 speech sounds. Ask her if she knows another way to spell it for sounds with alternate spellings like *k* and *c* for the /k/ sound. These two routines should only take about five to ten minutes to finish and you will have a fairly good picture of what she knows and doesn't know. This informal exercise will confirm what you see as her error patterns in the DIBELS booklet.

Assume that Karen is struggling with all the short and long vowels. She knows a few short vowels, including *a* and *o*, but can't differentiate short *e*, short *i*, and short *u*. Make sure that she is able to spell the beginning and ending consonants of CVC words, and the vowel is represented by a picture card. Once you are sure that she can do this, it's time to move to instruction on the vowels. This is where intervention will begin.

- Word Chains with Short Vowel Sounds—Using magnetic letter tiles or pocket charts with letter cards, ask Karen to spell CVC words by selecting from five or six consonants and one vowel. Give her a word chain in which one consonant changes and the vowel is the same. After practicing with all five short vowels, ask her to choose between two vowels at a time. Select vowels that are fairly different in sound from one another, such as *i* and *o*. Then choose two other vowels. Finally, after she is proficient at spelling words when she can select from only two vowels, give her more choices. Eventually she will be able to select the appropriate vowel without any scaffolding from the interventionist. It is helpful to teach students a key word to associate with each short vowel, such as *itch* for /ĭ/, *echo* for /ĕ/, *apple* for /ă/, *octopus* for /ŏ/, and *up* for /ŭ/.

Table 6.2

Lesson Plan for Karen

Phonics Lesson Plan			
Lesson Plan #	I		
Date	January 12, 2004		
Group Members	Karen, Raphael, and Adrienne		
Instructional Focus	Phonemic Awareness—segmentation and blending		
Skill Area	Name of Activity	Number of Minutes	Activity Number
Letter-Sound Correspondence	Letter-Sound Cards: card drill —show letter, ask for sound Note letters students miss	7	10–2
	Beach Ball	5	10–4
Spelling	Karen—Word Chains: word chain practicing /ĕ/ and /ŭ/ Raphael—word chain practicing changes in initial consonants Adrienne—word chain practicing changes in final consonants	10	10–14
Applying at Word Level	Read lists of words with target skills Read words in sentences	8	10–10 & 10–19
	Decodable Text: work on high frequency nonphonetic sight words		

Lesson Plans for Groups

These examples of lesson planning for our kindergarten student, José, and our first grade student, Karen, demonstrate how to plan daily lessons. In most cases the interventionist will be planning lessons for a small group and not one individual student. The process and lesson plan format is the same for a group as for an individual student. However, you will need to adapt instruction to differentiate it for each of the three students in the group. Hopefully, the needs of all three students in the group will be similar enough that they can all be working on the same activity.

Skilled interventionists differentiate what they ask students to do based on the needs of each child. For example, if the students are all working on the sound train activity for phonemic awareness, the task can be changed slightly for each student. Each child has a train and is matching picture cards based on a target sound, but the target sound each student is assigned may be varied. One student who is still working on consonants in the initial sound position can be matching pictures that begin with the initial sound /m/. A second student who has mastered initial sounds and is working on sounds in the final position in a word can be asked to select pictures to add to his train if they end with the sound /p/. The third student, who is furthest along in phonemic awareness, can be matching pictures on his train based on whether they have the target sound /ă/ in the middle position of the word.

Skilled intervention instructors are able to differentiate nearly any activity as long as they know each student's instructional level in phonemic awareness, reading, spelling, or language. Creating lesson plans takes time, but is essential for effective instruction. After the first few weeks, planning becomes easier and the same format can be used for multiple groups. Table 6.3 lists phonological awareness activities. The activities are described in detail in Chapter 9.

Table 6.3

List of Phonological Awareness Activities		
Level	**Activity # and Name**	**Short Description**
Segmenting Sentences Into Words	9–1 Just Say Part	Drop one word at a time from the end of a sentence
	9–2 Clapping Words in a Sentence	Students repeat a sentence, and then clap each word
	9–3 Word Chairs	Teacher taps head of students and they stand and say their word
Segmenting Words Into Syllables	9–4 Clap, Snap, or Tap	Student decides if others will clap, tap, or snap syllables in his name

Table 6.3

continued

	9–5 Break It in Half		Start with hands out and fists closed. Turn hand over and open for each syllable
	9–6 Syllable Puzzles		Pictures of 2-syllable words are cut into puzzle pieces
Segmenting Words Into Onset-Rime, Rhyming, and Alliteration	9–7 Rhyming Picture Sort		Select pictures of pairs of words that rhyme
	9–8 Rhyming Picture Puzzles		Select 2 pictures of rhyming words that fit together as a puzzle
	9–9 Rhyme-Away Story		As teacher reads poem, students erase part of picture that rhymes. Gradually erase entire picture.
	9–10 Oops! Wrong Rhyme		Point to body part and say word that rhymes
	9–11 Stand Up Rhyme Time		Touch part of body that completes phrase with a rhyming word
	9–12 Say It and Take It		4 picture cards are lined up. Teacher says onset, and student takes card if can complete rime for one of pictures
Phonemic Awareness— Isolation	9–13 Isolate That Sound		Teacher asks what the first sound in a word is
	9–14 All Aboard!		Students add picture cards to a train which has same initial sound as picture on engine
	9–15 Saying Silly Sentences		Repeat alliterative sentence and fill in last word that has same initial sound
	9–16 Where's That Sound?		Point to position on body of animal to identify whether target sound is at beginning, middle, or end of word
	9–17 Thumbs Up		Give thumbs up sign if sound in spoken word matches target sound
Phonemic Awareness: Identity	9–18 Sound Dominos		Picture cards on end of sticks are lined up together if initial sound matches
Phonemic Awareness: Categorization	9–19 Picture Card Sort		Place picture in proper column to match initial sounds
	9–20 Sort Objects Into Piles		Objects are sorted into piles by same initial sound
Phonemic Awareness— Blending	9–21 Turtle Talk		Holding picture of turtles, take a step for each sound to blend elongated sounds in words

Table 6.3

continued

	9–22 Blending Animal Names in Old McDonald's Farm	Teacher says sounds for animals and students blend to give name of animal
	9-23 Tap and Sweep, or Tapping the Sounds	Tap each sound with fists and then sweep fist back over area to blend—tap sounds with 2 fingers on arm & sweep as blend to say word
	9-24 Blending Phonemes	Phoneme pieces for words are pushed together while pronouncing them—also can use unifix cubes
Phonemic Awareness: Segmentation	**9-25** Head, Waist, & Toes	Hands on head for first sound, waist for second, and toes for last sound
	9-26 Say-It-and-Move-It	Move an object for each sound in a word
	9-27 Let's Count Sounds	Count phonemes in the word by raising a finger for each sound
Phonemic Awareness: Deletion	**9-28** Deleting a Sound	Teacher says a word. Students repeat. Teacher asks to say it again without a specific sound.
	9-29 Take Away a Sound	Start with an object for each sound. Then remove the object for the sound deleted.
Phonemic Awareness: Addition	**9-30** Make a New Word	Teacher says word and students repeat. Now add a sound and say new word.
Phonemic Awareness: Substitution	**9-31** Change That Word	Say a word. Change one sound in the word and say the new word.

Note: These activities are described in detail in Chapter 9.

Progress Monitoring and Record Keeping

> *DIBELS has been valuable tool for me to find who needs immediate attention for intervention. The progress monitoring is equally valuable for me to see at a glance who has improved or reached benchmark, and who needs more intense instruction that hadn't been at risk or progressed at too slow of a rate.*
>
> Kindergarten teacher

Overview of Progress Monitoring

What Is Progress Monitoring?

Perhaps the most important characteristic of using DIBELS is its capacity to monitor the progress of students while they are receiving intervention instruction. Yet many times schools that are using DIBELS for benchmark screening three times a year are not regularly monitoring progress of the students receiving extra help. Given how much teachers value progress monitoring, this is a lost opportunity.

The Reading First Assessment Committee provided a definition of progress monitoring, as follows:

> *Assessments that determine if students are making adequate progress or need more intervention to achieve grade level reading outcomes (U.S. Department of Education 2002).*

If the purpose of administering a screening assessment is to predict which children are at risk of later reading difficulties, then we must monitor to see how well our intervention efforts are doing in helping the student reach critical reading milestones.

When a student's DIBELS scores indicate that he is at risk of failing to learn to read, teachers are compelled to respond by planning extra help in the form of intervention instruction. Knowing exactly what type of instruction will work for each individual student is not always simple. The DIBELS data, along with other information about the student, help teachers decide on a focus for the intervention instruction. Additionally, data from different students is reviewed to determine which students should be placed together in a small group. The person or team that oversees the intervention instruction, whether at the classroom or school-based level, must determine several additional things:

- Amount of time for intervention instruction

- Instructional materials or programs

- Instructor

All of these factors add up to make the decision about the course for an individual student complex. As with any complex decision, it is not always possible to balance all the factors correctly every time. One of the greatest benefits of using DIBELS is that, through repeated administrations of the alternate forms of the indicators, it is possible to track a student's progress in reaching benchmark goals over time. Through this continual monitoring it is possible to make adjustments if things aren't progressing.

Separate booklets are provided for progress monitoring. For each student whose progress you are monitoring, you will have a separate progress monitoring booklet that contains 20 alternate forms of a single indicator (ISF, PSF, NWF, ORF & RTF, and WUF), as well as a chart for tracking scores. Whereas a student's benchmark booklet provides the various indicators needed for each assessment period, the progress monitoring booklet contains multiple alternate forms for one specific indicator. The chart in the progress monitoring booklet appears on the outside cover (or just inside the cover on the Sopris West 2004 edition of DIBELS) and enables the examiner to record the scores each time the measure is administered to the student. A sample chart appears in Table 7.1.

Why There Isn't an LNF Progress Monitoring Booklet

The research team that developed DIBELS views letter naming as a less important skill for instruction than the skills that are based on knowledge of sounds (ISF, PSF, and NWF). Letter naming is included as an indicator because it is a predictor of reading success. Some of the teachers in schools that have implemented early reading screening and intervention programs wish to monitor progress in LNF. When asked, the research team says that they don't object to teachers doing this. However, they don't encourage it, and therefore don't provide a progress

Chapter 7 • Progress Monitoring and Record Keeping

154   *I've DIBEL'd, Now What?*

Table 7.1

Example of Progress Monitoring Chart for a Single Student

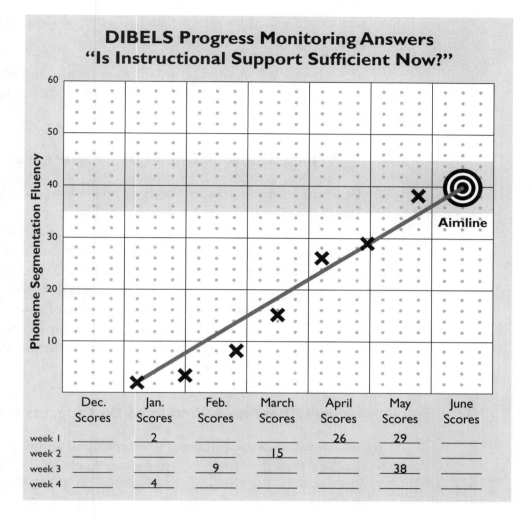

DIBELS Progress Monitoring Answers "Is Instructional Support Sufficient Now?"

Phoneme Segmentation Fluency

	Dec. Scores	Jan. Scores	Feb. Scores	March Scores	April Scores	May Scores	June Scores
week 1		2			26	29	
week 2				15			
week 3			9			38	
week 4		4					

monitoring booklet for this purpose. The reason is that they encourage teachers to devote their intervention instruction to teaching students the sounds and letter-sound correspondences rather than the names of the letters.

If you wish to monitor the progress of students using LNF from DIBELS, it is possible to create your own progress monitoring materials.

- If working with a first grade student, copy the three LNF pages from a kindergarten benchmark booklet for the examiner to use for scoring. Use the student materials page from the kindergarten kit to place in front of the student during the assessment.

- If working with a kindergarten student, use the fifth edition pages for LNF from the DIBELS Web site.

- If the student scored below 40 on LNF, then he didn't reach the last six rows on the LNF page. You can cover the rows at the top that he read previously and use the bottom half of a page from an earlier benchmark screening.

You can create a chart to track the student's progress by copying a chart from the front of another booklet and labeling it LNF.

Again, although it is easy to create progress monitoring materials for LNF, teachers need to be aware that the research team discourages emphasizing instruction in letter naming.

Which Students Should Be Progress Monitored?

Progress monitoring is primarily for students who are below benchmark on the DIBELS *and* are receiving intervention instruction. For all the students who are at benchmark and are reaching important milestones in reading, there is no need to monitor progress more often than the three times a year they participate in the benchmark screening. Progress monitoring is designed for the students whose scores are below benchmark; therefore, you will only be administering progress monitoring to a portion of your class. As the year progresses, more and more students will be exited from intervention groups back to core instruction only, and therefore the number of students receiving progress monitoring decreases over time.

How Often Should Students Be Progress Monitored?

We recommend assessing students in intervention groups at least every three weeks. The *Three-Tier Reading Model* manual published by the University of Texas Center for Reading and Language Arts (UTCRLA) recommends that progress monitoring assessment for students in Tier II and Tier III occurs every two weeks (University of Texas Center for Reading and Language Arts 2003). Some experts suggest that the lowest students who are in Tier III intervention be assessed weekly, and the intermediate students in Tier II be assessed every two weeks. While there are circumstances that suggest assessing this often is beneficial, my preference is for this to be the exception rather than the rule. The purpose of progress monitoring is to check on the rate of progress of each student in order to make changes in a timely fashion.

My recommendations to do progress monitoring every three weeks is based on the following observations:

- Unless you are ready to respond by changing the instruction or the group members every week, weekly progress monitoring is not necessary.

- The trend line of rate of progress can be observed for nearly all students through assessing every three weeks, rather than weekly or bi-weekly.

- It is more important to spend time instructing rather than assessing.

Since most of the time, the person who is instructing the intervention group is also administering the progress monitoring assessment, it is critical to minimize any activities that take away from time devoted to instruction. Although it only takes a little over a minute per student for each indicator, assessment still distracts from instruction time. Since most schools don't systematically analyze data every week and act upon it weekly, it seems that weekly progress monitoring may be wasted time.

Assessing every three weeks generally allows the instructor to see a good trend line of progress after nine weeks. Monitoring progress every three weeks, within nine weeks of the fall benchmark, allows plotting of three points—the initial benchmark in which the student was flagged for intervention instruction and two progress monitoring scores.

There are several circumstances in which weekly or biweekly progress monitoring makes sense. If a student's scores are bouncing around rather than following a line, then you may need to assess more often to understand why. Also, if a student is placed in a group that is a little bit of a stretch for him, then you will want to monitor his progress more often to make sure that the group placement is appropriate. If you assess every three weeks, you can always increase the frequency for any student for any reason. If you opt for more frequent intervals for progress monitoring on a case-by-case basis, you will avoid wasting time unnecessarily.

A sample calendar for assessment is shown in Table 7.2. There are nine assessment periods planned for progress monitoring, along with the three benchmark periods.

Table 7.2

Sample Assessment Schedule*

September	December	March
Week 1	Week 1	Week 1
Week 2—Fall Benchmark	Week 2—PM #4	Week 2
Week 3	Week 3	Week 3—PM #7
Week 4	Week 4	Week 4
October	**January**	**April**
Week 1—PM #1	Week 1	Week 1
Week 2	Week 2—Winter Benchmark	Week 2—PM # 8
Week 3	Week 3	Week 3
Week 4—PM #2	Week 4	Week 4
November	**February**	**May**
Week 1	Week 1—PM #5	Week 1—PM # 9
Week 2	Week 2	Week 2
Week 3—PM # 3	Week 3	Week 3
Week 4	Week 4—PM #6	Week 4—Spring Benchmark

* PM = Progress Monitoring

Which Indicators Are Assessed for Progress Monitoring?

Although a student may be below benchmark in several indicators, you may need to monitor progress on only one or two skills at a time. Select the skills that you are currently teaching to monitor progress. For example, let's explore what to assess for a student in the fall of second grade whose scores are below benchmark in NWF, ORF, RTF, and WUF. If the current instructional focus for this student is on teaching unknown letter-sound correspondences and blending words fluently at the CVC level, then you only need to monitor progress on NWF for now. Once the student gets closer to the benchmark of 50 on NWF, you can begin assessing both NWF and ORF until eventually you will drop NWF and only monitor ORF and RTF. If the intervention instruction is not addressing vocabulary, there is no reason to administer the WUF progress monitoring indicator. Therefore, the rule of thumb is to assess only one or two indicators at a time, and only the ones that measure the skill or skills you are explicitly teaching in your intervention group.

Using Progress Monitoring Data

Informing Decisions for an Individual Student

When you look at the data from progress monitoring assessments for an individual student, your concern is not only whether he is making progress, but also if the rate of progress is adequate for him to catch up to benchmark in time. We want a student to reach benchmark in the skill area, and also to reach the benchmark level on time. Therefore, whenever a student is in intervention instruction, our goal is to catch him up on the deficient skill as soon as possible so that he won't lag behind on the next skill as well. There is no time to waste. We should not be satisfied merely with progress; we need to relentlessly focus on catching him up as fast as possible.

Because catching a student up to benchmark is an urgent concern, one of the most important things to review on the progress monitoring chart is the slope of the line. For example, if you have three data points plotted during the first nine weeks the student received intervention instruction, extend the line out to the end of the year and observe whether the student will make it to the benchmark range at this rate of progress. Depending upon how far behind the student is, achieving benchmark range by year-end may not be good enough. If he will still be behind in the next skill along the continuum, then he has to reach benchmark in both skills by year-end.

For example, if a first grade student is below benchmark at the beginning of the year in both PSF and NWF, he needs to reach benchmark in PSF as soon as possible, or he will not make the benchmark of 50 for NWF by the middle of first grade. The success of intervention instruction depends upon accelerating his rate of progress rather than settling for some degree of improvement.

What to Do if the Student's Rate of Progress Is Too Slow

It was great because you could switch your groups around and be reflective with it. The testing shows we will have to take this one out of here because he's stronger now—he's moved up in that area. Another student can come down to this group. So the groups were changing a lot. And that was neat to be able to do that.

Kindergarten teacher

In the quote above, a kindergarten teacher spoke about the decisions that she learned to make about her students in intervention groups based on DIBELS data. She had just learned to administer and score the DIBELS assessment in September. By May of that same academic year, she was comfortable making data-informed instructional decisions, as revealed by her comments during a focus group interview.

If the rate of progress is too slow for the student to catch up to benchmark at a reasonable point, some possible adjustments are:

- Lengthen the amount of intervention time for the group. If all the students in the 30-minute group need a more accelerated rate of growth, then change the schedule to enable the group to receive intervention instruction for 45 minutes daily until the rate of progress is better.

- Change the student to a group that meets for a longer period of time. For example, place the student in a group that meets for two 30-minute sessions daily. In the Three-Tier Reading Model, this may represent a move from a Tier II to a Tier III group.

- Change the intervention materials. Have the instructor use a more systematic and explicit instructional program. For some skill areas, this may mean changing materials. For other areas, it may be possible for the instructor to change the way she uses the materials.

- Change instructors, or provide more coaching to the instructor. If the entire group's progress is not as strong as desired rather than just one individual student's progress, this may signal that the group should be reassigned to a different teacher. Alternatively, if the school has a reading coach, it may be possible for the coach to spend more time helping the instructor use techniques that increase the intensity of instruction.

The *Three-Tier Reading Model* from the UTCRLA suggests that students stay in Tier II instruction for ten to twelve weeks. At the end of the first cycle in Tier II, a student may enter another round of ten to twelve weeks in Tier II. If the student has not made enough progress at the end of the second round, he can be moved to Tier III. Although this model is a useful framework, most schools implement a more flexible version of this model within the first year. Students can be moved between levels of intensity on schedules that aren't tied to the ten to twelve week cycle, and intensity within a group can be increased at any point it is needed.

One way to analyze whether a student is in an appropriate group is to view the progress monitoring data on a single indicator for the three to five students in a group all on one chart. It will be apparent if they should stay together because the rate of progress will be about the same for the students (see Table 7.3).

Table 7.3

Sample
Progress
Monitoring
Graph for an
Intervention
Group

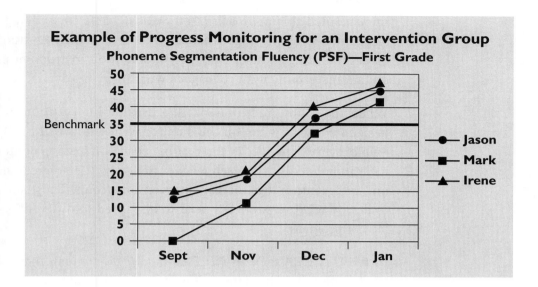

Example of Progress Monitoring for an Intervention Group

Phoneme Segmentation Fluency (PSF)—First Grade

Similarly, if one student's rate of progress is much slower than the other two, it will be obvious on this chart. The student making slower progress should be considered for placement in a different group.

When to Exit a Student From Intervention Instruction

When a student's progress monitoring score reaches benchmark on two consecutive assessments, or for six weeks, it is time for him to exit the group. He has caught up to benchmark and may only need core reading instruction at this point. One of the most interesting things to observe is that teachers have a hard time exiting the students out of intervention. One possible reason is concern about whether the student's skills will continue to progress. If that is a concern, the teacher can progress monitor the student for a few weeks after he is exited from the intervention group just to be sure that he stays on track. If at any point his skills aren't continuing to make progress, he can reenter the intervention group. In my experience, very rarely does a student who is exited from the intervention group have to re-enter it. Generally, with effective and early intervention, once the student catches up, he continues to make progress with core reading instruction alone.

Procedures to Analyze Data Periodically

At least during the first year of using the DIBELS data, some schools prefer to institute a systematic procedure for when and how data is analyzed. One of the best processes is for a team of teachers to study the data regularly at grade-level meetings. Most teachers did not enter the profession knowing how to implement data-driven instruction. Therefore, they have to learn how to use data in new ways through ongoing support and dialogue. Schools that have implemented this approach often dedicate time to studying student data at each grade-level meeting. Teachers take turns bringing a student's data to the team, analyzing it, discussing the intervention instruction provided to date, and brainstorming with colleagues what to try next.

When the school first organizes to provide intervention, it may be best to designate a time when all the data for each group will be examined. For example, every nine weeks the reading coach or reading content leader would meet individually with each teacher to review the progress monitoring charts and intervention logs for her intervention group. They could work together to decide whether students need to be moved to different groups because of lack of progress.

In the UTCRLA's *Three-Tier Reading Model* manual, there are some helpful suggestions about how to implement a plan in your school. One recommendation is that criteria be stated for entry and exit from Tier II and Tier III.

Many schools state explicit goals for their early intervention programs. The overarching goal is typically to improve student reading outcomes, or to reduce the number of students not at benchmark. Some sample school goals are:

- No more than 5% of students will be below benchmark by the end of the first year of implementation.

- All students below benchmark will receive at least 30 minutes of intervention daily in a group no larger than five students.

- All students in the lowest 10% will receive two 30-minute intervention lessons daily for as many weeks as needed in groups no larger than three students.

- Data for each student and group receiving intervention instruction will be analyzed at least every nine weeks.

- If after nine weeks a student is not making an adequate level of progress to reach benchmark by year-end, his intervention will be intensified.

- Students will remain in intervention instruction until they reach DIBELS benchmark on two consecutive progress monitoring assessments (or six weeks).

The *Three-Tier Reading Model* manual recommends that a campus assessment team be assigned the responsibility for evaluating the progress of the students in Tier II and Tier III interventions. A pre-referral team can also evaluate the progress of an individual student to determine when to refer him for further diagnostic testing.

Analyzing the Effectiveness of the School's Intervention Program

Another use for the progress monitoring data is to analyze how effective the school's intervention instruction is in catching up struggling readers. If you are using the University of Oregon's data management system, one of the best ways to see this is to review some of the reports from this system. There are bar graphs displaying the entire grade level reading outcomes for each DIBELS indicator. By comparing the proportion of students requiring intervention at the beginning of the year with the end of the year, the effectiveness of the instruction is visible. Keep in mind that there is no way to separate out the effectiveness of the core instruction from the intervention instruction since the students who were below benchmark received both. However it doesn't really matter which instruction contributed the most to catching the students up to benchmark; what is important is that the combination of services helped the students. The box plot charts show graphically not only how much the entire school is progressing, but also whether the lowest students are making progress.

Record Keeping for Intervention Groups

Intervention Lesson Plans

Chapter 6 provided some sample lesson plan forms. Most schools have a three-ring binder for the intervention groups and keep a copy of the lesson plans filed for each group. These lesson plans provide documentation about the types of materials used in the intervention and what level of intensity the student has already received. It is important to keep this information for analysis. When the reading coach or content leader meets with a teacher to decide if the intervention should be changed for a student who didn't make adequate progress, these plans provide critical information.

After completing separate lesson plans for a group for the first couple of weeks, it is possible to plan more efficiently across a two-week period by using a chart similar to the one shown in Tables 7.4 and 7.5.

Table 7.4

**Two-Week
Lesson Plan**

Intervention Activities Schedule

Group _____

Students in Group _____

Weeks _____

NAME of Activity	Week 1					Week 2				
	M	T	W	Th	F	M	T	W	Th	F

Table 7.5

**Sample
Two-Week
Lesson Plan**

Intervention Activities Schedule

Group ___Kindergarten—Group 1___

Students in Group ___Shenoa, Jeremy, Adrienne___

Weeks ___October 18 & 25, 2004___

	Week 1					Week 2				
NAME of Activity	M	T	W	Th	F	M	T	W	Th	F
Isolate That Sound	X	X				X	X	X		
All Aboard!	X	X	X				X	X	X	
Saying Silly Sentences	X	X	X						X	
Where's That Sound			X	X	X			X	X	X
Thumbs Up				X	X	X				X
Sound Dominos						X	X			X

Each activity is repeated for three days in a row. By rotating to a limited set of different activities, children experience variety, and teachers avoid investing unnecessary time in planning new activities and teaching students more new routines.

Intervention Logs

In addition to the lesson plans, most intervention teachers keep some kind of log so they can make notes about students' attendance, attentiveness to the task, progress on specific skills, and any apparent difficulties. These notes also provide important information, especially when the student isn't making progress. In some schools where the intervention instructor is not the classroom teacher, a copy of this log is placed in the teacher's mailbox weekly to help keep the teacher informed about the student's intervention instruction. A sample form is provided in Table 7.6.

Table 7.6

Sample Intervention Log No. 1

Intervention Log

Week of _____

Teacher _____

Students _____

Focus of Group's Instruction _____

Intervention Instructor _____

Major skills—focus this week (check all that apply)

☐ Listening Skills

☐ Letter Recognition   Letters: _____

☐ Sentence segmenting

☐ Syllable

☐ Onset-Rime/Rhyming

☐ Phonemic Awareness   Phonemes: _____

   ☐ Isolation

   ☐ Identity

   ☐ Categorization

   ☐ Blending

   ☐ Segmentation

   ☐ Deletion

   ☐ Addition

   ☐ Substitution

Major progress/accomplishments this week:

More work needed on:

Other observations:

Table 7.6

Sample
Intervention
Log No. 2

Group Information:

Instructional Focus of Group _____

Week of _____

Names of Students in Group & DIBELS Scores: _____

School / Teacher _____

	Name	ISF	LNF	PSF	NWF	ORF	RTF	WUF	Date:
1.									
2.									
3.									
4.									

Time—Intervention Provided:

Monday	Tuesday	Wednesday	Thursday	Friday

Times Met:

Total Minutes/Day: _____

Instructor: _____

Curriculum / Materials:

Attendance and Observation Records:

Student Name: Attendance:(circle if present) M T W Th F	Student Name: Attendance:(circle if present) M T W Th F
Student Name: Attendance:(circle if present) M T W Th F	Student Name: Attendance:(circle if present) M T W Th F

Add more boxes on back if more than 4 students

Part II

Sample Intervention Activities

Chapter 8

Intervention Activities for Letter Naming Fluency (LNF)

Overview on Letter Recognition and Naming Skills

Why Letter Naming Is Important

English has an alphabetic writing system; letters in written words represent sounds in spoken words. The awareness that letters represent the sounds in spoken words is called the alphabetic principle. One of the basic steps in learning the alphabetic principle is recognizing and naming the letters of the alphabet. Children will also have to learn the sounds in words (phonemic awareness) and the letters that represent those sounds. Most strong readers acquire a working knowledge of the alphabetic principle by the middle of first grade. It is also helpful for children to learn to sequence the letters from A to Z because alphabetical order is the way we organize our letters.

Not all researchers agree on the importance of learning the names of the letters in learning to read. The DIBELS research team believes that teaching letter knowledge is not an important instructional goal. It's not that instructing in letter knowledge is harmful, but rather that it may not be an important goal in teaching reading. They believe that children need to associate the sounds with letters, and may not need to know the letter names, for reading.

Other researchers believe that letter knowledge plays a more significant role in the realm of language arts—enough to make it an instructional goal even if it is not the most important goal. Why might learning the names of the letters be helpful in learning to read? Two of the researchers who work in this area found that children who did not know letter names had more difficulty learning letter sounds (Ehri & Wilce 1979). Letter names are closely related to the letter-sound relationships, and knowing the letter names helps children associate sound with many of the letters. It seems obvious that children who can easily recall the letter names instantly on sight, to an extent that we might say is "automatic," can easily form an association between a symbol and its name.

Letter naming knowledge has long been recognized as a potent predictor of later reading ability. Some studies suggest that although letter naming predicts the ability to read later on, it does not cause a child to learn more readily. Ehri and Wilce, however, suggested that letter name knowledge may be inseparable from letter-sound knowledge because so many letter names sound a great deal like the sound that is associated with them (for example, /m/ for the letter m). Gail Gillon describes a "bi-directional" relationship between letter-name and phoneme awareness, where knowledge of one enhances knowledge of the other (Gillon 2003).

For some children, knowledge of the alphabetic principle develops almost naturally as they interact with books, observe signs in the grocery store and labels on products, etc. These children begin to ask questions about letters, sounds, and words, and with exposure to a few examples, their brains start to connect which letters represent which sounds. But for many other children, those connections are learned primarily through instruction and sufficient practice with many examples.

Over the past few years, kindergarten teachers in schools serving families from all socioeconomic levels are reporting that more of their students are entering kindergarten knowing less about the alphabet, with many children unable to name even five letters. While teachers in urban schools who serve families with little print material at home have faced these problems for years, kindergarten teachers in affluent suburbs are attributing children's lack of alphabet knowledge to the increasingly busy lifestyle of many American families and the time children spend on electronic and computer games. This trend toward students entering kindergarten with lower alphabet and book knowledge means that more of the kindergarten curriculum must be devoted to teaching the alphabet.

Importance of Teaching Early Reading Skills in Kindergarten

Because the topic of this chapter is teaching letter naming and since basic alphabetic instruction usually begins in kindergarten, it is imperative to discuss the kindergarten curriculum at this point. Kindergarten teachers have often expressed concerns about the pressure to shift their curriculum from social to academic goals. These teachers wonder whether it is advisable to be teaching kindergartners pre-reading and early reading skills, when those children seem immature and unready to learn. My view, which is based on many studies of early reading development, is that children at the kindergarten level need to attain the following minimum goals because they strongly predict later reading success.

- A strong sense of phonemic awareness

- Fluency in naming uppercase and lowercase letters

- Knowledge of how a book is read

- Realization that reading is comprehending (taught through read-alouds)

- Strong oral language skills

- An expansive vocabulary

With the increased emphasis on reading instruction in kindergarten, many children are learning to read by the end of their kindergarten year. However, whether children actually learn to read in kindergarten is less important than their preparedness to read in first grade. Children must learn to read by the end of first grade or their entire academic career may be jeopardized. What children learn in kindergarten does significantly affect how well children will read and spell in first grade. The more kindergarteners know about phonemic awareness and the alphabet, and the stronger their oral language skills, the more easily they will learn to read from systematic and explicit instruction in first grade. The minimum mandatory goal for the kindergarten year must be to prepare *all* students to learn to read.

When Letter Naming Isn't Mastered in the Early Grades

Although letter naming and alphabetical order are skills that are generally mastered at least by the middle of first grade, many children reach the upper elementary grades without being able to fluently and automatically name and alphabetize the letters. Children who experience reading difficulties in first grade and beyond are commonly found to lack secure skills with letter naming and alphabetizing. These problems can be discovered by giving the LNF measure to older students. If they cannot name 40 randomly arranged letters in a minute, they may need additional instruction and practice on their letters.

Do I Teach Uppercase or Lowercase First?

Teachers often ask if they should teach uppercase or lowercase letters first. My recommendation is to teach uppercase first because fewer uppercase letters are confusable. Most children easily make the transition from uppercase to lowercase. It is not necessary to repeat the entire instructional approach to teach the lowercase letters, once the uppercase is known. Rather, children can easily learn to match uppercase and lowercase once the uppercase is known.

Overview of Types of Intervention Activities

The instructional strategies and activities to learn the alphabet in this manual are playful, fun, engaging, and active. They should be taught in short, ten to fifteen minute increments as part of intervention instruction for students of any age who need to improve their letter naming and alphabetizing skills. These activities can also be integrated into the core curriculum as supplemental strategies.

The activities are organized under four categories, as follows:

- Learning the Alphabet With Songs
- Matching Letter Shapes to Letter Names
- Letter Sequencing (Alphabetizing)
- Building Fluency in Letter Recognition and Naming

Intervention Activities

Learning the Alphabet With Songs

8-1: *Singing the Alphabet Song With Varying Pace and Rhythm*

Brief Description

Children sing the alphabet song at various paces, from very slow to very fast. A very slow pace is most important so that children are forced to articulate the letters LMNOP, which are often run together when the song is sung at its normal tempo.

Materials Needed

Three pictures for the teacher: a turtle, a person walking, and a rocket or jet.

Alphabet strip with uppercase letters for each student.

Step-by-Step Directions

1. The teacher holds up one of the pictures to indicate the pace at which the song is to be sung (turtle = very slow; walking person = normal; rocket or jet = fast).

2. The students sing the song at the appropriate pace.

3. The teacher holds up the turtle picture for the LMNOP letters so that the students realize these are separate letters.

4. VERY IMPORTANT: As students begin matching letters with letter names, and the students can sing the song at the slow or normal pace, they should touch each letter as they sing the song.

Additional Information

Many children learn the letter names before the shapes of the letters by singing the alphabet. When children know how to say the alphabet before they learn the names for each symbol, they can anchor the name to the visual representation of the letter.

8-2: Singing Only Part of the Alphabet Song

Brief Description

Children sing only part of the alphabet song, starting and ending at given letters..

Materials Needed

Pocket chart, a magnetic board, or some other way to display letters.

Letter cards or magnetic letters.

Three pictures: a turtle, a person walking, and a rocket or jet.

Alphabet strip with uppercase letters for each student.

Step-by-Step Directions

1. The teacher places the start and stop letters in the pocket chart or the magnetic board.

2. The teacher holds up one of the pictures to indicate the pace at which the song is to be sung (turtle = very slow; walking person = normal; jet or rocket = fast).

3. The students sing the song at the indicated pace from the starting letter to the stopping letter.

4. Students touch each letter as they sing the song.

8-3: Singing the Alphabet Song to Other Tunes[1]

Brief Description

Sing the alphabet song to other common tunes to help students realize that LMNOP are five separate letters.

---

[1] Neuhaus Education Center 2002, 4.

Materials Needed

Large cards with the letters displayed for the songs (see examples below).

Detailed Description

Make a large song card that students will be able to see. This song card shows the letters arranged as they will be sung to match the tunes. Table 8.1 shows two examples that are provided in the Neuhaus Education Center's publication called *Reading Readiness Manual.* This manual is an excellent resource, and other activities from it will be included in later chapters.

Table 8.1

**Singing the
Alphabet
Song to
Other Tunes**

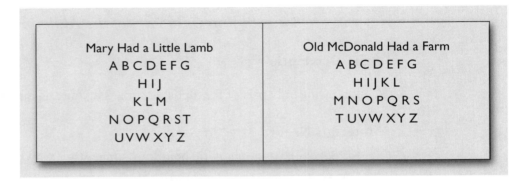

Mary Had a Little Lamb	Old McDonald Had a Farm
A B C D E F G	A B C D E F G
H I J	H I J K L
K L M	M N O P Q R S
N O P Q R S T	T U V W X Y Z
U V W X Y Z	

Matching Letter Shapes to Letter Names

8-4: Pre-Arc Cards [2]

---

[2] Neuhaus Education Center 2002, 1.

Brief Description

Teach the alphabet to students who have little knowledge of the letters using cards containing five letters at a time and plastic letters that match the size of the letters on the cards.

Materials Needed

For each student:

Five cards, with the following letters on them, in a size that matches the plastic letters (use cardstock and laminate, if possible):

ABCDE   FGHIJ   KLMNO   PQRST   UVWXYZ

Individual plastic letters (all 26 letters).

Step-by-Step Directions

1. Teacher gives each student the individual letters A, B, C, D, and E and the card with ABCDE on it.

2. Teacher introduces each letter by holding up the letter and pointing to it on the card.

   a. Teacher says, "This is the letter A. Touch the letter A on your card and say A."

   b. Students touch the letter and say, "A."

   c. Teacher says, "Find the plastic letter A and put it on top of the A on your card." Students find the individual letter and put it on the correction position on their cards.

   d. Repeat steps a-c for all five letters.

3. Teacher then asks students to scramble the letters, and arrange them on the mat as they say the name of each letter.

4. After students have mastered the first five letters, teacher repeats the exercise with the next five letters.

5. When students have learned more than one card, they can review all the letters they know.

Additional Information

This activity is a precursor to one of my favorite activities for improving letter recognition skills, the Alphabet Arc. Alphabet Arc activities, developed at the Neuhaus Center in Houston, Texas, involve naming each letter and placing a plastic letter over the spot where the letter is outlined on a mat. The 11 × 17-

inch mat has the traced letters arranged in an arc from the lower left corner of the page to the lower right corner.

In spite of the fact that the letters appear on the arc in alphabetical order, this arc can be overwhelming for some children who enter kindergarten knowing fewer than 10 letters of the alphabet. They need to work with a smaller group of letters to master a few at a time before working with all 26 letters.

For these students, the first step is to work with the blue plastic letters, five at a time per card. I call these cards "pre-arc cards"; the master for these five cards (there are six letters on the last card) is in the Neuhaus Center's *Reading Readiness Manual*. Try copying these cards on different colors of cardstock so when children move from one card to the next, you can celebrate moving to the "blue card." Blue plastic letters that exactly fit the letters on the arc are available from a company called Abecedarian for $1 per set. (Teachers can also make their own materials if they prefer.)

Make this as multisensory as you can. Ask the children to feel the plastic letters and tell you about which ones have straight lines, curvy lines, circles, or a combination. Also, always remember to review after the children have learned two or more cards. Check for mastery by playing a game with all ten letters. For this activity, be sure to review the letter names and not the sounds.

8-5: *Alphabet Arc Side I*[3]

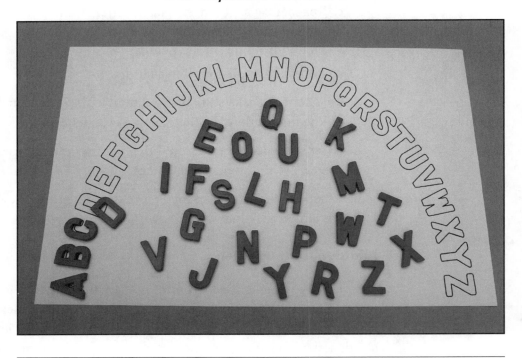

---

[3] Neuhaus Education Center 2002, 2.

Brief Description

Students learn to name and identify each letter by placing a plastic letter over the matching letter on an arc.

Materials Needed

Alphabet Arc, preferably copied on yellow 11 × 17-inch cardstock.

Uppercase letters to match the letters on the Alphabet Arc.

Detailed Description

After the children in the intervention group have mastered all five pre-arc cards, introduce the Alphabet Arc Side I. This is the side of the Alphabet Arc mat where all the letters are traced on the arc, in contrast to Side II where only the A, M, N, and Z appear on the arc. Generally, the Side I mat is copied on yellow cardstock and Side II on blue cardstock. The blackline master for these mats is in the *Reading Readiness Manual*, and the blue plastic letters that exactly fit the letters on the arc are available from a company called Abecedarian for $1 per set. (See Table 8.2 at the end of this chapter for contact information.) These materials are so inexpensive that teachers can feel comfortable sending sets home with children. When first introducing the Arc Side I, it's best to start with five or ten letters and let the student become familiar with using the same blue plastic letters on a new format. When a student can say the names of all the letters and place them on the mat in two minutes, he has reached the goal. Don't be surprised if it takes several months for some kindergarten intervention students to reach this goal. Some teachers ask the children to time themselves with a timer and chart their progress in reducing their own "personal best" time.

8-6: Matching Letters Game

Brief Description

Children use movable alphabet letters to match uppercase and lowercase letters.

Materials Needed

One set of uppercase letter cards or tiles for each student.

One set of lowercase letter cards or tiles for each student.

Step-by-Step Directions

1. The teacher gives one student (the moderator) a set of uppercase letters in a paper bag. The rest of the students (contestants) get a set of lowercase letters. Use only the letters that have been or are being taught.

2. The contestants place the letters face up in front of them.

3. Moderator reaches into the bag, holds up a letter and says its name.

4. One contestant is "on the spot" and the other contestants are the "checkers."

5. All contestants say the name of the letter and find the matching lower-case letter, hiding it in their hand.

6. The "on the spot" contestant shows his letter. He gets one point if he is correct.

7. The "checkers" show their letters. If the "on the spot" contestant is incorrect, all the checkers who have the right answer get a point.

8-7: *Matching Uppercase and Lowercase Letters*

Brief Description

Students arrange movable alphabet letters on top of a template that has the opposite case of letters.

Materials Needed

One set of uppercase letter cards or tiles for each student.

One set of lowercase letter cards or tiles for each student.

One template with the uppercase letters on it.

One template with lowercase letters on it.

Step-by-Step Directions

1. The teacher gives each student a template with the uppercase or lowercase letters on it and a set of movable alphabet letters that is the opposite case.

2. The teacher times the students as they place the movable alphabet letters on top of the corresponding letters on the template.

Additional Information

This activity works especially well with magnetic letter tiles because the letters don't move after the student places them on the template. Also, the students can hold up their whiteboard with the tiles on it when they finish, enabling the teacher to check their answers. They are also good for activity centers because children can create their answers and carry their "answer sheet" (the whiteboard with magnetic letter tiles on it) to the teacher to be checked.

Letter Sequencing (Alphabetizing)

8-8: Alphabet Arc Side II [4]

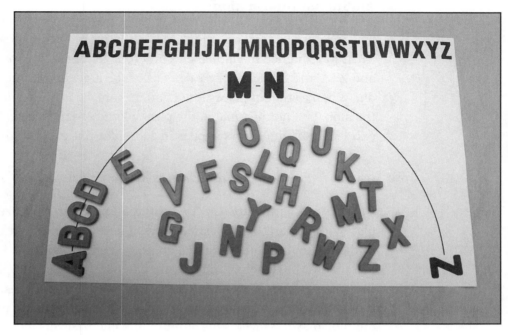

Brief Description

Practice in sequencing the letters in alphabetical order on an arc that has only the beginning, middle, and end of the alphabet provided.

Materials Needed

Alphabet Arc Side II, preferably copied on blue 11 × 17-inch cardstock.

Uppercase letters.

Step-by-Step Directions

1. Ask the student to find the A and place it on the arc.

2. Then find the Z and place it, and finally the M and N and place them.

3. The student continues by placing all the letters in the correct alphabetical order while naming them.

4. When the child has finished placing all her letters, ask her to check the order by touching and naming each letter, starting with A and moving to Z.

---

4 Neuhaus Education Center 2002, 5.

5. Repeat this activity frequently until the child can consistently place all the letters in the proper order within two minutes.

Additional Information

The purpose of this arc, which is slightly more challenging than Side I, is to learn to sequence the alphabet. Only four letters appear on the arc: A, M, N, and Z. A and Z anchor the two ends of the arc, and M and N anchor the middle. When a student places letters on this arc, he is forced to know the order of the alphabet, not just match the plastic letters to the traced letters. To provide extra support the letters appear in a straight line at the top of the page.

8-9: *Other Games With the Alphabet Arc*

In the *Reading Readiness Manual* there are at least a dozen other games to play with the arcs and plastic letters. These can be found in the first section of the manual. In one of these games, two students in the intervention group can play, or the teacher and student can play. Each player places all his letters in a brown paper bag. The players reach in their own bags, grab a letter, slap it down on the mat, and try to be the first to move it to its proper place on the arc. The player who gets his letter on the mat first gets to keep the letter on the arc and the other player returns the letter to his bag. The game is over when one player has all his letters properly placed on the mat.

Building Fluency in Letter Recognition and Naming

8-10: *Instant Letter Recognition Charts*

Brief Description

Use chart with random arrangement of letters to build fluency in identifying and naming letters.

Materials Needed

Set of cards with rows of letters arranged in random order.

Detailed Description

Another activity for building fluency in letter naming is to read letters on a chart as quickly as possible. The *Reading Readiness Manual* provides blackline masters of over ten pages of letter charts at the end of the first section of the manual. Letters are arranged ten to a line on these charts, in either uppercase or lowercase. If you wish to make a chart with a different font or one that mixes uppercase and lowercase, there is a blank chart at the end of the masters.

8-11: Letter Naming Flash Cards

Brief Description

Student reads letter names as teacher (or another student) flips a deck of cards with letters on them.

Materials Needed

Cards with letters on them (these can come from a kit or the teacher can make them).

Decks can include duplicates of some or all of the letters.

Step-by-Step Directions

1. Teacher shuffles the deck.

2. Teacher flips a card and student names the letter.

3. Teacher continues flipping cards as fast as student names the letter.

4. Correctly named letters are placed in one pile.

5. Misnamed letters are placed in a different pile to be reviewed later.

Note: Students can work in pairs for this activity. This activity can be timed.

8-12: Closer to Z[5]

Brief Description

Students practice alphabetic order by identifying whose letter is closer to Z.

Materials Needed

One set of plastic letters.

Brown paper bag.

Step-by-Step Directions

1. Each student works from one set of letters in a brown paper bag.

2. Both students choose a letter without looking and simultaneously place the letters on a desk.

3. Each student names his letter.

---

[5] Neuhaus Education Center 2002, 9.

4. The player with the letter closer to Z wins and picks up both letters.

5. The winner says, "I win because ___ is closer to Z than ___."

8-13: *Missing Letter Decks*[6]

Brief Description

Cards with a sequence of two to five letters in alphabetical order, in which one or two letters are missing; students name the missing letter(s).

Materials Needed

Four decks of index cards with letters missing from the sequence (see detailed description below).

Detailed Description

The activity for developing fluency with letter naming is called the "Missing Letter Deck." It can start with the simpler task and then increase in difficulty. Students see cards with two letters plus a line to indicate a letter is missing. As the cards in the deck are flipped, students name the missing letter on each card. Teachers can make these cards by using 3 × 5-inch cards. When working on the early part of the alphabet, the cards might look like this:

Set 1:

Make a deck for the entire alphabet and practice it in order first before shuffling the deck. Then increase the difficulty. Set 2 and Set 3 each are more difficult than Set 1 and also provide variety for this activity.

Set 2:

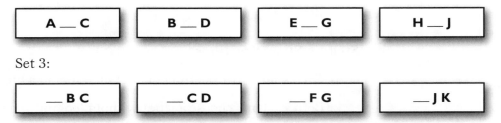

Set 3:

As the student becomes more proficient working with the cards in Sets 1–3, he is ready for Set 4, in which one middle letter is provided between lines for letters missing before and after the target letter. Set 4 cards would look like this:

[6] Birsh 1999, 100.

Set 4:

| __B__ | __E__ | __I__ | __N__ |

For a Friday game, cards from all four sets can be mixed. This activity, along with over a dozen others, is described in the fourth chapter of a book called *Multisensory Teaching of Basic Language Skills* (Birsh 1999). The chapter on letter recognition was written by Kay Allen and Marilyn Beckwith from the Neuhaus Education Center.

Commercially Available Products for Developing Letter Naming Fluency (LNF)

All the activities described in this chapter can be made with minimal expense. A list of commercially available products is included for two reasons. Many times teachers prefer to purchase rather than make materials. Additionally, interventionists like to vary their routines for lesson plans. The Alphabet Arc, which is emphasized in this chapter, is well-liked by both students and teachers. It can serve as the primary activity for building letter naming fluency. It is helpful to have some other materials that can be used to bring variety to the intervention sessions.

The first place to check for additional materials is your core reading curriculum. Many core reading programs (also called basals) have an audiotape with a song for each letter of the alphabet and letter cards than can be used for teaching the alphabet. It is best to check the kindergarten materials because they most often have the letter cards that contain only the upperccase and lowercase letters. At this point, since we are not yet teaching letter-sound associations, it is best to find the cards with only the letter and not the keyword picture. A list of some commercially available products is included in Table 8.2.

Table 8.2

Recommended Commercially Available Materials for Letter Naming Intervention

Name	Description	Contact Information*
Alphabet Songs & Books		
	Audiotape with songs about each letter of the alphabet.	ABC Sing-Along Flip Chart and Audiotape www.etacuisenaire.com IN61894 $24.95
	Collection of 26 alliterative stories—one for each letter of the alphabet.	AlphaTales www.etacuisenaire.com IN62140

Table 8.2

continued

Teaching Letter Names		
Alphabet Arcs	Master for Arc in *Reading Readiness Manual* (Neuhaus Education Center 2002).	Neuhaus Education Center www.neuhaus.org $35
Alphabet Arc Letters	Set of 26 plastic alphabet letters in self-sealing plastic bag. Blue uppercase and red lowercase. English and Spanish.	Abecedarian www.alphabetletter.com Uppercase English alphabet letters $1 per set plus shipping
Paper for Alphabet Arcs	11 x 17″ —67 lb. Wausau Exact Vellum Bristol	Available at paper, art, and office supply stores
Developing Fluency in Letter Recognition		
Tactile Letters Sorting Set	Set with divided plastic trays containing letters. Cards for uppercase and lowercase, and plastic letters to match.	www.etacuisenaire.com IN61753 $64.95
Clever Catch ABC Ball	24″ inflatable vinyl ball with letter and keyword pictures.	www.etacuisenaire.com IN61674 $10.95
Lakeshore Alphabet & Number Beads	Brightly colored plastic beads with alphabet letters to use to string.	www.lakeshorelearning.com LA11 $29.95
Hands On Literacy Phonics Cubes	Color-coded soft cubes that are like medium size dice with letters on all sides.	www.etacuisenaire.com IN62726—uppercase IN61109—lowercase $12.95 for set of 6
Hands-On Soft Alphabet Dice	Small alphabet dice that are foam so they are quiet.	www.etacuisenaire.com IN62740 $7.50
Toss 'N' Play Alphabet Bean Bags	Beanbags that are 4½ inches square in assorted colors. Upper and lowercase on same bag.	www.etacuisenaire.com IN61709 $37.95
Alphabet Sorting Kits Lakeshore Learning	Vinyl mat with colored dots with alphabet letters. Includes chunky plastic letter that match.	www.lakeshorelearning.com TT845—upper $24.95 TT846—lower $24.95

Note: Prices at time of printing. Please contact vendor for current information.

Chapter 9

Intervention Activities for Initial Sound Fluency (ISF) and Phoneme Segmentation Fluency (PSF)

Phonological awareness is well documented as an important skill that good readers have and many struggling readers lack. Research shows that 80 to 90 percent of students with reading difficulties have deficiencies in phonological awareness. Some students have other deficient skills and some lack only phonemic awareness, a critical subset of phonological awareness.

Phonological and Phonemic Awareness Defined

It is important for teachers to understand the relationship between phonological awareness and phonemic awareness. As Table 9.1 shows, phonemic awareness is a subset of phonological awareness, with phonological awareness encompassing phonemic awareness and many other skills.

Table 9.1

Phonemic Awareness Is a Type of Phonological Awareness

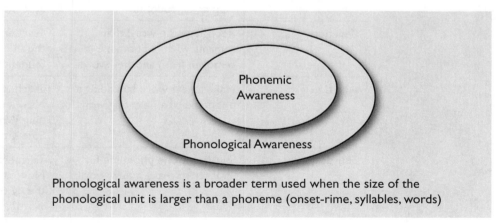

Phonological awareness is a broader term used when the size of the phonological unit is larger than a phoneme (onset-rime, syllables, words)

Phonological awareness is the ability to identify and manipulate word parts, such as syllables, onset and rime, and phonemes. Phonemic awareness, the highest level of phonological awareness, is the ability to identify and manipulate phonemes. Table 9.2 shows the continuum of types of phonological awareness activities and illustrates the difference between activities that teach phonemic awareness and activities that teach other aspects of phonological awareness.

Table 9.2

Sample
Activities
on the
Phonological
Awareness
Continuum

Phonological Awareness Level	Description of Skill	Sample Activity
Word	Distinguish and manipulate words in a sentence	Walk one step for each word in this sentence: *The cat is black.* (4 steps)
Syllable	Distinguish and manipulate syllables in a word	Clap the syllables in your name. *Davon* (2 claps)
Onset-Rime/ Rhyming	Recognize, identify, and produce words that rhyme	Which word rhymes with *dog? Log* or *bat?* (*log*) Tell me a word that rhymes with *frog.* (*log* or *dog*)
Phonemic Awareness		
Isolation	Recognize individual sounds in a word	Teacher: What is the first sound in *bat?* Student: /b/
Identification	Recognize the same sounds in different words	Teacher: What sound is the same in *man, mat,* and *mouse?* Student: /m/
Categorization	Recognize that one word in a set has an "odd" sound	Teacher: Which word doesn't belong? *cap, car, bat* Student: *bat*
Blending	Listen to a sequence of sounds and combine them to say a word	Teacher: What word is /m/ /o/ /p/? Student: *mop*
Segmentation	Break a word into its separate sounds, saying each sound while tapping or counting	Teacher: what are the sounds in *hat?* Student: /h/ /a/ /t/
Deletion	Recognize the word that remains when a phoneme is removed from another word	Teacher: What is *his* without the /h/? Student: *is*
Addition	Make a new word by adding a phoneme to an existing word	Teacher: Say the word *top.* Now add /s/ to the beginning. What's the new word? Student: *stop*
Substitution	Substitute one phoneme for another to make a new word	Teacher: Say the word *bus.* Now say it again and change the /s/ to /n/. What's the new word? Student: *bun*

Resources

Two types of resources are described in this section. First, a list is provided of curricula that offer reasonably comprehensive sets of activities and strategies to use when teaching phonological awareness. Second, a list of books that have phonological awareness activities is provided.

The seven comprehensive programs are described in Table 9.3.

Table 9.3

Resource List: Comprehensive Programs for Phonological Awareness

---

More Complete Phonological Awareness Training Curricula

Phonemic Awareness in Young Children
- By Marilyn Adams, Barbara Foorman, Ingvar Lindberg, and Terri Beeler
- 1998, Paul H. Brookes Publishing Company, 1-800- 638-3775, www.brookespublishing.com, $29.95.
- This spiral-bound manual provides a curriculum that can be delivered in 15-20 minutes daily to complement a prereading program for kindergarten, first-grade, or special education students. It is organized in tabs relating to the different skills, building generally from the simple to the complex. The manual is composed of pages of activities organized in the following sections: listening games, rhyming, words and sentences, awareness of syllables, initial and final sounds, phonemes, and introducing letters and spellings. A schedule is provided at the back of the manual (pages 139–141) showing how to schedule the activities across 140 days. One of the benefits of this book is the clear organization by type of skill. One thing that makes this book slightly less appealing to teachers is that it doesn't include the black line masters of cards, pictures, and other materials that many other books have.

Phonological Awareness Training for Reading
- By Joseph Torgesen and Brian Bryant
- 1994, ProEd, 1-800-897-3202, www.proedinc.com, $139.
- This program was designed for use with children in the second half of kindergarten, or with students in first and second grade who are at risk. It can be provided in four weekly 20–25 minute sessions either individually or in small groups. Each lesson is divided into four segments, including a rhyming warm-up, sound blending, sound segmenting, and then eventually the lessons build to reading and spelling with letters. Each lesson uses a set of words. This program comes in a box with game boards, picture cards, a spiral-bound manual, an audiotape, and all the materials needed.

Reading Readiness Manual
- By Neuhaus Education Center
- 2002, Neuhaus Education Center, (713) 664-7676, www.neuhaus.org, $35.
- Manual of activities for 20- 30-minute lessons that can be used in the classroom or in intervention groups. There are five sections in the manual: letter recognition, phonological awareness, oral language, multisensory letter introduction, and handwriting. Each section contains a series of activities and includes the black line masters at the end of the section. A deck of letter-sound cards is included, as well.

Note: Prices listed are at time of publication. Please contact vendor for current information.

Table 9.3

continued

Road to the Code
- By Benita Blachman, Eileen Whynne Ball, Rochella Black, and Darlene M. Tangel
- 2000, Paul H. Brookes Publishing Company, 1-800- 638-3775, www.brookespublishing.com, $49.95.
- The Road to the Code program is an 11-week curriculum to help kindergarten and first grade students who are having difficulty learning phonemic awareness and some letter-sound correspondences. In the spiral-bound manual, a series of 44 sequential lessons is described, and a script is provided for these 15–20 minute lessons. The final third of this nearly 400-page manual is black line masters containing Say-It-And-Move-It cards, Alphabet Picture Cards, Sound Categorization Cards, Sound Bingo Cards, and Elkonin Cards. Although only eight letters are introduced (a, m, t , i, s, r, b, and f) during this 44-day program, the picture cards and jingles for all 26 letters are included.

Teacher-Directed PALS: Paths to Achieving Literacy Success
- By Patricia Mathes, Jill Howard Allor, Joseph K. Torgesen, and Shelley H. Allen
- 2001, Sopris West, 1-800-547-6747, www.sopriswest.com, $29.95.
- This spiral-bound manual includes 57 lessons designed specifically for use by paraprofessionals and teachers providing supplemental or intervention instruction to small groups of struggling readers. Within each 20–30-minute lesson, students practice phonemic awareness, letter-sound recognition, and phonological decoding. Each lesson also includes applying skills in decoding connected text, including practicing comprehension strategies while reading a trade book aloud in a section called "Story Sharing." The formats for the lessons, along with some scripts, are included in the first couple of chapters of the manual. One of the best things provided is the Mastery Monitoring Form in Chapter 4, which is used to keep track of each student's progress while completing the six activities to learn a new sound. A scope and sequence appears in Chapter 2 on pages 12 and 13, along with a list of recommended books for the story sharing.

The Sounds Abound Program
- Developed at the Stern Center for Language and Learning by Orna Lenchner and Blanche Podhajski
- 1998, LinguiSystems, Inc., www.linguisystems.com, 1-800-776-4332, $109.95.
- This program is distributed in a kit with a spiral manual, page-size cards, and a videotape to help teachers learn how to introduce this curriculum into their classroom. The program contains a sequential series of classroom activities to develop phonological awareness in children. The 20 activities are divided into three sections—rhyme, syllable, phoneme.

Scott Foresman Early Reading Intervention
- By Deb Simmons and Ed Kame'enui.
- Formerly called the Optimize Program.
- 2003, Scott Foresman, www.scottforesman.com, 1-800-841-8939, ISBN 0-328-05045-8, $999.
- This program is a complete kit with teacher guides that contain scripted lesson plans, cards, game boards, and books. The lessons are complete and offer a sequential program for phonological awareness, letter naming, and early phonics.

Note: Prices listed are at time of publication. Please contact vendor for current information.

Table 9.3

continued

Other Resources

Ladders to Literacy: A Kindergarten Activity Book
- By Rollanda O'Conner, Angela Notari-Syverson, and Patricia F. Vadasy
- 1998, Paul H. Brookes Publishing Company, 1-800- 638-3775, www.brookespublishing.com, $49.95.
- The kindergarten curriculum described in this spiral-bound manual includes three sections, including Print Awareness, Phonological Awareness, and Oral Language. Although there are not enough activities specifically for phonological awareness as some of the other programs listed here, it is included on this list because it includes activities to use in developing the other critical kindergarten skills of oral language and print awareness. Take-home activities for teachers to give to parents are included in the Appendix.

WatchWord: a Multisensory Reading and Writing Program
- By Karen Lacey and Wendy Baird
- 2005, Sopris West, 1-800-547-6747, www.sopriswest.com, $95.00 for the complete set.
- Teacher's guide includes an explanation of how to teach students to associate the sound with a key object. Each student uses a pattern to make a personalized object for each sound. Students pick objects from their sound boxes to represent the sounds in simple words. For example, a mitten for /m/, an apple for /ă/, and a slice of pizza for /p/ are placed on a board with a green, yellow and red box to correspond to the beginning, middle, and ending sounds. A CD-ROM with demonstration lessons is included.

Note: Prices listed are at time of publication. Please contact vendor for current information.

Each of the seven comprehensive programs contains activities to use with students, but what differentiates them as "more comprehensive" than the activity books described later in this section is that these programs also explain how to organize the activities into a fully sequential curriculum. These more comprehensive curricula also provide a description of a lesson and a progression of lessons across a time period. Each program either supplies the materials or cards to teach the activities or provides blackline masters for teachers to make the materials easily. Some of them also include information about research that was conducted using the program.

These comprehensive programs can be used to enhance the kindergarten or first grade core curriculum, or they can be used in an intervention group setting. They are included in this manual because they are each well-suited for teachers or aides to use when teaching at-risk students in small intervention groups.

The second type of resource is activity books that provide ideas for developing a student's phonological awareness. Because of the extensive recent attention to phonological awareness, many books have been published about this topic since 2000. Recommended books are listed in are listed in Table 9.4.

Table 9.4

Phonological Awareness Activity Books

Blevins, Wiley, *Phonemic Awareness Activities for Early Reading Success* (New York: Scholastic, 1997), ISBN 0-590-37231-9.

Catts, Hugh, and Tina Olsen, *Sounds Abound: Listening Rhyming and Reading* (East Moline, IL: Linguisystems, 1993), www.linguisystems.com, 1-800-776-4332, book ISBN 0-7606-0238-7 and Multisensory Phonological Awareness Program.

Fitzpatrick, Jo, *Getting Ready to Read: Independent Phonemic Awareness Centers for Emergent Readers* (Cypress, CA: Creative Teaching Press, 2002), ISBN 1-57471-936-X.

Fitzpatrick, Jo, *Phonemic Awareness: Playing with Sounds to Strengthen Beginning Reading Skills* (Cypress, CA: Creative Teaching Press, 1997), ISBN 1-57471-231-4.

Jordano, Kimberly, and Trisha Callella, *Phonemic Awareness Songs and Rhymes* (CA: Creative Teaching Press, 1998), ISBN 1-57471-694-8 (available for fall, winter, spring—includes CD of songs).

Yopp, Hallie Kay, and Ruth Helen Yopp, *Oo-pples and Boo-noo-noos: Songs and Activities for Phonemic Awareness* (Orlando, FL: Harcourt), ISBN 0-15-325786-5.

Zgonc, Yvette, *Sounds in Action: Phonological Awareness Activities and Assessment* (Peterborough, NH: Crystal Springs Books, 2000), ISBN 1-884548-32-6.

Some of these activity books are written by teachers and have more of a practitioner focus than the seven programs listed in Table 9.3. Other activity books are written by academics. No matter the author or the apparent teacher-friendliness of the book, these materials must be reviewed carefully because activities are not always as simple as they are presented to be in the book. It is not uncommon to discover a lowest level activity that should be placed in the highest level instead. For example, in one of my favorite activity books, there is a game that is played by changing the first sound in each student's name to a sound of the day. (For example, if the sound of the day is /m/, the name Jerry would be changed to "Merry.") The author has placed this phonemic substitution activity in Level 1 (easiest) whereas, according to most experts, it should be placed as a Level 5 (most difficult) activity to indicate that it is at the highest level of phonological awareness skills, not the beginning level.

This example illustrates how important it is for teachers to be informed about how to teach reading. It takes a deep understanding of phonological awareness to evaluate each activity and to sequence it properly within a curriculum. The need for professional development in early reading has been discussed previously in this book. Neither a sequence nor a selection of activities is provided in the activity books. When using the activity books, teachers will have to figure out the sequence of activities they want to use and how to create a strong lesson plan using the activities they select.

Why Activities Are Included in This Manual

This section provides an overview of different kinds of activities for teaching various levels of phonological awareness skills. A few activities for each section are included, and they are meant to serve as examples rather than to provide an exhaustive list. The main reason these activities were selected is to demonstrate the types of activities that teach a specific skill. The activities and teaching strategies included in this book are not intended to represent a comprehensive intervention curriculum.

The activities below are described in brief terms. For more detailed instructions on how to teach a specific activity, teachers should refer to the activity book or program manual that is the source for the activity.

Sample Intervention Activities for Developing Phonological Awareness

Details about the resources cited for these activities are in Table 9.3. For more information and detailed instructions about an activity, refer to the book or manual for that resource.

Segmenting Sentences Into Words

9-1: *Just Say Part*

Brief Description

In this teacher-directed activity, a student says a complete sentence and then drops off one word from the end each time until down to only the first word.

Materials Needed

None

Step-by-Step Directions

This activity is found in Neuhaus Education Center's *Reading Readiness Manual* (2002), page 1 of the phonological awareness section.

9-2: Clapping Words in a Sentence

Brief Description

One popular activity to call a student's attention to the separate words in sentences is to ask students to "clap the words" in a sentence.

Materials Needed

None

Step-by-Step Directions

1. The teacher says a complete sentence.

2. Students repeat the sentence while clapping for each word.

9-3: Word Chairs

Brief Description

Seated in chairs, students stand on cue and say one word at a time to speak a sentence.

Materials Needed

One chair for each word in a sentence.

Step-by-Step Directions

The teacher sets up four chairs in the front of the room. She asks one student to sit in each chair, and then tells each student that they will "be" a specific word. As she moves along behind the line of chairs, the teacher taps the head of each student one at a time, and the students stand up and say their designated word in a four-word sentence. This activity can be found in the Neuhaus Education Center's *Reading Readiness Manual,* page 2 of the phonological awareness section.

Segmenting Words Into Syllables

9-4: Clap, Snap, or Tap

Brief Description

When it is his turn, a student decides whether to ask his classmates to clap, snap, or tap the syllables in his name.

Materials Needed

None

Detailed Description

As each student has a turn, ask him to decide if he wants to clap, tap, or snap his fingers to the syllables in his own name. This activity is described in more detail in Jo Fitzpatrick's book, *Phonemic Awareness* (1997), on page 25.

9-5: Break It in Half

Brief Description

Use hand signals to indicate syllable division of two-syllable words.

Materials Needed

None

Detailed Description

Model breaking two-syllable words apart by starting with both fists closed and down, and as each syllable is pronounced, turn your hand over and open your fist. This is also described in Jo Fitzpatrick's *Phonemic Awareness* (1997) book on page 29 with a nice illustration.

9-6: Syllable Puzzles

Brief Description

Pictures of two-syllable words are divided into two puzzle pieces.

Materials Needed

Pictures of words cut into pieces for each syllable.

Detailed Description

In Jo Fitzpatrick's book, *Getting Ready to Read* (2002), on pages 32 and 33, she includes blackline masters to make 20 puzzles for demonstrating and practicing dividing words into syllables. She includes two-syllable pictures that are divided into two puzzle pieces that connect to make the picture whole. Some of the words she has used for this activity include *basket*, *pizza*, *monkey*, *pumpkin*, *dollar*, and *apple*.

Segmenting Words Into Onset-Rime, Rhyming, and Alliteration

9-7: *Rhyming Picture Sort*

Brief Description

Students select pairs of rhyming words from among a set of picture cards.

Materials Needed

Sets of picture cards for words that rhyme.

Detailed Description

Many activity books provide pictures of words that rhyme. Sets of cards can be laminated and placed in baggies that can be resealed. Some teachers create ways to make the cards self-correcting, like mounting the rhyming pairs on different colors of card stock or using colored stickers. Some of my favorite blackline master pictures are in Jo Fitzpatrick's book, *Phonemic Awareness*, on pages 77–88.

9-8: *Rhyming Picture Puzzles*

Brief Description

Rectangular pieces with two words that rhyme are cut into puzzle pieces.

Materials Needed

Puzzle pieces for pairs of words that rhyme.

Detailed Description

Another common activity is for students to select pictures of words that rhyme and when placed together, they fit like a puzzle. To make these puzzles, take a rectangular piece of paper with two pictures that rhyme. Cut the pictures apart with a jagged edge so, when put together, they fit. An illustration of this activity can be found in *Ladders to Literacy* on page 107 (O'Conner et al. 1998). This activity is also included in Jo Fitzpatrick's book, *Getting Ready to Read,* with a blackline master to make ten puzzles, on page 24.

9-9: *Rhyme-Away Story*

Brief Description

Students erase a section of a picture for a word that rhymes in a poem.

Materials Needed

Picture drawn on a chalk or whiteboard.

Eraser.

Detailed Description

One activity that is a favorite among kindergarten teachers is called Rhyme-Away Stories, found in Jo Fitzpatrick's book, *Phonemic Awareness*. The author provides a story that is written as a poem. The teacher draws a picture on the chalkboard as closely as possible to that provided in the book. While the teacher reads the poem aloud, the students have to orally guess the missing word to complete the line with a rhyming word. As the students answer with each rhyming word, the teacher erases the corresponding portion of the picture on the chalkboard. The poem and erasing continue until the drawing is completely gone. For example, on page 103, there is a picture of a boy. The first line of the poem says:

"He can't smell a rose, if you erase his <u>nose.</u>"

There is also a description of a related activity called "Draw a Rhyme Stories" on the University of Virginia Curry School of Education's PALS Web site (http://pals.virginia.edu/scores/Activities) under the rhyming section.

9-10: Oops! Wrong Rhyme

Brief Description

Teacher says a word that rhymes but doesn't make sense, and students must change it to the rhyming word that does fit in the sentence.

Materials Needed

List of sentences.

Detailed Description

Children love silly activities and this activity from Neuhaus' *Reading Readiness Manual* (phonological awareness section, page 11) is sure to be well-liked. Teachers read a sentence and students fill in the appropriate rhyme. Here's how it goes:

(Point to hand.) "This is my <u>sand.</u> Oops! Wrong rhyme! I mean this is my <u>hand.</u> *Sand* and *hand* rhyme."

Other examples with body parts include: nose/rose, chin/pin, eye/pie, ear/cheer. This activity can be extended to other themes, including objects in the room (bear/chair, etc.).

9-11: Stand-Up Rhyme Time

Brief Description

Students complete a rhyming line that says what part of their body they are supposed to touch.

Materials Needed

Stand-up Rhyme Time poem.

Detailed Description

This activity comes from J. K. Montgomery's *Building Phonological Awareness Skills in Young Readers* (2002, 13).

Table 9.5

Stand-Up Rhyme Time

To develop phonological awareness skills, auditory attention to vowel sounds, vocabulary, and practice the concept of syllable rhyming. Read the first sentence, wait for the child to repeat. Read the second sentence omitting the last word. Child repeats the missing word adding a gesture of locating the body part. Begin at the head or the toe. Change the initial rhyming words from time to time. Children make up their own rhyming words to match the body parts.

1.	Say pup. Now please stand (up).	16.	Say drum. Now find your (thumb)
2.	Say snow. Now find your (toe).	17.	Say linger. Now find your (finger).
3.	Say meat. Now find your (feet).	18.	Say check. Now find your (neck).
4.	Say steel. Now find your (heel).	19.	Say grin. Now find your (chin).
5.	Say giraffe. Now find your (calf).	20.	Say snip. Now find your (lip).
6.	Say free. Now find your (knee).	21.	Say south. Now find your (mouth).
7.	Say fly. Now find your (thigh).	22.	Say beneath. Now find your (teeth).
8.	Say paste. Now find your (waist).	23.	Say clothes. Now find your (nose).
9.	Say jelly. Now find your (belly).	24.	Say sneak. Now find your (cheek).
10.	Say nest. Now find your (chest).	25.	Say shy. Now find your (eye).
11.	Say folder. Now find your (shoulder).	26.	Say cow. Now find your (brow).
12.	Say crack. Now find your (back).	27.	Say appear. Now find your (ear).
13.	Say farm. Now find your (arm).	28.	Say aware. Now find your (hair).
14.	Say kissed. Now find your (wrist).	29.	Say bed. Now find your (head).
15.	Say grand. Now find your (hand).	30.	Say clown. Now please sit (down).

Source: Adapted by Montgomery (2002) from Fagen & Prouty, *Language Strategies for Little Ones* (1998).

9-12: Say It, Take It

Brief Description

Teacher says an onset, and the student says the rime that completes the word for one of four pictures.

Materials Needed

Picture cards.

Detailed Description

An excellent activity for segmenting words into onset-rime can be found in Jo Fitzpatrick's *Getting Ready to Read*. In this activity, children lay out four picture cards in a row. The teacher starts by saying an onset for one of the pictures. The child who can say the rime that completes the name of one of the pictures gets to pick up that picture card. On pages 49 and 50 of the book there is a set of blackline masters for the picture cards to make 8 sets of cards.

Phonemic Awareness: Isolation

9-13: *Isolate That Sound*

Brief Description

Students isolate a sound in a word in a target position.

Materials Needed

None

Detailed Description

The most common strategy for isolating initial sounds is to say a word and ask the student what sound it begins with. This can also be done with the final and middle sounds as the student becomes more familiar with how to isolate one sound from the rest of the sounds in a word. Here's an example:

Teacher	What's the first sound in *bat*?
Students	/b/
Teacher	What's the last sound in *wig*?
Students	/g/
Teacher	What's the middle sound in *bag*?
Students	/ă/ (short *a*)

9-14: All Aboard!

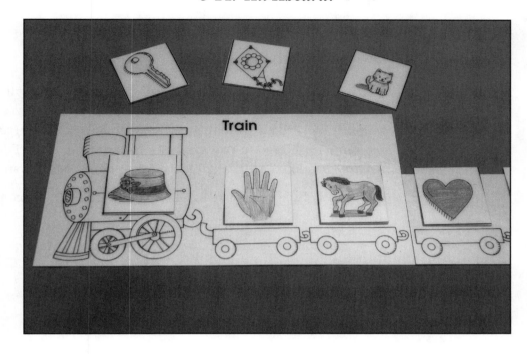

Brief Description

Cars of a train are used for students to sort pictures that match initial sounds.

Materials Needed

Trains.

Picture cards for initial sounds.

Detailed Description

Jo Fitzpatrick uses the cars of a train to create an activity where a student must isolate the initial sound in a word and then line up the picture cards for all the words that begin with the same sound. In Fitzpatrick's book, *Getting Ready to Read*, she includes the blackline master for the train on page 89 followed by 100 beginning sound picture cards.

9-15: Saying Silly Sentences

Brief Description

Teacher reads an alliterative silly sentence, leaving off the last word, which students have to fill in.

Materials Needed

Silly sentences for teacher to read.

Detailed Description

The teacher says a sentence where all the words begin with the same initial sound, leaving off the last word. The students are asked to repeat the partial sentence and fill in a word that begins with the same initial sound to complete the sentence. Here are two examples from the Neuhaus Education Center's *Reading Readiness Manual,* page 9, of the phonological awareness section.

- Lively little lambs like to lick luscious _____. (lemons, licorice, lollipops)

- Many messy monkeys make muddy _____. (mudpies, messes, mush)

9-16: *Where's That Sound?*

Brief Description

Students point to the beginning, middle, or ending of an animal that has an elongated body to indicate where a sound appears in a word.

Materials Needed

"Long animal" pictures taped to sticks.

Craft stick for pointing.

Detailed Description

A favorite activity for isolating the sounds in words is on page 36 of Jo Fitzpatrick's book *Phonemic Awareness.* The alligator, snake, and dachshund can be copied on card stock, laminated, and taped to a craft stick. Students each choose one animal and then use a colored craft stick to point to where the sound is positioned in the word by pointing to the animal's body—at the beginning, middle, or end. Blackline masters of three "long" animals are provided on page 113.

9-17: *Thumbs Up*

Brief Description

Student gives the "thumbs up" sign if he hears a sound in a word in a specified position.

Materials Needed

Stickers for thumbs (optional).

Detailed Description

A common activity that appears in the teacher's guide of many reading programs is to ask students to give the thumbs up sign if they hear a target sound at the beginning of a word. Then the teacher reads a list of words, and students respond accordingly. Once the students are ready, you can increase the difficulty by changing the task to isolate and match the ending sounds, and then eventually the middle sounds.

Phonemic Awareness: Identity

9-18: *Sound Dominos*

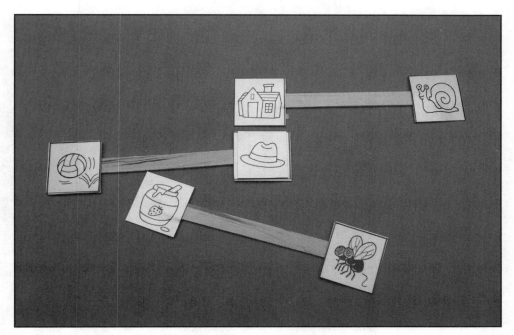

Brief Description

Students play the game of initial sound dominos using pictures taped on craft sticks.

Materials Needed

Picture cards taped to each end of a craft stick.

Detailed Description

This activity helps students identify the initial sound in words. As described on page 36 of Jo Fitzpatrick's book *Phonemic Awareness,* students use picture cards taped to each end of a craft stick to connect the initial sounds in words. The book provides blackline masters for this activity on page 112. (My experience is that it is best to enlarge the pictures slightly and color them before laminating and taping on the ends of craft sticks.) One teacher I saw facilitating this activity with a group of three kindergarten students identified for intervention did a great job of scaffolding this activity by holding the stick beside a picture and saying the names of each word, and then asking the student whether the first picture and the new picture begin with the same sound. She continued trying the new picture around the board until a match was reached.

Phonemic Awareness: Categorization

9-19: *Picture Card Sort*

Brief Description

Picture cards are sorted into columns by initial sound.

Materials Needed

Set of picture cards sorted by initial sound in the word.

Detailed Description

Most classrooms contain a box of picture cards. These can be used to create an activity with about six to eight cards per sound for two beginning sounds. At first it is best to select sounds that are continuant rather than stop sounds and to make sure that the sounds are different and easily distinguished from one another. After a while, you can extend this activity to focus on the ending or middle sounds in words.

9-20: Sort Objects Into Piles

Brief Description

Students sort miniature objects into piles that correspond with the initial sound in the name of the object.

Materials Needed

Six to eight miniature objects for each sound.

Detailed Description

Students pick a miniature object, say its name, determine the initial sound in the word, and then place the object in the appropriate pile. Teachers can create or purchase this activity. Lakeshore Learning Materials sells a set of tubs called *Alphabet Sounds Teaching Tubs* that have multiple objects for each initial sound. It is expensive at $129 per set, but one set can be used by the entire kindergarten or first grade team as most of the time a teacher will be working on only a few sounds at a time. Lakeshore also has a similar activity called *Match-A-Sound! Phonemic Awareness Boxes.* There is a box for rhyming, beginning, and ending sounds. Each box has several mats and multiple objects.

Phonemic Awareness: Blending

9-21: *Turtle Talk*

Brief Description

Students practice segmenting and blending the sounds in words by stepping forward while holding a stick with a picture of a turtle.

Materials Needed

A turtle picture on a craft stick, one for each student.

Detailed Description

One of the most clever activities for blending sounds is called "Turtle Talk." Each student holds a picture of a turtle taped to a craft stick. The teacher asks students how turtles move. "Slowly," they all say. When it's Turtle Talk Time, all the students in the group hold their turtles up and step one slow step at a time to segment the sounds in words. This activity, along with the blackline masters to use for copying the turtles on green card stock, can be found online at the University of Virginia's PALS Web site at http://pals.virginia.edu/scores/Activities/ or in Jo Fitzpatrick's book, *Phonemic Awareness*, on pages 30 and 108.

9-22: *Blending Animal Names in "Old MacDonald" Song*

Brief Description

Song to emphasize the sounds in the names of animals.

Materials Needed

Copy of the song for the teacher.

Detailed Description

On the PALS Web site under "Blending" there is an activity that was included in a Virginia Department of Education publication on early intervention resources for teachers. From the PALS Web site at http://pals.virginia.edu/scores/Activities, click the section on Blending Activities under Phonological Awareness. While singing the children's song *Old MacDonald Had a Farm*, instead of saying the name of the animal, the teacher says the sounds and asks the students to blend the sounds and give the animal's name.

9-23: *Tap and Sweep, or Tapping Out the Sounds*

Brief Description

Students tap the sounds in words.

Materials Needed

   None

Detailed Description

In Jo Fitzpatrick's book, *Phonemic Awareness,* on page 45, there is an activity called "Tap and Sweep" where students are asked first to tap the separate sounds in a word on a tabletop, and then sweep their fist back over the sounds while they blend them together. This same technique is used in many programs, including Wilson Language Training (see www.wilsonlanguage.com), where children are taught to tap with two fingers on their other arm for each sound and then sweep down their outstretched arm while blending the sounds into a word.

9-24: *Blending Phonemes*

Brief Description

Pictures of words are divided into the number of pieces that correspond to the number of sounds in the book.

Materials Needed

   Picture puzzles.

Detailed Description

Each picture is separated into the number of pieces as there are sounds in the word. For example, the picture of a shoe is divided into two pieces, and the fish and cheese into three pieces. The Catts and Olsen book called *Sounds Abound* includes blackline masters (1993). A total of 16 pictures are provided, starting on page 166. One of the other strategies suggested on page 174 of this book is to use a hand puppet to pronounce the sounds separately, and then ask the student to combine them to say the word.

Phonemic Awareness: Segmentation

9-25: *Head, Waist, and Toes*

Brief Description

Students practice segmenting phonemes by touching their head for the first sound, waist for the middle sound, and toes for the final sound in a word.

Materials Needed

None

Detailed Description

One of the most common activities to segment the sounds in words is to place your hands on your head for the first sound in a word, then on your waist for the middle sound, and finally to your toes while saying the final sound in the word. This activity is described in Jo Fitzpatrick's *Phonemic Awareness* book on page 51.

9-26: *Say-It-and-Move-It*

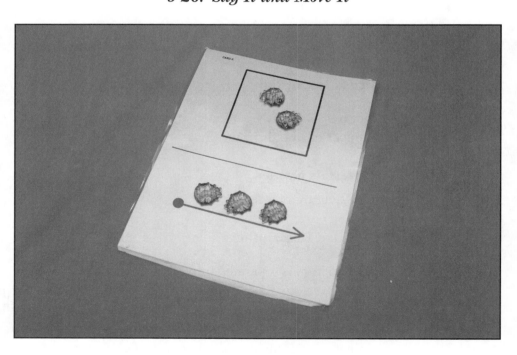

Brief Description

To practice segmenting sounds in a word, a student moves an object while saying each sound.

Materials Needed

Say-It-and-Move-It card.

Manipulative objects (such as blocks or counters).

Detailed Description

If teachers had to choose only a handful of activities to use, this would certainly be on that list. One of the most effective ways to teach students to become aware of the separate sounds in words is to have them move a token or object as they say each sound. For example, with the word *mop*, the students moves a token while saying /m/, moves a second token while saying /ŏ/, and a third token for /p/. I like the description of how to teach this strategy provided in the *Reading Readiness Manual* on pages 24–27. This manual also provides a list of words, as well as the blackline masters to use in creating the cards. What is nice about the cards in the Neuhaus manual is that there is a spot for children to keep their tokens and also a line to move them to, with an arrow to remind them to blend the sounds back together at the end. The *Ladders to Literacy* book has the same activity, and the PALS book by Mathes et al. emphasizes it as well. There are many variations of this activity. One variation is to give the students a paper with the number of boxes that correspond to the number of sounds. This is like using Elkonin boxes. For this activity, no print or letters are visible. A variation of this activity is shown where students place an object into the box where they hear the target sound (beginning, middle, or end of three-phoneme words). Another wonderful variation of this strategy is for students to use colored blocks or felts, where the color of the object corresponds to whether the sounds are the same or different. Don't forget to use nonsense words for this one, as well.

9-27: *Let's Count Sounds*

Brief Description

Students count sounds in words by raising a finger for each sound.

Materials Needed

None

Detailed Description

In this activity, the students learn how to count the sounds in a word by raising a finger each time a new sound is segmented.

Phonemic Awareness: Deletion

9-28: *Deleting a Sound*

Brief Description

Students repeat a word that a teacher says, except without one sound.

Materials Needed

None

Detailed Description

The most classic phoneme deletion activity is for the teacher to say a word, ask the students to repeat the word, and then say it again without a specific sound. For example:

Teacher	Say *hand*.
Students	*Hand*.
Teacher	Now say it again without the /h/.
Students	*And*.

Often teachers start by teaching this activity using compound words. After students know how to do it, you can move to segmenting a sound from the word. The *Reading Readiness Manual* has a list of compound words on page 17 and a list of words to use to omit a sound on page 39 (both in the phonological awareness section). In *Sounds Abound* (Catts & Olsen), there is a list of words for deleting the initial sounds on page 163 and another list for deleting final sounds on page 164.

9-29: *Take Away a Sound*

Brief Description

Students delete a sound by showing with blocks which sound was taken away.

Materials Needed

Colored blocks or counters.

Detailed Description

Phonemic Awareness in Young Children describes an activity where students delete a sound by removing the block that represents that sound (Adams et al. 1998). For example, with the word *ham*, the student can remove the first block and then blend the new word, which is *am*. This activity is also described on the PALS Web site under the Sound-to-Letter Segmentation Section (http://pals.virginia.edu/scores/Activities/). On page 84 of *Phonemic Awareness in Young Children*, this strategy is also used to teach students that consonant blends are two separate sounds.

Phonemic Awareness: Addition

9-30: *Make a New Word*

Brief Description

Students add a sound to a word to make a new word.

Materials Needed

> None

Detailed Description

Phoneme addition is the opposite of deletion. The teacher gives the child a word, then asks what word it will become when another sound is added. Here's an example:

Teacher	Say *pot.*
Students	*Pot.*
Teacher	Add /s/ to the beginning. What word is it now?
Students	*Spot.*

Phonemic Awareness: Substitution

9-31: *Change That Word*

Brief Description

Students create a different word by changing one sound.

Materials Needed

> None

Detailed Description

The most common way to use phoneme substitution is to ask children to say a word, and then say it again with a different sound in one position. This is how it goes:

Teacher	Say *mop*.
Students	*Mop*.
Teacher	Now change the /m/ to /k/.
Students	*Cop*.

There are many activities that use this strategy. When children are asked to sing "Oopples and Boonoonoos" in place of "Apples and Bananas," this requires phoneme substitution. Another game is to substitute sounds at the beginning of children's names to create silly names.

A list of recommended materials to use for phonological awareness intervention is presented in Table 9.6.

Name	Description	Contact Information
Rhyming		
Rhyming Words Skills Puzzles	Approximately 25 chunky 2-piece puzzle that self-corrects to match 2 rhyming words and pictures.	Lakeshore Learning www.lakeshorelearning.com CV202 $10.95
Rhyming Sounds Teaching Tubs	Set of 10 plastic tubs, each with at least 4 miniature objects that rhyme.	Lakeshore Learning www.lakeshorelearning.com LA588 $49.50
Phonemic Awareness		
Alphabet Sounds Photo Library	300 cards with photos arranged in a file box by letter. Use for initial sound card sorts	Lakeshore Learning www.lakeshorelearning.com RR993 $49.95
Alphabet Sounds Teaching Tubs	Tub for each letter with 6 miniature objects. Also available for vowels, and blends & digraphs.	Lakeshore Learning www.lakeshorelearning.com LC856 $129–$139 per set
Match-A-Sound! Phonemic Awareness Boxes	Each set contains 10 mats and 30 manipulatives.	Lakeshore Learning www.lakeshorelearning.com AA411 Beg—413 Ending $29.95 per box
Beginning Sounds Activity Kit	Using a starter strip in a pocket chart, students add pictures to match initial sounds.	Lakeshore Learning www.lakeshorelearning.com RR502 $19.95
Beginning Sounds Match & Clip	Activity board to insert pictures. Students clip matching sound. Letter can be used for phonics.	Lakeshore Learning www.lakeshorelearning.com RR715 $19.95

Note: Prices listed are at time of publication. Please contact vendor for current information.

Chapter 10

Intervention Activities for Nonsense Word Fluency (NWF): Planning Phonics Intervention

Overview of Phonics Instruction

Phonics and Phonemic Awareness Defined

The goal of phonics instruction is different from phonemic awareness instruction. Phonemic awareness instruction focuses the child on the speech sounds in words, while phonics instruction focuses the child on the letters and letter patterns used to represent those speech sounds. Phonics instruction occurs when students are taught the relationships between sounds and letters, and they then apply those associations to blending sounds and reading words. An expert teacher may integrate both goals by using letters to reinforce awareness of speech sounds, and using speech sound awareness to help children recall letter sequences.

Generally, phonemic awareness instruction begins in kindergarten and continues, with waning emphasis, throughout first grade as an integral part of a comprehensive curriculum. In some curricula simple phonics instruction begins in middle kindergarten, with single consonant and short vowel, one-to-one letter-sound correspondences, along with reading three-sound words that have those letter-sound correspondences. In most curricula, instruction in all the common letter-sound correspondences occurs during the first half of first grade. More complex letter-sound relationships, including digraphs, blends, and common multiple spellings for long vowel sounds, are taught throughout first grade. Instruction in more advanced phonics concepts, such as silent letters and unusual vowel spellings, is generally introduced in first grade and continues throughout second grade. Beginning in second grade, syllabication, word endings, compounds, contractions, and up to 300 high frequency words are typically emphasized.

Nonsense Word Fluency (NWF) is the DIBELS measure that provides information about a student's skill in phonics. Initial Sound Fluency and Phoneme Segmentation Fluency are the measures that provide information about phonemic awareness. Students who fail to achieve benchmark scores on PSF as well as NWF should receive intervention instruction to improve phonological and phonemic awareness skills before they concentrate on phonics instruction.

Why Nonsense Words Are Important

Often teachers wonder why nonsense words are used in DIBELS instead of real words. First, from an assessment perspective, nonsense words are used to explore whether children can apply their sound-symbol knowledge in sounding out a word. Real words cannot be used for this purpose because it is unclear whether a child has previously memorized the word.

For nearly all instructional time, real words are emphasized: students practice words and learn them through multiple exposures. Yet, later in this chapter, we recommend nonsense words for one instructional strategy because there is one point in a student's development when instructing with nonsense words is particularly helpful.

Students who can read nonsense words fluently and accurately are more likely to read real words well. Once students have learned the letter-sound associations but need more fluency in applying these associations in reading words, an effective type of brief practice is for students to read one-syllable nonsense words with the patterns that have been taught. The objective is to build fluency with blending sound-symbol relationships using letter patterns where it is impossible to read the word from sight as a previously memorized word.

Systematic and Explicit Phonics Instruction Is Recommended

Phonics has been one of the most controversial topics in the field of reading. Educators argue about whether or not to teach phonics, and even when they agree that phonics should be taught, they argue about the most effective way to teach it. The National Reading Panel (NRP) gave a strong recommendation in their report that phonics be included as a component of reading instruction. Furthermore, the NRP addressed how to teach phonics when they stated that phonics is most effective when taught in an *systematic* and *explicit* manner. In order to be consistent with the scientifically based reading research, the techniques suggested in this book are systematic and explicit.

Put Reading First, a publication that summarizes the NRP results for teachers, describes systematic and explicit phonics (Armbruster et al. 2001).

> *The hallmark of programs of systematic phonics instruction is the direct teaching of a set of letter-sound relationships in a clearly defined sequence. The set includes the major sound/spelling relationships of both consonants and vowels.*

The NRP report emphasizes the importance of giving students an opportunity to practice applying their knowledge. It also states that students need books that contain a large number of words that they can decode from the letter-sound relationships they have learned. (These are called "decodable" books.) The report defines *explicit instruction* as a program that provides teachers with precise directions so that the relationship between letters and sounds is made clear to students.

Early Reading Programs Emphasizing Systematic, Explicit Phonics Instruction

Often teachers ask for recommendations for programs they can use to teach phonics. The list in Table 10.1 shows phonics programs that are sold separately from a core reading curriculum. All include sound-symbol cards, a sequence for teaching the letter-sound correspondences, decodable text that relates to the sequence, and extensive notes and instructions for teachers. The programs all can be used as part of a core curriculum in kindergarten or first grade, or they can be adapted for to use in intervention groups for students of all ages.

Table 10.1

Comprehensive Phonics Programs Sold Separately

Name of Program	Contact Information
Benchmark Phonetic Connections StartUp Phonics BuildUp Phonics	Benchmark Education Co. www.benchmarkeducation.com $1,125 for StartUp Phonics kit $1,435 for BuildUp Phonics kit
Open Court Phonics Kits By Anita Archer, James Flood, Diane Lapp, and Linda Lungren	SRA/McGraw Hill www.sraonline.com ISBN 0-07602-132-7 $630 for first grade phonics kit. Phonics program from Open Court Reading. Available by grade level.
Phonics for Reading By Anita Archer, James Flood, Diane Lapp, and Linda Lungren	Curriculum Associates www.curriculumassociates.com $15 for teacher's guide $35 for 5-pack of student workbooks
Read Well – Level K – Level One	Sopris West www.sopriswest.com $1,999 for Level K kit, $1,499 for Level One
Reading Mastery Plus	SRA/McGraw Hill www.sraonline.com $828 for Level 1
Reading Rods Phonics—Grade 1 Program	ETA Cuisenaire www.etacuisenaire.com RSP-60101 $545 for Grade 1 program
Road to the Code	Paul H. Brookes Publishing Co. www.brookespublishing.com $49.95 for book

Note: Prices listed are at time of publication. Please contact vendor for current information.

Table 10.1

continued

Saxon Phonics and Spelling	Saxon Publishers www.saxonpublishers.com Product 3020 $650 for the Grade I kit, 24-student. Available by grade level.
Scott Foresman Early Reading Intervention	Pearson Scott Foresman www.scottforesman.com ISBN 0-32814-675-7 $1500 Early phonics.
The Literacy Center	LeapFrog SchoolHouse www.leapfrog.com $1,895–2,595 per grade level

Note: Prices listed are at time of publication. Please contact vendor for current information.

In any core reading program, often called a "basal program," instruction in phonics that is systematic and explicit has a common pattern of lesson design. A typical phonics lesson begins with instruction in a few new letter sounds, including practicing them to fluency; reading words that contain these new letters; writing words that include the new correspondences; and concluding with reading text. Early in the program sequence of teaching phonics, the teacher usually teaches a group of four to five consonants and one short vowel. Most well-designed phonics programs explicitly teach the articulation of a sound and show the letter symbol associated with that sound. After introducing the letter-sound associations for this first set of consonants and one short vowel, children read and write simple words that contain these sounds. Students read words, sentences, and short decodable books using the previously introduced sound-symbol correspondences. In order to read simple text, the programs teach some common nonphonetic words concurrently with the letter-sound introductions. The process of reading and writing words is important in mastering the letter-sound associations, which is why the better programs teach children to blend sounds into words and to write words as soon as they have introduced several correspondences.

After the first set of letter sounds is mastered, instruction continues with another set of four or five consonants and another short vowel. With ten consonants and two short vowels, it is possible to read and write a large number of words. As the introduction of new letters continues, the inventory of words to use for reading and spelling practice grows. The decodable text becomes more interesting as the letter-sound patterns expand and the number of known nonphonetic sight words increases. Eventually the student is more and more fluent in blending letter-sounds and can read more authentic text. Although the major emphasis on letter-sound correspondences is usually in the fall of first grade, instruction in more advanced phonics concepts continues throughout the second half of first grade and somewhat during second grade as well.

Creating Intervention Activities and Programs

Some schools decide not to purchase complete phonics curriculum programs, either because they don't have adequate funding to do so or because their teachers are accustomed to creating their own curriculum materials. Creating your own phonics curriculum is extremely difficult to do because it requires a great deal of knowledge and time to design an effective program.

The first place that teachers who develop their own intervention instruction should look for materials is the school's core, comprehensive reading curriculum. Often students who need intervention actually need to learn the same skills that are typically taught in the first grade core curriculum. Intervention instruction can be delivered using the same materials provided by the core curriculum if your core program includes sound-symbol cards, a specified scope and sequence for teaching sounds and letters, and decodable word lists and books. The intervention instruction may simply need to be more explicit and delivered in smaller groups at a slower pace so students have more time to practice, and so that they can receive immediate and extensive corrective feedback. A close match between the core curriculum and the intervention program is ideal.

If a school has a core reading program that lacks a systematic and explicit approach to teaching phonics, it will not work for struggling readers, no matter how slowly it is delivered. In this case, the teachers providing intervention instruction will need additional materials and strategies. Some ideas to get you started are described in the next section of this chapter.

After you review the activities and begin using them in your intervention groups, you will need to assess whether these activities are enough to accomplish your goal of teaching children the skills they are missing and enabling them to read at least on grade level. If, after using these activities, the students in intervention groups are not demonstrating progress by improved DIBELS scores, your school may need to purchase a more comprehensive and thorough phonics program to use for intervention.

Intervention Lesson Structure

Intervention instruction is the 15 to 60 minutes a day of *extra* instruction for students who are behind in mastering early reading skills, as measured by DIBELS. Fifteen minutes is very short; 30 minutes is preferable, but some schools use 20-minute blocks. The students who are most behind may need a total of 60 minutes of intervention instruction, divided into two, 30-minute sessions instead of one session, which would be too much at one time. Intervention instruction occurs in small groups of three to five students, and it may sometimes be offered one-on-one to students who need more concentrated attention. The point cannot be overemphasized that intervention instruction is provided *in addition to* instruction in a well-researched core reading curriculum that includes phonics as one component.

The structure of a beginning phonics lesson for an intervention group in which a new letter-sound relationship is taught might include the following components:

- Review letter-sound correspondences previously taught.

- Introduce new letter-sound correspondences.

- Read words using Touch and Say (see activity 10-7, following).

- Spell words using Say and Write (see activity 10-15, following).

- Read real and/or nonsense words from word cards or using word decks.

- Read words from word lists.

- Read decodable sentences.

- Spell words and sentences from dictation.

- Read decodable text.

In order to read even simple text, students need to know some high frequency non-phonetic words. These words are usually taught and reviewed before the student reads them in decodable text. However, some children who have difficulty with phonics have already mastered a number of these non-phonetic high frequency words in their core curriculum, so the amount of time spent teaching non-phonetic words will vary depending on the group's ability with these words.

It is important to note that for intervention instruction, students are not required to master all the basic letter-sound relationships before beginning phonics instruction. Students should begin reading words as soon as they know sounds for as few as three or four consonant letters and one vowel letter. For example, with the three consonants *m, s,* and *t* and the short vowel sound for the letter *a*, students can read the real words *am, at, Sam, sat,* and *mat* and the nonsense words *tam, tas, mas.* (Yes, *tam* is a real word, but not to most beginning readers.)

With ten consonants and two short vowels it is possible to read and write a large number of words. For example, with *m, s, t, g, n, f, b, d, h,* and *l* plus short *a* and short *o,* the real words that students can read are: *mat, sat, fat, bat, hat, man, fan, ban, Dan, tan, Sam, bam, dam, ham, sag, tag, nag, bag, hag, lag, gas, tab, dab, gab, nab, lab, mad, sad, fad, bad, had, lad, gal, Hal, hot, lot, Don, mom, Tom, sod, pod,* and *nod.*

As more new letter-sound combinations are introduced, the inventory of words to use for reading and spelling practice grows. Decodable text becomes more interesting as the letter-sound patterns expand and the number of known high frequency non-phonetic sight words increases. Eventually the student becomes more and more fluent in reading real and nonsense words, achieves a DIBELS benchmark score in Nonsense Word Fluency and Oral Reading Fluency, no longer needs intervention instruction, and is able to learn adequately by participating only in the core curriculum.

Intervention Activities

This section provides activities and techniques that can be used to teach phonics during small group intervention instruction. All the activities listed are examples of explicit instructional techniques that can benefit students receiving intervention instruction. The activities are divided into the following categories:

- Introducing and Practicing Letter-Sound associations

- Blending Letters Into Words

- Building Fluency When Reading Real and Nonsense Words

- Spelling Simple One-Syllable Words

- Reading and Spelling Multisyllabic Words

- Techniques for Teaching Nonphonetic Sight Words

- Practicing With Text

Some intervention lessons will include activities from each of the categories. Other intervention lessons may include activities from only two or three of the categories. The exact structure of a lesson will depend on the skills the students need to be taught and on the time allotted for the lessons.

Introducing and Practicing Letter-Sound Associations

10-1: *Using Letter-Sound Cards to Introduce Letter-Sound Associations*

Brief Description

Teachers use cards to introduce letter-sound correspondences.

Materials Needed

Letter-sound cards large enough to be viewed by the students when they are placed on a wall. The complete letter sound package will have one card for each letter and one card for the digraphs *sh*, *ch*, *th*, *wh*, and *ck*. Each card will have the letter or digraph, typically displayed in uppercase and lowercase, plus a picture representing the key word for the sound being taught. Some cards include alternate ways to spell the sound.

Detailed Description

Each letter-sound card has a letter and a picture that represent the key word for the letter-sound correspondence (for example, *a/apple* and *m/mop*). Generally, a teacher introduces one or two new letter-sound correspondences at a time in an intervention group, but this number varies depending on the level of the group.

Step-by-Step Directions

1. When introducing a sound, the teacher says the name of the letter, the sound for the letter, and explains how the sound is contained in the key word. For example, "This is the letter *a*. The sound for the letter *a* is /ă/. The word *apple* begins with the sound /ă/."

2. The teacher reviews all new sounds introduced by having the students repeat the sound and the key word—"/ă/ as in *apple*"—while he points to each card in random order.

3. The teacher presents the next sound, repeating steps 1 and 2.

4. The teacher places the new cards in a prominent place so that students can refer to the cards to remember the sound for the letter.

Additional Information

Letter-sound cards are an important tool in teaching children how to associate the sounds in our language with the letters that are used to spell the sounds. Children use these cards to help remember the letter and the sound it represents. Most teachers hang the cards above the chalkboard or in some other prominent location in the classroom so that children can look at the cards when they need to figure out the way a sound is spelled in a word they are reading or writing.

When using letter-sound cards for intervention instruction, it is best to use a common keyword between core classroom and intervention instruction. This avoids confusing the students who are learning from both the core curriculum and the intervention instruction. Most of the comprehensive core reading programs, including SRA's *Open Court Reading* and Harcourt's *Trophies,* include a set of sound-spelling cards. If your core curriculum doesn't include keywords and sound spelling cards, this will not be a problem because the cards are available from several sources.

Reading Readiness Manual (Neuhaus Education Center 2002) is an excellent source for early reading instruction, including letter-symbol cards. The manual includes cards that show the letter and a picture for the associated keyword. For example, an apple appears on the *a* card. Although the *Reading Readiness Manual* letter-sound cards don't show the alternate spelling for a sound, they are ideal for initial instruction in the letter-sound associations.

Under the section in the *Reading Readiness Manual* called "Multisensory Letter Introduction," there is a sample dialogue for introducing each sound, including examples for discussing the articulation. Ideally, students will have learned to articulate sounds during phonemic awareness instruction. However, some students will need further instruction in the place and manner of articulation of the sound when they learn to match the sound to the letter.

The *Reading Readiness Manual* also describes multisensory techniques, such as skywriting, and some techniques for teaching students how to blend sounds. Each lesson in the *Reading Readiness Manual* includes words to use for practice that include only letters previously taught in the sequence of instruction. There is a chart of the sequence of letter-sound correspondences introduced in Section Four on page 1.

10-2: *Reviewing Letter-Sound Relationships With Letter-Sound Cards*

Brief Description

The teacher uses a deck of cards that have only the letter or letter combinations previously taught to review the letter-sound relationships.

Materials Needed

Cards with each of the letters and letter combinations. These cards need to be small enough to place in a "deck," generally from 1.5 × 2 inches to 3 × 5 inches. These can be purchased or easily made by the teacher. Some teachers place multiple cards for each letter or letter combination in the deck so that students cannot assume that once a card has been shown, it will not be shown again.

Step-by-Step Directions

1. The teacher stacks the cards in a deck and places them face down.

2. The teacher turns each card over, asking the students as a group or an individual student to name the sound for each letter or letter combination as fast as possible. The teacher can set fluency goals, with the ultimate goal being to name 50 sounds in one minute.

10-3: Fill in the Initial Letter

Brief Description

Practice applying letter-sound correspondences by filling in a missing letter in a simple three-letter word.

Materials Needed

Elkonin boxes with two of the three letters completed in a simple word.
Letter cards.

Detailed Description

When a student is beginning to learn letter-sound associations, one excellent activity for practicing the new letters is to ask the student to fill in the missing letter in simple words by selecting a letter from three or four possible letters. In this activity, it is essential that you ask the student to identify both the sounds and the letter names after they have read the word. Because the middle vowel and ending consonant in the CVC word are provided, and you are asking the child to choose the missing letter from a small set of options, this activity offers sufficient support to use early in your phonics instruction. One example of this activity appears on pages 182–186 in *Sounds Abound* book (Catts & Olsen 1993). Three boxes are shown. The second and third boxes have the letters filled in, and the first box is blank. Four or five alternative letters are provided below in boxes so they can be cut out and set over the first blank box. For example:

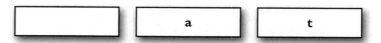

The teacher cuts out the letters *s*, *f*, *m*, *p*, and *r* and places them under the box. The student places each letter in the first box and reads the word it spells. *Sounds Abound* provides four other examples that are ready for use, along with a blank form and letters to use in spelling more words.

10-4: Beginning Sounds—Beach Ball

Brief Description

In order to review letter-sound associations, the teacher tosses a beach ball with letters written on it, and students have to say the letter sound, letter name, and a word that starts with the selected letter.

Materials Needed

Prepare a beach ball for this activity by writing a letter on each section of the ball.

Detailed Description

Students in the intervention group sit in a circle on the floor with the teacher. The teacher throws the ball to a student and the student looks at the letters where his fingers are positioned. The student chooses one of these and says the letter, the sound it makes, and a word that begins with this sound. Then the student throws the ball back to the teacher, who throws it to another student.

10-5: *Mystery Picture*

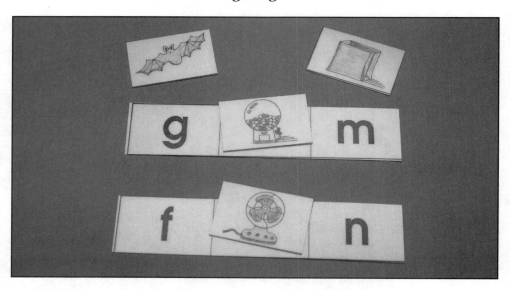

Brief Description

Students practice letter-sound associations by identifying which picture re-lates to a word strip that contains only initial and final letters and placing the picture in the blank middle space that represents the missing vowel.

Materials Needed

Word strips and picture cards.

Detailed Description

An activity called "Mystery Picture" from Jo Fitzpatrick's book *Getting Ready to Read* (2002) helps students associate beginning and ending letters with words. Students match a picture with a word strip that has beginning and ending letters and a blank box in the middle. For example, if a strip has b __t, the student would place a picture of a bat in the box between the letters. The teacher can make up letter strips and pictures, or use the blackline masters for 18 word strips on pages 86–90 of *Getting Ready to Read*.

10-6: Scavenger Hunt

Brief Description

This is an advanced activity for practicing letter-sound correspondences for initial and final sounds in which students write the letters in blank boxes in front of and after a picture.

Materials Needed

Word strips with three boxes and pictures of three-sound words.

Detailed Description

Scavenger Hunt is another activity from *Getting Reading to Read* that is similar to, but more advanced than, Mystery Picture. In Scavenger Hunt, the child places a picture on a middle box and writes the letter for the beginning and ending sounds on lines on each side of the picture. The teacher can make the word strips to match pictures, or use the blackline masters from pages 81 and 82 of Jo Fitzpatrick's book, *Getting Ready to Read*.

Blending Letters Into Words

10-7: *Touch and Say*

Brief description

The teacher spells a real or nonsense word with a movable alphabet. The student touches each letter and says the sound at the same time he touches the letter. The student then blends the sounds into a word, moving his or her hand across the word from left to right.

Materials

Movable alphabet (each letter or digraph is on a separate piece, such as a magnetic tile or paper; most teachers laminate pieces and sometimes attach them to magnetic sheets; you can also use the letter-sound cards from reading programs for this activity).

Step-by-Step Directions

1. The teacher spells a word with the tiles. This should begin with two- and three-sound words, and continues with words that have as many as six sounds.

2. The student touches each letter and says the sound. The student pauses at least one second before each sound to demonstrate that he understands the sound is discreet and matches the letter he is touching.

3. The student blends the sounds into a word and reads the word while running his finger under the letters from left to right.

Say and Write, described in 10-15 of this chapter under *Spelling Simple One-Syllable Words,* is a good activity to immediately follow Touch and Say.

Additional Information

This is one of the most powerful activities to help children who are having difficulty with reading. The teacher should select words that begin with continuant sounds (sounds such as /m/, /z/, /s/, /f/, /l/, /n/, and /v/) because these sounds are easier to blend into the vowel. Once the student can read words that begin with continuants, the teacher can use the activity with all sounds.

Building Fluency When Reading Real and Nonsense Words

10-8: *Detective Game With Real and Nonsense Word Cards*

Brief Description

Students read real words that the teacher has written on index cards. The words should stress the letter-sound combination being taught, but should also include words with all the letter-sounds that have been introduced to date.

Materials Needed

Fifteen to 20 index cards with real words, one word per card, prepared by the teacher.

Optional: Index cards with nonsense words, one word per card, different color of paper from the real word cards, prepared by the teacher.

Step-by-Step Directions

1. The teacher has the students read each word as she shows the card. This is most effective if the students read the cards individually. For example, if the teacher makes 15 cards and three students are in the group, each student would read 5 cards.

2. The teacher places each card on the table after the student correctly reads it.

3. When all the cards are on the table, the teacher asks each student questions and the students find the card or cards that answer the questions. Questions can be various types:

   definitions—What is an animal that says quack? (*duck*)

   fun about the class—What color is Brenda's hair? (*red*)

   sounds—Which words begin with /m/? (*mop, mom, met*)

4. The student reads the word before he picks it up.

5. The teacher also can time the students reading the words as fast as they can as she flips them from the stack.

Additional Information

Some teachers, from time to time, mix real and nonsense words into one deck. Make sure that real and nonsense words are on different color index cards. The teacher asks the children to read the words as she flips them. The purpose of this activity is to keep children from memorizing the relatively small number of real words and to make sure that they are reading the words using letter-sound correspondences. Mixing real and nonsense words ensures that the student who has a good memory for real words is not simply relying on his memory to read the words.

Some children with poor vocabularies may view many "real" words as nonsense words. This activity is a good indicator of students' oral vocabularies. In such cases, it is best to emphasize phonic reading of real words and contextualizing their meanings into phrases and sentences.

10-9: Sorting Real and Nonsense Words on Cards

Brief Description

The teacher writes real and nonsense words on index cards, using the same color for real and nonsense words. The students read the words and sort them into real and nonsense words.

Materials Needed

Ten to 15 cards with real and nonsense words, one word per card, prepared by the teacher; each child has different words.

Step-by-Step Directions

1. The teacher gives each child a set of index card words.

2. Each child reads the words silently and sorts the words into two piles: real words and nonsense words.

3. The children are encouraged to ask questions if they are unsure; the teacher helps them think of a sentence into which the word might fit if it is a real word.

4. When the children are finished sorting, the teacher asks each one to read the words and the rest of the group verifies that the sort is correct.

10-10: Timed Reading of Word Lists

Brief Description

The student reads three columns of words; the list in each column has the same words arranged in a different order and includes about 50% high frequency words. The goal is to read the words accurately while improving time from the second to the third reading.

Materials

A sheet of paper with three columns of words arranged in a different order in each column.

Stopwatch.

Pencil.

Step-by-Step Directions

Prepare by selecting 10 to 25 words to practice, including at least 50% high frequency words. Type words on a sheet of paper arranged in three columns, repeating exactly the same words in each column but in a different order.

1. Teacher gives each student the word lists.

2. When reading the first word list, the student says each sound and underlines the spelling for the sound, then reads the word.

3. The second and third time students read the lists, the teacher times them as they read the words only.

4. The person timing records the number of errors and the elapsed time.

10-11: *Three Sound Word Deck*

Brief Description

The teacher flips cards from three decks, one card at a time, while the student reads the word to practice blending sound-symbol correspondences.

Materials

A set of letter cards, sorted into three decks—two consonant piles and one vowel pile.

Detailed Description

The teacher sets three decks of cards, including two decks of consonant letters, face-down on the table, with a deck of vowel letters in the center. The teacher selects the letters that the student needs to practice.

As the teacher flips a single card from one of the three decks, the student reads the word. Most of the words will be nonsense words. This activity works well with about five to eight consonants in each pile. The purpose of this activity is to increase fluency with making the sound-symbol associations and blending the sounds together, so it is important to include only letters the students have mastered. This is a fluency drill in applying sound-symbol associations and blending them to read words, not a time to instruct on the associations.

Spelling Simple One-Syllable Words

10-12: Elkonin Boxes With Pictures

Brief Description

Children begin learning to spell simple three-letter words on cards with a picture and boxes or lines to indicate the number of letters needed.

Materials Needed

Cards with a picture and Elkonin boxes below for the number of letters required.

Letter cards or plastic letters to place in the empty boxes.

Detailed Description

One common way to start children spelling words is to provide a picture and then either lines or boxes to indicate the number of letters needed to spell the word. As you introduce the concept of spelling words, you can scaffold the instruction by first modeling the process of starting by isolating the initial sound, and then selecting the letter that represents that sound. This modeling continues by isolating the second sound, followed by the third sound. By offering the students only the three letters needed to spell the word and supporting their choice about which letter goes in which box, students can do this task more easily. The *Reading Readiness Manual* from the Neuhaus Center provides pages to fold to create simple books to use when students are beginning to spell common phonetic words with three sounds. Each word is carefully selected so that it only takes one grapheme, or letter, to spell each of the sounds. In the manual there are five books, each with four pictures and words. Examples of the words in these books are *pig*, *lip*, *dog*, and *rug*. Teachers can laminate these books for writing and erasing or ask students to place plastic letters on the lines if they prefer to reuse the books rather than have the students write on them and take them home. To help teachers, there is a list of six to ten letters at the top of the page to have ready as options for spelling each word. The same type of cards can be found in the *Road to the Code* curriculum, where there are about 20 cards starting on page 355 (Blachman et al. 2000).

10-13: *Sound Boards*

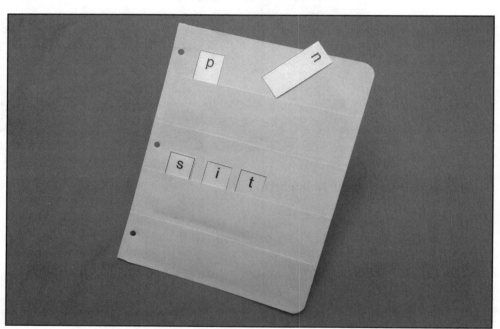

Brief Description

Students use individual pocket charts for spelling simple words.

Materials Needed

> Pocket charts (make your own or purchase stamp collector pages from stamp shops).
>
> Individual cardboard letters.

Detailed Description

Once students understand how to match sounds and letters to spell words with the Elkonin boxes or lines, the next step is to give more options in spelling. One of the most traditional ways to help children begin spelling is to model how to spell an initial word, and then ask students to change one letter at a time to spell a new word. One of my favorite formats for this activity—because it keeps the letters from falling off a student's desk and scattering on the floor—is in Neuhaus' *Reading Readiness Manual* (2002). The stamp collector pages Neuhaus recommends work well because they have four pockets across a page and are very inexpensive. The ordering information is provided on page 30 of Section 3 of the manual. The student can put selected letter cards in the top pocket and then move the letters down to the bottom pocket to spell words. The top pocket provides a place to hold the letters not currently in use. The manual provides a script for the teacher or aide, letters to copy on cardstock and cut out, and a list of the five to seven letters needed to spell specific sets of words. The sequence of letter presentation is predetermined, so only previously taught letters are used to spell words. The first set of letters introduced is *i, p, n, s, t,* and *d.* With these six letters, you can guide students to spell and read the following words: *sip, tip, dip,* and *nip.* I have given these materials to aides, who have used them effectively in intervention groups with struggling readers. There is a more extensive version of this activity in another Neuhaus publication, *Language Enrichment* (2000).

10-14: Word Chains

Brief Description

Word chains for early spelling should start with a simple word and then change one letter-sound at a time.

Materials Needed

Letter cards, magnetic letter tiles, or plastic alphabet letters.

Detailed Description

In the Sound Boards activity described in 10-13 above, teachers use simple word chains. Many teachers use pocket charts or sounds boards for word chain activities. An example of this activity can be found on the PALS Web site (http://pals.virginia.edu/scores/Activities) in the Letter Sounds section, called *Change That Vowel*.

Designing a word chain activity takes some careful planning. Depending upon the instructional strategy you are practicing, the chain is different. When you are first instructing students in letter-sound associations, the word chains typically include a single short vowel. First the student is changing the initial sound only and leaving the middle vowel and ending sound the same for the words in the sequence. Once the student masters this, the focus shifts to the ending consonant. Again, the words in the chain are selected to vary the ending sounds only while leaving the initial sound and vowel the same. Next you can alternate the beginning and ending sounds in the chain. This same routine can be repeated multiple times while learning new consonants. A chain that focuses on a single vowel helps the child practice using that one vowel blended in different words. After you have introduced a couple of vowels, the focus of your instruction changes. Now you can create word chains using two or three vowels. The progression is summarized in Table 10.2.

Table 10.2

Word Chain Progression

Target Sound That Changes

Focus on Consonants (use one short vowel at a time)
- Beginning sound only
- Ending sound
- Beginning and ending sounds
- Continue until all consonants mastered

Focus on Short Vowels
- Alternate middle sound—two vowels
- Alternate middle sound—three vowels
- Continue until all short vowels mastered

More Advanced Word Chains
- Change only one sound at a time, yet alternate between beginning, middle, and ending
- Ask student to think of new word to spell that changes one sound from current word
- Increase the number of letters
- Add more complex letter-sounds, including consonant digraphs, consonant blends
- Expand from short to long vowels, including vowel blends and r-controlled vowels

One of the areas in which students often need the most help is in mastering the vowels. Table 10.3 shows an example of a word chain to practice spelling words first with the same vowel, and later with three alternate vowels.

Another way to practice using the letter tiles, especially at the beginning of spelling words, is to use a combination of letter tiles and an erasable marker. The teacher can begin by placing letter tiles for the beginning and middle sounds in a word, and leaving the final sound blank. The student then fills in a final sound that makes three different words. For example, the teacher places three rows of letter tiles that spell 'ba' and then draws a line at the end of each row to indicate a space to fill in the final sound with a letter tile. When students are just beginning to spell words, you can provide support by placing a few letter tiles at the top that might make words. Later the student will be able to think of the words and look for the letter tile to complete the word.

Table 10.3

Word Chains to Practice Vowels

Word Lists to Practice Blending Words with Short Vowels				
Short o	**Short a**	**Short i**	**Short u**	**Short e**
mop	mat	sit	fun	jet
hot	ham	fin	hug	yes
cop	wax	win	bun	fed
hop	mad	big	hum	net
dot	bag	dip	nut	pet

Word Chains for Teaching Short Vowel Sounds		
a-o-i	**o-u-a**	**e-a-i**
mat	not	pet
map	nut	pat
mop	cut	sat
top	cat	set
tip	cot	let
tap	cop	lit
rap	cap	fit
rip	cup	fat
		fan
		fin

Note: These vowel activities were provided by Linda Farrell of Accent on Reading. Used with permission.

10-15: Say and Write

Brief Description

The student spells words with the movable alphabet, and then writes the words.

Materials Needed

Movable alphabet.

Pencil and paper, or dry erase board and marker.

Step-by-Step Directions

1. The teacher gives the student a word to spell.

2. The student segments the word into sounds. As he identifies each sound, he finds the movable alphabet piece that spells the sound and puts it in front of him (on his paper or on the dry erase board).

3. Next, the student writes each letter, saying the sound as he writes the letters.

4. When he finishes writing the word, he reads the word and spells it with letter names.

Reading and Spelling Multisyllabic Words

10-16: Spelling Words With Two or More Syllables

Brief Description

Students use "syllable boards" to spell words by syllable. Then they spell the word on a piece of paper.

Materials Needed

"Syllable boards" are 3 × 5-inch pieces of laminate; purchase a large sheet of laminate that accepts dry erase marker at a home improvement store and ask them to cut it into 3 × 5-inch pieces.

Dry erase markers and eraser.

Lined pencil and paper.

Spelling list, with each word spelled in its entirety and by syllable.

Step-by-Step Directions

1. The student has a list of the spelling words in front of him, with each word spelled in its entirety and by syllable.

2. The teacher reads the spelling words to the students.

3. The students read the spelling words to the teacher from the spelling list.

4. Without looking at the word, the students orally break each word into syllables, and they place one syllable board in front of them for each syllable in the word.

5. The students say each syllable as they write the spelling for each syllable on a separate syllable board.

6. The students check their spelling of the word against the spelling list.

7. If they had difficulty with any syllable, they discuss the spelling with the teacher.

8. After changing the spelling on the syllable boards, the student turns the syllable boards over and writes the word on paper.

9. The student checks his spelling against the syllable boards.

10. If a student still missed the spelling, he writes the word on an index card and practices spelling the word on syllable boards every day.

Additional Information

This technique is imperative for students with spelling difficulties. They often try to memorize the spelling of words, rather than breaking them into syllables and spelling by the smaller units in the word.

Teachers can teach their students to use the same technique when they are writing and need to spell an unfamiliar multisyllabic word. They can use their syllable boards until they are in the habit of spelling unfamiliar or seldom used words by syllable.

10-17: *Flexing Syllables for Multisyllabic Words*

Brief Description

This technique helps students move from single to multisyllablic words.

Materials Needed

Syllable boards (small erasable white boards; see "Materials" under 10-16 for details).

Different colors of dry erase markers.

Whiteboard eraser.

Detailed Description

After students are comfortable spelling short consonant-vowel-consonant (CVC) words, they may still be hesitant to attempt to work with multisyllabic words. One technique that may help is to use something called syllable boards and "flexing" the syllable.[1] For this activity, use erasable whiteboards cut to the size of 3 × 5-inch cards so you can work with students in learning to "flex" the vowel until the word is pronounced correctly.

Write a multisyllabic word such as *document* on a board. First, ask the student to divide the word and pronounce it. If that doesn't sound right, then divide another way by moving a letter in question to the other syllable and try pronouncing it again. In order to determine the number of syllables in a word for spelling, here are the steps:

Teacher:	How many vowels are there in the word?
Student:	3
Teacher:	Are they together or apart?
Student	Apart
Teacher:	Do you see a *silent e*?
Student	No
Teacher	Okay, then how many syllables are there in the word?
Student	3
Teacher	Okay, now please write them on the syllable boards.

If the student writes *do-cu-ment*:

---

[1] Teaching technique credited to Linda Farrell of Accent on Reading.

ask him to pronounce it. Assuming that he has been taught rules for syllable division, he would know that the *do* is pronounced with a long o because it is an open syllable. Therefore the word doesn't make sense. So let's try to "flex" the syllable by erasing the *c* from the second syllable board and writing a *c* on the first syllable board. On second reading, the first syllable would be closed, with a short vowel, and the word would be syllabicated correctly. One reason to use white boards and markers for this exercise is that often children don't like to erase work they do with pencil and paper.

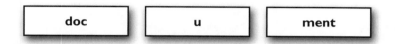

This technique can be used both for reading and spelling multisyllabic words.

Techniques for Teaching Nonphonetic Sight Words

10-18: *Heart Words*

Brief Description

This technique teaches students how to memorize nonphonetic sight words.

Materials Needed

Magnetic letter tiles or letter cards.

Detailed Description

"Sight words" is a term that most teachers use to mean the phonically irregular words that children must memorize because the words don't follow the rules for spelling. Teachers use many different techniques for helping students learn to read and spell these common irregular words. Some of the most common techniques include repeatedly writing the words, including them on the weekly spelling list, giving students a personal dictionary to reference at their desks, and placing these words on the word wall. One of the most unusual and effective approaches to teach nonphonetic words appears in a DVD series distributed by Sopris West called *Colleague in the Classroom.* In this series an approach called "heart words" is demonstrated. The teacher conducts a dialogue with the student about which sounds in the word are spelled as expected and which part is not spelled as expected; that part is signaled with a heart placed over the letters. Students see that in most of these words, there are some predictable letters. Only part of the word must be memorized by heart. For example, in the word *said* the s and the d are spelled as expected. It is the *ai* that must be memorized by heart. The process of analyzing the word for what sounds are spelled regularly and irregularly helps focus the student's attention on the exact spelling of the word. The process continues with a game of concentration to help memorize the spelling. The teacher turns the letter tiles over and asks the student to remember what is on each one backwards and forwards. I've seen teachers cut hearts out of red cellophane to cover the letters that don't follow the rules.

Practicing With Text

10-19: Decodable Text

Brief Description

Practice reading letter-sound correspondences and nonphonetic sight words previously taught by reading text that requires these skills.

Materials Needed

Decodable text that aligns with the sequence of previously learned letter-sounds and nonphonetic sight words.

Detailed Description

Once students begin reading simple words, they need to practice this skill with connected text. One of the most important types of text to make available for this early reading practice is decodable text. The aim of decodable text is that students will be successful at sounding out new words as they come to them. For that to happen, the decodable text must be tied to the sequence of letter-sound associations you are teaching. Ideally you will be able to use books from your core reading curriculum in your intervention groups, and then teach the letter-sounds in the order of the curriculum. Yet not all core reading curricula have an adequate supply of decodable books, so teachers often ask how to locate some books they can use in intervention instruction. The most difficult part about finding decodable text is that it is only decodable if it is designed to correspond with the instructional sequence of letter-sound associations, including explicit teaching of the nonphonetic sight words. Therefore in designing an intervention curriculum, you either need to start with the text and then establish the sequence of the presentation of the sound-symbols, or the text has to be written to go along with the order in which you are teaching sound-symbol associations. Writing and illustrating decodable text is a huge undertaking that few teachers have time to accomplish, so additional resources should be on any teacher's bookshelf.

Additional Information

Critics often claim that decodable books are boring, stilted, and contain "unnatural" language. Consider decodable texts a stepping stone to other types of text with more appealing language and information. They are texts to be used until the student becomes proficient at making the letter-sound associations and blending them together to read words. Decodable text is used to practice reading a large number of words with the sound-symbol patterns and sight words being taught and to enable the reading of uncontrolled text as soon as the child is ready. When the student has learned all the letter-sound correspondences, can blend them to read simple text where the control over the words helps him decode successfully, and knows a set of common nonphonetic sight words, he is ready to read more diverse types of text. Although the enjoyment of authentic children's literature is a desirable goal, a child may be discouraged by text that contains words that he cannot sound out, and he will be forced to guess and use other clues that are less effective. Tables 10.4 through 10.6 include lists of recommended decodable books and commercially available materials for phonics intervention.

Table 10.4 **List of Recommended Decodable Books**	• *Reading Series 1 to 3* written by Laura Appleton-Smith. Flyleaf Publishing Company, 1-800-449-7006, www.flyleafpublishing.com. Each series is a set of five to eight books available in paperback for $45-$72 per set. • *Dr. Maggie's Phonics Readers*, by Margaret Allen. Available from Creative Teaching Press and Lakeshore Learning, www.creativeteaching.com and www.lakeshorelearning.com. $69 for a set of 24 books. See Table 10.6 for the scope and sequence of this series. • *Bob Books*. Available through book retailers or Lakeshore Learning, www.lakeshorelearning.com. Each set contains 12 books for $16.95. Levels A and B each have two sets, and Level C has one set. • *Power Readers*, written by Susan Ebbers. To be published in 2006 by Sopris West, www.sopriswest.com. • *Phonics First Readers*. Available from Lakeshore Learning, www.lakeshorelearning.com. Item SK80, $89.50 for a set of 40 books.

Note: Prices listed are at time of publication. Please contact vendor for current information.

Table 10.5

Recommended
Commercially
Available
Materials for
Phonics
Intervention

Name	Description	Contact Information
Letter-Sound Associations		
Alphabet Rings, Class Set	Alphabet cards with keyword picture to create take-home rings for up to 20 students.	Lakeshore Learning www.lakeshorelearning.com TT-378 $49.95
Alphabet Reading Skills Puzzles	Set of puzzle cards with keyword picture on top. Letter fits below picture.	Lakeshore Learning www.lakeshorelearning.com CV-201 $10.95
Spelling Words		
Magnetic Letter Tiles	Each kit contains 8 of each sound-letter tile. Basic and Advanced sets available.	Accent on Reading www.accentonreading.com $135 per set
Make-A-Word Student Kit for 6	Magnetic boards and letters for 6 students	Lakeshore Learning www.lakeshorelearning.com AA454 RR-252 $79.95
Reading Rods Reading Specialist Kit-Comprehension	Color-coded manipulatives that interlock	ETA Cuisenaire www.etacuisenaire.com R5P-60099 $299.95
Spell-The-Word Picture Game	24 cards with pictures and boxes below to spell simple words. Letter cards also provided.	Lakeshore Learning www.lakeshorelearning.com FS-786 $19.95
Beginning Sounds		
Beginning Sounds Word Building Kit	75 cards with a picture and a word with the initial sound missing. Letters also included.	Lakeshore Learning www.lakeshorelearning.com RR-981 $19.95
Lakeshore Giant Learning Letters	Jumbo stuffed cloth letters and 3 pictures that stick with Velcro.	Lakeshore Learning www.lakeshorelearning.com LA-440 $69.50
Beginning Phonics Picture Card Library	Over 490 picture cards arranged by 40 phonics sounds. Good for use in pocket charts.	Lakeshore Learning www.lakeshorelearning.com TT-732 $29.95
Sight Words		
Sight-Word Take-Home Rings	Set includes 20 copies of 45 high-frequency words on rings to take home.	Lakeshore Learning www.lakeshorelearning.com AA-601 & 2 $49.95 per set (2 sets)

Table 10.5

continued

Other Materials		
Phonics Word Card Library	Over 600 word cards arranged by 79 sound-spelling patterns. Focus sound in red.	Lakeshore Learning www.lakeshorelearning.com AA-139 $59.95
Phonics Flip Books	Set of 34 color-coded flip books to practice words with specific vowels, blends, and digraphs.	Lakeshore Learning www.lakeshorelearning.com AA-902 $49.95
Phonics from A to Z	Book written by Wiley Blevins. Excellent lists of words for each sound.	New York, NY: Scholastic, 1998. ISBN 0-590-31510-2

Note: Prices listed are at time of publication. Please contact vendor for current information.

Table 10.6

Dr. Maggie's Phonics Readers: Scope and Sequence

Book #	Title	Focus Skills	Sight Words
1	I spy	m, f, s, r, h, t, c, short a	a, and, i, in, no, on, the
2	Hap and Cap	p, n, short a	but, have, here, of, said, to, was
3	Top Job, Mom!	b, d, g, l, j, short o	is, it, new, put, so
4	Pom-Pom's Big Win	w, k, short i	day, gets, you
5	Pug's Hugs	v. y, short u	come, plays, then
6	Jet It, Get It	z, x, short e	do, for, off, take
7	Click, Click	qu, ck	we
8	The ABC Bags	double f, l, and s	asks, one, this, what
9	Sing-Song Sid	-ing, -ong, -ang	likes, sees, things, your
10	Draw and Share	consonant digraphs: sh, ch, th	now
11	Truck Tricks	consonant blends: tr, gr, dr, cr, fl	go, look, out, time
12	Dave and Jane's Band	long a: ay, a-e, ai	her, into, she, they, very
13	Pete's Street Beat	long e: ee, e-e, ea, ending e	sounds
14	Twice as Nice	long i: i-e	are, good, my
15	The Little Green Man Visits Pine Cone Cove	long o: o-e, oa, ow, ending o; -old	from, head, little
16	Mr. Noisy at the Dude Ranch	long u: u-e, /oi/ sound: oi, oy	when
17	Sad Sam and Blue Sue	oo, ue	
18	Out to Gumball Pond	ew; ou as in out; ow as in now	does, girls, their
19	Splish, Splash	3-letter blends: str, spl, scr	learns, move, watch
20	Barney Bear's Party	r-controlled vowels	asked, once, open
21	The Rainy Day Band	contractions	family, family's, great, two
22	Cat and Dog at the Circus	question words, soft c and g	began some
23	Jo Jo in Outer Space	simple word endings: -er, -ed, -l, -y	talk, want
24	Riddle and Rhyme with Apron Annie	rhyming words, 2-syllable words	because, school, words

Chapter 11

Intervention Activities for Oral Reading Fluency (ORF)

Overview on Fluency

Why Fluency Is Important

Reading fluency has sometimes been called the "neglected" component of reading. Until recently core reading curricula gave little attention to the need to build passage fluency. This all is changing now. Fluency is gaining attention and is receiving additional research funding. According to the 1992 National Assessment of Educational Progress (NAEP) Report, 44% of the fourth graders were not fluent in their reading. This finding came from a component of the NAEP assessment in which examiners listened to students read passages orally and rated their reading on a scale. The examiners described the 44% of readers who were not fluent as reading in a slow and choppy manner.

In spite of the increasing recognition of the importance of fluency in reading instruction, there is no universally accepted definition for it. Some educators and researchers emphasize that fluency is accuracy and automaticity in recognizing words while reading. Others assert that fluency is best described as occurring when a reader reads so rapidly and effortlessly that he pays little attention to mechanics such as decoding. Still others focus on the appropriate use of prosody, or the expressiveness of the reader who reads fluently. A description of fluency from *Put Reading First* follows:

> *Fluency is the ability to read a text accurately and quickly. When fluent readers read silently, they recognize words automatically. They group words quickly in ways that help them gain meaning from what they read. Fluent readers read aloud effortlessly and with expression. Their reading sounds natural, as if they are speaking.* (Armbruster et al. 2001, 22)

Fluent reading sounds natural because it is divided into meaningful chunks, with appropriate pauses at the end of phrases, clauses, and sentences. One reason skilled readers achieve this prosody is that they recognize a high percentage of words automatically. Automaticity is a term used to describe how a skill can be applied without having to devote attention to it. Fluency requires automaticity, although more than automaticity is required to achieve prosody and expression.

Many times automaticity and speed are connected with regard to fluency. Indeed, speed when reading is important, but extreme speed is not necessary to be an excellent reader. In order to read fluently, the reader must be able to read rapidly enough to hold the meaning until the end of the sentence. Yet if the speed is too fast, meaning can suffer. So reading must be automatic, and at a pace that is above some minimum level in order to process meaning and below an overly speedy level in order not to lose meaning.

Importance of Rapid and Automatic Word Recognition

Instant word recognition has long been recognized as a critical task in efficient reading. There are at least two tasks that compete for the emerging reader's attention—word recognition and comprehension. Achieving accurate and automatic reading at the word level is a skill needed to be able to devote adequate attention to making meaning (comprehension). Readers who are accurate at reading words can devote attention to making connections between what they read and their background knowledge, as well as to other ideas in the passage.

What Causes Dysfluent Reading?

There are a variety of problems that can cause students to lack fluency. Readers who read dysfluently often lack underlying skills, such as phonemic awareness or an understanding of phonics. It is important to understand why a student isn't reading fluently in order to figure out which problem to address. According to Louisa Moats in Module 5 of the *LETRS* curriculum (Moats 2002, Book 2, 71), some possible underlying problems that can cause a lack of fluency include:

- Low proportion of words recognized "by sight"
- Variations in processing speed of known words
- Low speed when reading unfamiliar words
- Using context to identify words
- Low speed when identifying word meanings

As discussed earlier in this book, intervention begins at the lowest point of failure. If a student is not reading fluently, then it is critical to understand which early reading skills are missing so that intervention instruction can be provided at the appropriate level. Too often teachers assume that a second grader knows the skills that have been taught, such as that a silent e assists a vowel to have its long sound, or even a skill as basic as being able to name the letters quickly and automatically. When these skills are missing and they are not taught, the student will never catch up.

When Is a Student Ready for Fluency Building?

Students are not ready for activities or strategies to build fluency with text reading until they can read words accurately. In other words, the other lower level skills have to be in place before it is time to begin building fluency at the passage level. Once a student has a sufficient level of phonemic awareness and letter knowledge, the alphabetic principle, where the letters and sounds can be connected, develops. Then from this base, the student is ready to learn phonics. Once he has learned the basic phonic relationships and can read word lists, it's time to build fluency at the word level. Learning how to blend at a sound-by-sound level precedes learning to identify an unknown word in "chunks" such as syllables, prefixes, suffixes, base words, and common letter combinations. Once rapid and accurate word decoding skills develop, then it's time to work at the sentence level. At this point, if the student has all these underlying skills in place, then it's time to build fluency in connected text or passages.

When a student cannot read words accurately, there is no point in beginning fluency activities at the passage level. It's like trying to work on speed in bike riding before the child has his balance completely coordinated or his pedaling skills mastered. Children who stumble over every few words and aren't able to bring a variety of skills together to decode unknown words are not ready for working on fluency at the passage level. In order to build fluency at the passage level, the student needs to be able to decode the passage fairly accurately, yet is not able to read it rapidly enough.

Students who are ready for fluency building activities read accurately, but haltingly or very slowly. They don't get stuck a long time on unknown words; they just go at a slow pace. Fluency activities are to improve speed, rhythm, and smoothness when reading, not to improve word reading accuracy.

Research-Based Interventions for Acquiring Passage Fluency Skills

One of the strongest research findings is the positive relationship between fluency and comprehension. Children who read fluently also comprehend well. That is because it is necessary to read fluently to have attention to dedicate to comprehension. While reading fluently doesn't automatically guarantee comprehension for every reader, only a few students can decode well and with appropriate speed but not comprehend as they read.

Studies have also demonstrated that measuring oral reading fluency can serve as a proxy for measuring overall proficiency in reading. One minute measures of oral reading fluency are known to be the best measures of reading ability.

The primary technique for building fluency is repeated readings, where the student reads the same passage aloud with an adult or a student partner who can provide guidance. A substantial amount of research supports that rereading the same passage helps build fluency not only in that passage, but other passages as well.

There are two common approaches for repeated reading. The first approach is to reread the same passage orally with guidance, individually or in groups. The second approach is to read aloud while listening to a passage on a tape recording for feedback on accurate decoding of the words. Both are described in activities 11-1, 11-2, and 11-3, following. There are other common group activities for developing fluency, including reader's theater, choral reading, and echo reading. Repeated reading and partner reading may be more efficient in improving fluency than reader's theater.

While independent silent reading may be useful for building vocabulary and other skills, at this point there is not adequate research to validate this practice for the purpose of building fluency.

Selecting the Appropriate Passage for Building Fluency

It is important to select appropriate reading materials for fluency activities. When working on fluency activities, the student should be able to read the passage with 95% accuracy (independent reading level). This means that the student only misses one out of every 20 words. To calculate reading level, simply divide the number of words read correctly by the total number of words read and multiply by 100. This gives the accuracy percentage.

For readers who have recently mastered phonics relationships, selecting a highly decodable passage is helpful. Decodable passages have a high percentage of words that follow regular phonics relationships and very few irregular words. Using decodable text in fluency exercises enables the student to practice reading words with sound-symbol correspondences he knows, and to use that knowledge when he encounters words he doesn't recognize automatically "by sight."

While practicing fluency with connected text, it is best to supply the word when a student struggles more than a couple of seconds on any given word.

This is because the purpose of these activities is to build fluency in passages, not to learn how to decode words. If the student is struggling with a few words, particularly frequent nonphonetic words that appear in the passage, it may be helpful to provide an opportunity to practice these words separately from the passage reading. (Remember that if the student cannot read 95% of the words accurately, the passage is too difficult for a fluency activity.) In some curricula, using a word list or a chart of words provides practice reading individual words. Other curricula suggest having the student make index cards to practice difficult words.

How Fluency Is Calculated

Fluency is generally represented as the number of words read per minute. Teachers have two choices for calculating fluency. They can either have students read a passage for one minute and count the number of words read correctly. The number of words read correctly in this case is also the number of words read per minute.

The second method is to have a student read an entire passage that is fewer or more than 100 words. The teacher records the student's time and calculates the words read correctly per minute using the following formula:

$$\frac{\text{words read correctly}}{\text{total reading time in minutes.}}$$

For example, a student who takes 2 minutes and 13 seconds (133 seconds, or 2.22 minutes) to read a passage with 237 words and makes 17 errors (a total of 220 correct words) has a rate of 99 words per minute. (Round a fraction to the nearest whole number.)

$$\frac{220 \text{ correct words}}{2.22 \text{ minutes}}$$

$$= 99 \text{ words per minute}$$

The DIBELS Oral Reading Fluency Measure uses a one-minute timed reading. Words pronounced incorrectly, substitutions, and omissions are all considered errors, and are indicated by marking a slash line through the incorrect word on the examiner's copy of the passage. Self-corrections within three seconds, repetitions, and insertions are not counted as errors, but they do negatively affect the fluency score by taking extra time.

Fluency Building Programs

Fluency instruction generally should begin once a student knows all the sounds and can accurately decode words with the following patterns:

- One-syllable words with digraphs and blends

- One-syllable CVC words

- The most common nonphonetic sight words

Decodable books are best for fluency work until the student can read this type of text somewhat fluently. After that the student may be ready for other types of fluency instruction.

Read Naturally is one of the most widely used fluency building programs. Candyce Ihnot, a former Title I reading specialist, developed this program for students experiencing reading difficulties. The program provides leveled passages and manuals with procedures. Some schools establish *Read Naturally* as a supplemental program that can be part of an intervention program, or used as part of an after-school program.

Read Naturally uses a procedure to place students in the appropriate leveled books. After they are placed in the appropriate book, students select a passage and, before they read the passage, write a sentence to predict what the passage may be about based on the title and the pictures. Then the student reads for one minute from a passage without rehearsal and underlines unknown words. After he finishes reading, he uses a blue pencil and graphs the number of words he read correctly in the minute for his "cold read" starting time.

After the initial reading, the student reads the same passage aloud softly while tracking with his finger and listening to a tape-recorded version of the story, timing each practice. After a number of practice readings and once he reaches his goal time, he answers some comprehension questions about the passage. Then the student invites the teacher to listen to him read the passage aloud. He records his score on the graph in red and moves to the next passage.

For more information on *Read Naturally,* see the Web site at www.readnaturally.com. A paper written by Dr. Marcia Davidson on the research supporting this program can be downloaded from the Web site. The paper also describes the *Reading Fluency Monitor*, which is a fluency assessment that can be used in conjunction with *Read Naturally.*

Intervention Activities on Fluency

Building Fluency With Repeated Oral Readings

11-1: *Repeated Oral Readings*

Brief Description

Students read the same story orally several times and chart their times.

Materials Needed

Passage at the student's independent reading level.

Timer.

Chart.

Step-by-Step Directions

1. Select a passage at a student's independent reading level and mark an asterisk after word 100.

2. On the first day, time each student individually while the student reads the first 100 words of the story. Record the story title, date, and number of minutes for this reading of 100 words.

3. Optional step—have student practice reading a list of as many as 30 selected words from the passage. These words should be high frequency or nonphonetic words.

4. On days two, three, and four, student rereads the same passage. Record times each day.

5. On the fifth day, student reads the passage again. Record the time and chart the student's progress across the five days. Select a different passage for the next five days.

Additional Information

Any set of passages can be used for this activity, yet they must be carefully examined to make sure that they increase in difficulty gradually, and that each student begins with a passage at his independent reading level. A collection of decodable passages is published in a manual distributed by the Neuhaus Education Center called *Practices for Developing Accuracy and Fluency* (2000). There are 30 passages in order of estimated grade level equivalents from first to fourth grade. Each story has an asterisk marked after the 100th word. Rapid Word

Recognition Charts are provided with about 30 words for each story, as well as student charts to record the day one and day five timings for each story. The first page of the manual gives directions on placing students in the appropriate starting passage, and also in how to calculate the student's fluency rate and accuracy.

11-2: Partner Reading

Brief Description

A stronger reader is paired with a weaker reader. They read a passage aloud together, either at the same time or sequentially (with the stronger reader going first).

Materials Needed

Two copies of a passage for the pair.

Step-by-Step Directions

Pairing students allows the stronger reader to help the weaker reader. A procedure is given below for how to pair students so that the distance between the student's reading skills is about right. You may also want to model how you want them to read and to establish some ground rules about when and how to help when your partner is struggling. Suggest that they wait a short time (five seconds is usually about right) before supplying an unknown word. It is important to discuss expectations with students so that no child feels that their partner is embarrassing them.

Steps for Determining Pairs in a Classroom:

1. On a piece of paper, list all students from highest to lowest reader.

2. Cut the paper in the middle of the list and place the two pieces next to each other.

3. Pair the top reader with the student at the top of the bottom half of the list, and so on.

4. Give both students a copy of a passage and ask the stronger reader to read first.

5. The weaker reader follows along and rereads the same part of the passage.

6. It is best if both students have a copy of the passage so they can follow along. Another possibility is to have the students point to the words as they are reading or listening.

Additional Information

While students are paired they can either alternate reading parts of the passage, such as a paragraph at a time before switching, or they can simultaneously read it orally. When simultaneously reading the passage, typically the stronger reader reads just a slight bit ahead of the weaker reader, almost "pushing" the weaker reader gently to keep up a slightly more appealing pace. The weaker reader can also benefit from hearing the phrasing of the stronger reader.

Other Strategies for Building Passage Reading Fluency

11-3: Audiotaped Stories

Brief Description

Student listens to an audiotaped recording of a story, while reading aloud along with the text.

Materials Needed

Copy of the story for each student.

Audiotape of same story.

Detailed Description

In order to build fluency with the text, children can listen to a reading of the story on an audiotape while reading along. It is important that the student follows along while listening, so encouraging him to move his finger with the reading while he reads aloud is a good practice. You can purchase audiotaped stories, check them out from the public library, or make tapes by recording the story yourself. Another idea is for older students to make the tapes for younger students. Parents can be encouraged to make tapes for their children who are receiving intervention instruction.

11-4: Echo Reading

Brief Description

The teacher reads a section of a passage, accentuating appropriate phrasing and intonation, followed by the students echoing it as they read their own copy of the passage.

Materials Needed

Copy of the passage for the student and the teacher.

Detailed Description

Struggling readers need to hear what fluent reading sounds like and then try to imitate it. This activity provides a very structured activity where the teacher reads a short section of the passage with expression and proper phrasing. Then the student immediately reads the same line, following the teacher's example. This echo reading continues for the entire passage.

Commercially Available Products for Developing Oral Reading Fluency (ORF)

The first place to check for additional materials is your core reading curriculum. Many core reading programs (also called basals) have books that can be used for fluency passages, as well as audiotapes of some of the books. A list of some commercially available products is included in Table 11.1.

Table 11.1

Recommended Commercially Available Materials for Improving Fluency

Name	Description	Contact Information
Fluency Programs		
Read Naturally Master's Edition (Software Edition also available)	Program to develop fluency. Blackline masters for stories in levels 1-8, as well as audio-taped versions.	www.readnaturally.com $95-$105 per level, including 24 stories and tapes
Fluency First!: Daily Routines to Develop Fluency	Fluency program developed by Tim Rasinski and Nancy Padak. Each grade level includes passages, word work, a CD-ROM with passages, etc.	Wright Group/McGraw-Hill, 2005 www.wrightgroup.com $299.97, Complete Kit, Grade 1
Practices for Developing Accuracy and Fluency	Manual with 30 graded passages, high frequency word charts, student timing charts, & CD with taped stories.	Neuhaus Education Center's fluency manual www.neuhaus.org $35, with CD
Resources for Teachers		
A Focus on Fluency: Research-Based Practices in Early Reading Series	30-page publication about fluency. Followed a summit in the fall of 2002.	Published by the Pacific Resources for Education and Learning; available online. www.prel.org
The Fluent Reader: Oral Reading Strategies for Building Word Recognition, Fluency, and Comprehension	Book by Tim Rasinski with tips on building fluency.	Scholastic Professional Books www.Scholastic.com ISBN 0-439-33208-7
Building Fluency: Lessons and Strategies for Reading Success	Book by Wiley Blevins with background information about fluency, as well as mini-lessons and activities	Scholastic Professional Books www.Scholastic.com ISBN 0-439-28838-X
Books on Tape		
Listening Center B	Books on audiocassette	www.etacuisenaire.com IN62686 $599.95
Also LeapPad and Quantum-Pad Learning System		Leapfrog www.leapfrog.com

Note: Prices listed are at time of publication. Please contact vendor for current information.

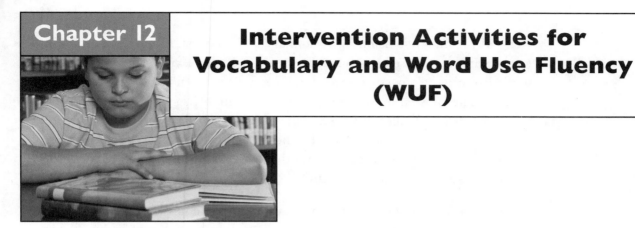

Intervention Activities for Vocabulary and Word Use Fluency (WUF)

Overview of Vocabulary Instruction

The Importance of Vocabulary and Oral Language

Oral language skills and vocabulary are two of the most important factors impacting a child's ability to comprehend passages. Consider the child who can decode words well but comes to a word he doesn't recognize in print. He may haltingly sound it out and try a pronunciation. But he is rightfully uncertain about any pronunciation when the word he is trying to read doesn't relate to any word he knows. This child can have excellent decoding skills and still not read fluently or with good comprehension because his limited vocabulary precludes accurate pronunciation and understanding the text.

Research shows that oral language skills and vocabulary are closely related. Additionally, a good vocabulary becomes more and more essential to comprehension as the student moves from grade to grade. In kindergarten through second grade, most of the words the student reads should be familiar to him, although some students struggle with the meaning of even the most basic words. Vocabulary and oral language are so important to successful reading that in DIBELS the measure called Word Use Fluency (WUF) is assessed at every benchmark testing period, kindergarten through third grade.

Some Terms to Know

There are four types of vocabulary knowledge: listening vocabulary, speaking vocabulary, reading vocabulary, and writing vocabulary. Listening vocabulary includes the words that a student can understand from listening to a conversation or a book read aloud. A student's speaking vocabulary includes all the words he uses in everyday speech. Reading vocabulary includes the words a student can successfully read and understand in print, and writing vocabulary includes the words he uses correctly when writing.

Chapter 12 • Intervention Activities for Vocabulary and Word Use Fluency (WUF)

I've DIBEL'd, Now What? **257**

Generally a student's listening vocabulary is the largest. Often a student will know what a word means when he hears it in context of conversation or while listening to a passage read aloud, even if he doesn't know the meaning well enough to use it in his own speech or writing. His speaking and writing vocabularies are smallest because there are many words a child may know to some extent, yet may not understand their meaning well enough to define the words clearly. Or indeed, he may not have access to them in the lexicon of words he uses in speech and writing.

A term that is gaining widespread attention in the education field is "word consciousness." According to the Teacher Reading Academy materials, word consciousness means an awareness of and interest in words and their meanings (University of Texas and Texas Education Agency 2002, 10). Bill Nagy and Judy Scott, two researchers in the area of vocabulary, write about the importance of developing a student's interest in learning words because it is impossible to teach students all the words they need to learn (Scott & Nagy 2004). They also suggest that word consciousness is a cluster of rather diverse types of knowledge and skills. These skills include the abilities: (1) to focus on the units in the word, (2) to be aware of the word's role in a sentence, and (3) to understand the difference between written and spoken language.

How Children Learn Words

Knowledge about the meaning of a word grows gradually over time and with multiple exposures to the word. Anyone learning a new word goes through the stages of not knowing the word, to becoming acquainted with it, to considering the word as part of his established knowledge. How does a child make this progression from encountering an unknown word to having it as an established part of his vocabulary?

Learning a word can occur in many different ways. Children who hear an extensive vocabulary at home and who read independently are more likely to have a robust knowledge of word meanings and language patterns. Likewise, children who are given explicit and systematic vocabulary and oral language instruction are more likely to have larger working vocabularies.

A Groundbreaking Study

One of the most significant books about the impact of home environments on vocabulary development is the groundbreaking *Meaningful Differences in the Everyday Experience of Young American Children* by Hart and Risley (1995). This book summarizes a study of conversations in 42 families in Lawrence, Kansas, from a range of socioeconomic levels over two and a half years. The goal of the longitudinal study was to discover relationships between family interaction patterns and vocabulary growth rates. Observers recorded and examined all the words children in these select families heard in one hour per month from the age of about ten months until they were three years old. The study found that:

- By the age of three, the children from the professional families had a larger spoken vocabulary than the parents in the welfare homes.

- Some children arrive at kindergarten having heard 32 million fewer words than their classmates.

- There is a difference of nearly 1,500 words spoken per hour between professional and welfare families.

- The parents in the welfare families used language for directive and punitive purposes rather than for encouragement or discussion of shared experiences.

These findings have gained extensive media attention. The findings related vocabulary to the family's socioeconomic (SES) level, which can be a very politically charged topic. Generalizations should be used cautiously because there are many low-income families that consider talking with their children and reading aloud a priority, and many "middle class" families that seldom interact verbally with their children. The message of this study for our purposes is that it is important to be concerned about children who are raised in homes that are not language rich, regardless of their income level or the reasons why. It is critical that children who enter preschool or kindergarten with low vocabularies immediately be placed in language-rich classrooms and that the emphasis on vocabulary is unrelenting throughout their schooling. Although the research on whether it is possible to completely close the gap is not definitive, the studies that have been done to date are not encouraging. However, that doesn't mean that our focus on the goal of improving all students' vocabularies, especially the student with limited word knowledge, can ever waiver.

Vocabulary Instruction

A team of researchers, Baumann, Kame'enui, and Ash, suggests that there are three objectives for vocabulary instruction (2003). These three objectives are:

- Teach specific words.

- Teach students to learn words independently.

- Help students develop an appreciation for words and to experience enjoyment and satisfaction in their use.

Research has long documented the enormous amount of vocabulary that students must acquire in order to keep up with grade level expectations in terms of growth each year. Students need to know at least 4,000 words by the end of first grade, and they must learn between 2,000 and 3,000 new words each year from third grade onward to be acquiring words at an average rate (Biemiller 1999, 11). Because it is impossible to teach all these words through classroom instruction, emphasis must be placed on teaching students *how* to learn new words. Teachers should consider modeling strategies for how to learn a word as an important part of vocabulary instruction.

Many times children are instructed to look up words in the dictionary. There is an instructional benefit for looking up definitions, but it is also helpful to think about the limitations of dictionary definitions. Dictionary definitions follow a very rigid format because of space limitations. Often a noun is defined by the category to which it belongs, followed by a specific distinguishing feature that makes the target word unique within the category. For example, in *Webster's New Collegiate Dictionary* a colonel is "a commissioned officer in the army, air force, or marine corps ranking above a lieutenant colonel and below a brigadier general." A colonel fits in the category of a commissioned officer in the armed services, and what distinguishes a colonel from other officers is where he fits in the ranking hierarchy. It helps students to appreciate the format so they can use the information more efficiently.

Rather than providing a formal dictionary definition, it may be more useful to simply give a "student-friendly explanation," which is to explain the meaning in everyday language that characterizes how the word is typically used (Beck et al. 2002, 35, 37). Start students off with a strong focused concept of what the word means, and then later include multiple meanings. An example of a student-friendly definition from Isabel Beck's book on vocabulary instruction, *Bringing Words to Life,* is to say that "*covert* describes something that is done in a hidden or secret way." This definition can be compared to one dictionary definition, "hidden or disguised" which could lead children to believe that covert means the condition of being covered rather than the quality of an action, which the teacher's definition makes clear.

In addition to helping students with a definition worded in easily understood language, teachers can provide synonyms and antonyms and use the word in a sentence that is meaningful to the students. After the student has moved from not knowing the word's meaning at all to becoming somewhat acquainted with it, the teacher can lead a discussion about multiple meanings. Examining how a word has different meanings in different contexts can help the student move the word into his or her "established" zone. It is critical to provide students many opportunities to use the word while learning its meaning. Learning is greatly enhanced when students are rewarded for finding occasions when the week's vocabulary words are used outside of school. Beck calls this procedure "word detectives."

It is common for teachers to think about whether to provide instruction in word meanings before, during, or after reading a story. Teachers also need to focus on whether specific vocabulary instruction is most effective in an explicit or implicit format. The National Reading Panel endorses both as important ways that students learn new word meanings (National Reading Panel 2000).

Implicit instruction occurs when a student reads a word independently and employs a strategy on his own to figure out a meaning for the new word. A student can implicitly learn a word while working in a group of students and hearing another child use a new word in such a way that he can deduce the meaning. Implicit instruction also occurs when a student reads a new word in a book or school assignment and is able to understand the word because of its context.

Explicit instruction actively involves the student in making the meaning of the word clear during the teaching. In *Bringing Words to Life,* Beck describes some active meaning-making activities. A good example is from a kindergarten teacher. Having selected the word *morsel* from a read-aloud story, the teacher gives her kindergarten class a student-friendly definition that "morsel is a very tiny piece of food." The teacher then says a list of foods and asks students to make choices about whether each is a morsel. For each item that is a morsel, the students are instructed to say "morsel" and to not say anything if it is not. The activity continues with the teacher saying the following list of foods: one cheerio, a whole pie, a raisin, a turkey dinner, a cake crumb (Beck et al. 2001, 61). During this activity, students are actively thinking about whether each food the teacher says is in fact a morsel or not and must choose an appropriate response.

One of the most important things that teachers can do during vocabulary instruction is to model how to use context to make sense of an unknown word and how to use information about the word part to help determine the meaning. Vocabulary instruction in third grade and beyond should emphasize studying the base word and the meanings of the prefixes and suffixes. Graphic organizers are very popular as teaching tools to help students organize what they know about a word's meaning. Some graphic organizers focus on the multiple meanings for words and how to use information about synonyms and antonyms to discover a more precise understanding of the meaning of a word.

Planning vocabulary instruction is important for all grades. Vocabulary instruction during the elementary years changes across time because of the nature of the vocabulary words in children's text. The words that appear in text students are reading in kindergarten through second grade are specifically selected to provide the opportunity to see printed representations of words students already know. The selection of words in early reading text is not intended to add vocabulary knowledge. During these grades, most of the words teachers choose for vocabulary instruction are taken from read-aloud text. Students practice most new words orally because they will be too difficult to read. As children progress from second to third grade, and their reading skills become more sophisticated, unfamiliar words can come from text that students read.

Teachers often ask how to choose which words to teach. In *Bringing Words to Life,* the authors recommend that teachers select words for instruction that are important for comprehension in the selected text and are also good general words that the student will encounter often. Words that are ripe for vocabulary instruction provide precision and specificity about a concept students already generally understand. Some excellent kindergarten words might be grumpy, prowl, annoy, and toppled. Examples of first grade words include coaxed, gleeful, devotion, detest, and dignified. A list of recommended instructional words from classic read-aloud books for grades kindergarten through second grade appears in the Appendix of *Bringing Words to Life,* pages 131–137.

Overview of Vocabulary Intervention Activities

Vocabulary intervention is different than any other domain measured by DIBELS. When a WUF score is low, it is a red flag that indicates the student may have low vocabulary and oral language skills. Even with the best intervention, the impact of instruction may not readily be seen over a short period of time. Vocabulary is learned over many years and does not follow a concrete sequencing of skills. Children need exposure to new words through oral discussion as well as reading. In spite of these challenges in assessing where to begin intervention, instruction is still needed. Intervention lessons for Word Use Fluency can include a combination of studying new words, learning about meaningful parts of words, and using the words correctly in oral and written expression.

Unlike some of the other measures in DIBELS, vocabulary deficits may not respond to instruction quickly and gains may not be evident on frequent progress-monitoring. For this reason, progress monitoring WUF may not make sense more frequently than every four to six few weeks because children with extremely low vocabularies will need continuous intervention throughout the year and are not likely to be moved in or out of intervention groups as with other areas.

For students whose vocabulary is well below benchmark, the ideal situation is for them to participate in a small group that receives 30 minutes of vocabulary and oral language instruction per day using a very structured program. One example of a vocabulary program that is often used successfully in a kindergarten intervention setting is called *Language for Learning*, which is distributed by SRA/McGraw-Hill. It is a direct instruction program that is carefully organized to introduce students to vocabulary that is commonly used in school. This vocabulary instruction is typically in addition to their work in an intervention group for other specific skill deficits.

If your school uses a core comprehensive reading program, it is likely to include a vocabulary strand. Some teachers wish to enhance the curriculum through providing additional instruction. For this reason, a few activities are provided in this chapter. However, it is important to realize that merely combining these activities is *not* likely to be sufficient to serve as an entire vocabulary curriculum because the most successful vocabulary programs are highly structured to provide children with information about words.

Intervention Activities

12-1: *Robust Vocabulary Instruction*

Brief Description

Teacher selects ten vocabulary words per week to teach using strategies that provide robust active experiences with these words.

Materials Needed

> Vocabulary words.
>
> Student friendly definitions.
>
> Additional materials as indicated in Directions, below.

Step-by-Step Directions

To Do Before

1. Select ten words for vocabulary instruction per week from read-aloud or student text.

2. Develop a student-friendly definition for each word.

3. Design an activity for each day for each word (see Additional Information, below).

To Do During

1. Introduce the word before, during, or after reading it in a story. Say the word and ask students to repeat it.

2. Provide a student-friendly definition.

3. Retell how the word was used in the story.

4. Discuss how the word can be used in another context.

5. Ask children to provide their own examples of how the word could be used.

6. Ask students to say the word again to reinforce its phonological representation.

7. Facilitate an activity using the word. See examples below.

Additional Information

Developing engaging and meaningful activities are the heart and soul of this form of robust vocabulary instruction. It takes time to think of these activities. Some examples from *Bringing Words to Life* include the following.[1] (The vocabulary word is italicized.)

- Questions and Reasons
  - Which of these things might be *extraordinary*? A dog that likes to play ball, or a dog that does the dishes?
  - What would an *immense* amount of snow look like outside your window?

- Making Choices
  - If I say something that could be done *leisurely*, say "Leisurely." If you'd need to be in a hurry, say "Hurry." *running a race, lying by the side of the pool*
  - Applaud to show how much you would like to be described by this word (not at all, a little bit, or a lot). *gloomy, stern, mischievous*

- Children Creating Examples
  - If you are *ravenous*, what do you want to eat for a snack?
  - If your friend is looking *forlorn*, what might have happened?

- Word Associations
  - Of the following five words we are studying this week, which one goes with *banter*? (*tease*)

---

[1] Based on activities suggested in Beck et al. 2002, 44, 56, 58–60.

- Have You Ever...?

  - Describe a time when you felt *complacent*.

12-2: The Colors and Shapes of Language [2]

Brief Description

Teacher engages students in a dialogue about vocabulary words that includes naming things, describing them, hearing the words in a story, retelling the story using the words, and then writing about them.

Materials Needed

Text.

Pictures of the topics to discuss.

Step-by-Step Directions

1. The teacher asks students to name words in the topic area. For example, if the topic is horses, then the discussion might begin by naming animals, animals that live in a barn, animals that live in the rain forest, etc.

2. The teacher holds up a picture of a horse and asks students to describe it. Then the students discuss:

   - Some categories that a horse would belong in (animals you can ride, large animals, animals that live in a barn);

   - The function of a horse. How do you use it? What is it for? (to ride, to compete in shows, to pull a carriage, etc.);

   - The color and size of a horse; and

   - How a horse compares to several other animals (elephant, sparrow).

3. The teacher reads a story about a horse to the students, and asks a few questions about the story when finished.

4. The teacher models retelling the story. Students retell the story to a partner using pictures, if needed.

5. Students make lists about animals or horses.

6. Students respond to the story by drawing an illustration about the story, dictating a story to the teacher, or writing their own story on the topic (depending on age).

---

[2] Based on activities suggested in Neuhaus Education Center, 2000.

12-3: Vocabulary Map[3]

Brief Description

To introduce new vocabulary in a story, the teacher helps students prepare a chart that helps them think about the meaning of words before and after reading.

Materials Needed

Text.

Three-column chart on a piece of paper.

Step-by-Step Directions

1. Before reading the story, select words that students are likely not to know well.

2. Make a chart with three columns labeled: Word, What I Think It Means Before Reading, and What I Think It Means After Reading.

3. List the words, and either ask students to fill in the second column or write it as the students dictate.

4. Read the story.

5. Complete the third column and discuss how the word was used in the story.

12-4: Semantic Feature Analysis[4]

Brief Description

Using two or three similar nouns, the teacher creates a chart that lists the objects across the top and the features that differentiate the objects down the side. Students place checkmarks in boxes to note which object has each feature.

Materials Needed

Two or three objects from a category.

Chart for semantic feature analysis.

Step-by-Step Directions

1. Teacher sets two or three objects that are similar in front of students (for example: boot, tennis shoe, slipper).

---

[3] Texas Education Agency, *Intervention Activities Guide*, provided in the kit for the Texas Primary Reading Inventory, 18.

[4] Based on activity on the University of Virginia's PALS Web site and in Moats 2002, Book 2, 25.

2. Teacher creates a chart that lists the three objects across columns at the top.

3. Teacher asks students to think of features of the objects to list down the side (soft sole, laces, made from leather, etc.).

4. Students add + or – signs in the column to note which objects generally have these features.

5. Students create a definition based on the features that differentiate the objects (a boot is something you wear on your feet and that is generally made from leather, has hard soles, and is often worn to protect your feet from the weather or danger).

12-5: Human Word Web [5]

Brief Description

Students arrange cards in a web showing the relationships between the words.

Materials Needed

5 × 7-inch cards with related words, one word per card.

Several pieces of string.

Step by-Step Directions

1. Teacher creates cards before activity begins.

2. Each student in the small group is given a couple of cards.

3. Students are asked to discuss how all the words relate to each other.

4. Students arrange the cards and use the pieces of string to make a web-like design that depicts the way the words can be connected or categorized.

An example is shown in Table 12.1.

Additional Information

When using this activity with a small intervention group, the students can lay the cards out on a table and arrange them. When this activity is done with an entire class, each student is given one card and then the students move around and discuss the words. Students then can arrange themselves in a hierarchy so that the person holding the card with the topic heading stands on a chair, the category headings can then stand, and the descriptive words that belong in the categories can kneel beside the person holding the category heading. After the

---

[5] Activity based on exercise No. 4 in Moats 2002, Book 2, 21.

Table 12.1

Human Word Web

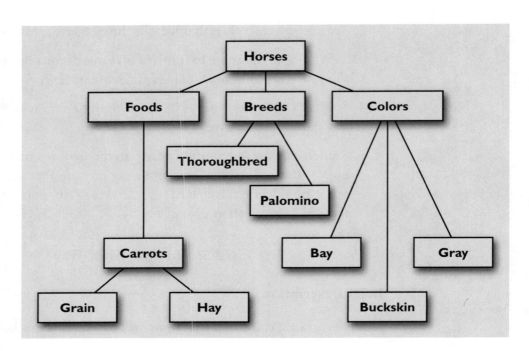

students have arranged themselves in the outline or web format, the teacher can tape the words on a wall so that the discussion can continue.

12-6: Scaling Antonym Pairs[6]

Brief Description

Students create a set of words and place them along a continuum from one antonym to another.

Materials Needed

List of antonym pairs.

A paper with a line with arrows on each end.

Pencil, dictionary, dictionary-style thesaurus.

Detailed Description

Students choose from a list of contrasting words whose meanings can be graded along a scale from one end to the other. Then students work together to think of many other words that might fall between the two along the continuous scale. For example, if the antonyms are *angry* and *delighted*, the words along the scale might include *furious, displeased, unhappy, happy,* and *pleased.* The exercise of discussing where along the continuum to place words helps students explore their definitions of words.

---

6   Activity based on exercise No. 8 in Moats 2002, Book 2, 29.

Commercially Available Products for Developing Vocabulary (WUF)

The first place to check for additional materials is your core reading curriculum. Many core reading programs have activities and curriculum specifically to help students develop a more robust vocabulary. A list of some commercially available products is included in Table 12.2.

Table 12.2

Recommended Commercially Available Materials for Improving Vocabulary and Oral Language

Name	Description	Contact Information
Vocabulary Programs		
Elements of Reading—Vocabulary	Comprehensive vocabulary program with teacher's guide, read-aloud anthology, and student books. Available for K–3.	Harcourt Achieve www.harcourtachieve.com $499 for classroom set Levels K, A, B, and C
Language for Learning	Systematic introduction to words used in school. Kit used with Pre-K–2.	SRA/McGraw-Hill www.sraonline.com $618 for set of teacher materials
Software	Software to help organize ideas for writing an outline. Can be used to create visual representations of the meanings of words.	Inspiration www.donjohnston.com $69 for 1–4 computers
Resources for Teachers		
The Colors and Shapes of Language, with CD	Spiral-bound manual for teachers to use in developing language. Includes activities on 21 topics.	Neuhaus Education Center www.neuhaus.org $25
Language and Literacy Units for Preschool: The Kitchen The Farm People People Everywhere Me & The World Around Me	Units developed for preschool but may be used for kindergarten intervention. Teacher manual plus magnetic manipulatives to develop oral language.	Neuhaus Education Center www.neuhaus.org $100 per set
Words Their Way: Word Study for Phonics, Vocabulary, and Spelling Instruction	By Donald R. Bear, Marcia Invernizzi, Shane Templeton, and Francine Johnston. Book for teachers on techniques for teaching students concepts using word sort.	Pearson Education $34

Note: Prices at time of publishing. Please contact vendor for current information.

Table 12.2

continued

Name	Description	Contact Information
Resources for Teachers		
Wordly Wise 3000	By Kenneth Hodkinson and Sandra Adams. Curriculum books for use with students. Lessons provide word list with definitions, plus sentence completion and multiple choice selection of meaning.	Educators Publishing Service www.epsbooks.com $117.50 per classroom set
Vocabulary from Classical Roots	By Norma Fifer and Nancy Flowers. Series of books that provide lessons on root words from Greek and Latin. 3rd grade and up.	Educators Publishing Service www.epsbooks.com $162.50 per set (too advanced for K–2)

Note: Prices at time of publishing. Please contact vendor for current information.

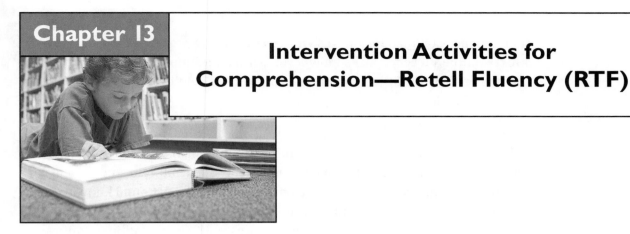

Chapter 13

Intervention Activities for Comprehension—Retell Fluency (RTF)

Overview of Comprehension Instruction

The Importance of Text Comprehension

Text comprehension appears last in this book because it is the reason for reading. Comprehension isn't an entity by itself, but rather occurs as the culminating result of all the skills operating efficiently. A student who reads with comprehension can tie his knowledge of phonemic awareness and sound-symbol correspondences together to decode unknown words, rapidly and automatically recognize a great number of words "by sight," and can instantaneously relate the meaning of the vocabulary words to his prior knowledge and connect the ideas within the text to make meaning. All this happens so efficiently that it appears effortless. The goal of all reading instruction is to help students ultimately be able to read fluently with comprehension.

Research has shown that good readers and poor readers differ in their approach toward comprehension. Good readers don't wait until the end of reading a text to comprehend; instead, they are actively thinking while reading. Additionally, they have a purpose for reading, and this purpose influences their reading process. Good readers also monitor their comprehension while reading and use strategies to fix problems in their understanding as they arise.

Are readers naturally born with the ability to actively engage in meaning as they read, or can this skill be improved with instruction? Effective instruction can improve a student's ability to self-monitor his comprehension and use fix-up strategies as needed.

Historical Perspective on Comprehension Instruction

More than two decades ago comprehension was viewed differently than it is today. We used to assume that if a student could read the words, he could comprehend. Comprehension was viewed as a passive process. A student read a text and then teachers asked low-level factual questions to test his reading comprehension. We tested comprehension, yet we didn't teach students *how* to comprehend.

Over the past ten to twenty years, new advances in cognitive science have influenced our view of comprehension. Now comprehension is viewed as an active, constructivist, meaning-making activity. While reading, a student must integrate new information obtained from the text with background knowledge he knew about the topic before reading. A reader summarizes and questions, sometimes clarifying within a sentence or paragraph if information is confusing or conflicting. While reading, a student must ask and answer questions and construct meaning beyond the words on the page. Often readers must draw inferences beyond the simple meaning of each word in the text.

As the education field has evolved in its thinking about what comprehension is, the perception of the role of the teacher has also evolved. The teacher's role is now seen as helping students make connections between their prior knowledge and experience and the text. For a while, it seemed that the teacher's role was to mention that a student should be making connections. But now the teacher plays an active role in helping students to bridge between their experience and the text. Additionally, an instructor teaches the student how to be strategic in understanding the text. It is not enough to mention what should be happening; now teachers must model and demonstrate what active construction of meaning looks like. Students need to know not only a variety of strategies to comprehend as they read, but also which strategy to use at what point during reading.

Explicit Comprehension Instruction

According to *Put Reading First,* effective comprehension instruction that is explicit, or direct, includes the following steps (Armbruster et al. 2001, 53):

1. Direct explanation—The teacher explains to students why the strategy helps comprehension and when to apply the strategy.

2. Modeling—The teacher models, or demonstrates, how to apply the strategy, usually by "thinking aloud" while reading the text that the students are using.

3. Guided practice—The teacher guides and assists students as they learn how and when to apply the strategy.

4. Application—The teacher helps students practice the strategy until they can apply it independently.

Children Who Have Trouble Comprehending

Within two years of the release of the National Reading Panel's report, another research summary was published, but this one focused specifically on comprehension. The Rand Corporation contracted a team of educators to comment on the topics that require future research (RAND Reading Study Group 2002). This study group presented a heuristic to think about reading comprehension. There were four components represented in the heuristic, each of which influences comprehension. The four components were the reader, the text, the task, and the context. Some of the characteristics of each of the four components are:

- Reader—natural ability in underlying processing skills including phonemic awareness, individual's understanding of language, attention, abstract reasoning processes, background knowledge about the topic;

- Text—how easy or complex the formatting of the text is, complexity at the single sentence level, whether the text is cohesive;

- Task—purpose for reading impacts how a reader reads, intrinsic vs. extrinsic motivators; and

- Context—whether there is support for the reader and the task, degree of scaffolding.

All of these factors influence how well a student comprehends the text he reads.

Overview of Comprehension Intervention Activities

Framework for a Comprehension Lesson Plan

This chapter provides a useful framework for thinking about how to design a lesson plan to teach comprehension. The teacher prepares a comprehension lesson by first previewing the text and designing the lesson. There are five sections in this lesson plan framework (see Table 13.1).

1. Summary of Understandings Students Should Extract or Construct
   - What are the most important learnings from the text?
   - What do you want students to understand from reading this text?

2. Text Problems to Be Addressed
   - Is any portion of the text incoherent? Does any portion require clarification?

- What inferences may cause problems for students?
- Is there any complex language structure to address?

3. Plan for Before Reading
   - What will you do to engender the student's interest in the text?
   - What questions will you ask?
   - How will you activate the student's prior knowledge?
   - What predictions do you want students to make?

4. Plan for During Reading
   - What queries or questions can you include in the plan to help students construct meaning?
   - How might a guided oral reading be used to scaffold the use of comprehension and metacognitive strategies?

5. Plan for After Reading
   - What experiences will you plan to enhance the students' understanding of the text, or to help them make appropriate connections to other text or knowledge?
   - What types of informal assessment will you use to provide information on the students' comprehension of the text?

Table 13.1

Framework for Reading Comprehension Lesson Plan

Understandings Students Should Extract or Construct
Text Problems to Be Addressed
Before Reading Preparation for Students
During Reading Preparation for Students
After Reading Preparation for Students

Source: Adapted from framework developed by the University of Texas Center for Reading and Language Arts, *Teacher Reading Academy* materials, and version developed by Marsha R. Berger.

Intervention Activities on Comprehension

13-1: K-W-L Chart

Brief Description

Using a chart with three columns, students are asked before reading to complete what they already know and want to know. After reading, they fill in what they learned.

Materials Needed

K-W-L chart (flipchart or paper with three columns).

Detailed Description

The instructor uses a flipchart or a paper with three columns labeled as follows:

What I Know (K)
What I Want to Know (W)
What I Have Learned (L)

This technique is used to help children activate prior knowledge and set a purpose for reading to seek information they want to know. They complete the first two columns before reading and fill in the third column after reading the passage. Donna Ogle initially developed this technique for use with expository text (Ogle 1986).

13-2: Write Predictions

Brief Description

Students learn to write predictions before reading and then check their predictions after reading.

Materials Needed

Flipchart or paper to record predictions.

Detailed Description

Before reading, students compose a list of their predictions about the passage based on the title and a picture walk (the teacher shows children the pictures before reading) of the book. After reading the story, they go back and place a checkmark next to all their predictions that were accurate. The purpose of this activity is to model for students that predicting what will happen is a purposeful strategy to use before and while reading.

13-3: Story Web

Brief Description

Students learn to think about the aspects of the story as they are reading.

Materials Needed

Story web graphic organizer.

Detailed Description

Students use a story web graphic organizer to record information about the story. The web can have separate circles or areas to record comments about the setting, characters, plot, etc.

13-4: Green, Yellow, and Red Question Cards[1]

Brief Description

A series of questions are written on three different colors of cards to signal that they are to be asked before (green), during (yellow), and after (red) reading.

Materials Needed

> Question cards on three different colors of cardstock paper (green, yellow, red).

Detailed Description

Students use a different set of questions to activate knowledge before reading, make connections during reading, and analyze the text after reading. Teachers can create these questions, which would vary depending upon whether the text is narrative or expository. Some sample questions for narrative text are provided below.

Before Reading (green cards)

- What does the title tell me about this story?
- What do the pictures tell me?
- What do I already know about....? (the topic of the story)

During Reading (yellow cards)

- Who? (tell who the story is about, or name the characters)
- What? (state the problem)
- When? (tell the time the story takes place)
- Where? (tell the place of the story)
- Why? (explain why something happened)
- How? (tell how the problem was solved)
- What do I think will happen next? (make predictions)

---

[1] University of Texas: Center for Reading and Language Arts, 2002. Narrative Cards Discussion, Handout 11 of First Grade Teacher Reading Academy materials.

After Reading (red cards)

- Who were the characters?

- What was the setting?

- What was the problem?

- How was the problem solved?

- Why did...? (elaborate on why something happened)

13-5: Comprehension Bookmark

Brief Description

A set of words are written on cardstock that is cut in the shape of a bookmark to use as a reminder while reading.

Materials Needed

Cardstock to make bookmarks.

Detailed Description

Words are written down in a column and copied on cardstock, which is then cut in the shape of a bookmark. The words represent reminders of what good readers think about while reading. Some sample words include *visualize, wonder, make connections, express feelings, predict, ask questions, reread,* and *clarify.*

13-6: Questioning the Author

Brief Description

A technique for comprehending is modeled by a teacher-led discussion during the first reading of a new passage. Teacher stops periodically while reading to ask queries of the author.

Materials Needed

Text.

Step-by-Step Directions:

To Do Before

1. Teacher previews the text and places an asterisk at each point to stop for a query.

2. Teacher writes a query/question for each stopping point (see examples below).

To Do During

1. Teacher begins reading the passage aloud while students follow along.

2. At the first asterisk, teacher stops and poses the query.

3. Students respond and discuss the topic of the query.

4. Reading continues until the teacher reaches the next asterisk.

5. Reading and queries continue until the end of the passage.

Additional Information

Isabel Beck and colleagues developed this approach to model what strategic readers do, and it is described in their book, *Questioning the Author* (Beck et al. 1997). Since students cannot see inside the mind to observe what good readers do, this approach highlights how readers stop during reading to ask questions and pose hypotheses to make sense of the text. The purpose is to model a guided discussion in which the teacher is questioning aloud along with the students. Together the teacher and the students construct meaning from the author's words. This approach is to be used occasionally rather than every time a text is read. Although the teacher prepares the activity ahead of time, for the students, it is planned to occur during a cold read of a new passage. Before beginning the process, the teacher tells the students that authors are not infallible and that sometimes they don't write clearly. Therefore we will stop and ask what the author intended us to understand. Examples of these types of questions, which are called "queries," are:

- What has the author told us about this topic?

- What does the author mean by…?

- How does this idea connect to what the author already told us?

- What is the author telling us here?

13-7: *Make a Movie*

Brief Description

Teacher directs students through process of "making a movie in their mind" while reading.

Materials Needed

Text.

Paper and colored pencils or crayons.

Detailed Description

Teacher first models this technique by thinking aloud about what her movie looks like, stopping periodically while reading a story aloud. After modeling this technique, she then begins reading a story aloud and stops from time to time to allow students to describe their mind movies. Students can tell about their movie orally, or they can draw a picture of what their movie looks like. Students are encouraged to think about what the character looks like, where he is standing, what is around him, what he is doing, and who else is in the scene.

13-8: Compare and Contrast

Brief Description

Students use a graphic organizer such as a Venn diagram to compare two aspects of the story, such as two characters for a narrative story or two events in an expository text.

Materials Needed

Graphic organizer.

Detailed Description

One technique for helping students interpret a text is to ask students to compare and contrast how two things are alike or different. A Venn diagram (two overlapping circles) is one useful graphic organizer for this discussion. If two events are compared, then things that are unique about each event appear in the circles outside of the overlapping area. Common characteristics of the two events are listed in the area where the two circles overlap.

13-9: Cause and Effect

Brief Description

A graphic organizer is used to help students think about the cause and effect relationships in a passage.

Materials Needed

Graphic organizer.

Detailed Description

As a way to teach students to look for cause and effect, the instructor can make a simple chart with two columns, one for "Cause" and the other for "Effect." Initially when modeling how to use this chart, the instructor can do this with the entire group. Later, each student can fill in his own chart.

13-10: Sequencing Events

Brief Description

As children read the story, they list the important events in sequential order.

Materials Needed

Graphic organizer.

Detailed Description

Children can list the events of a narrative story that lead up to the turning point in the story. This can be done on a graphic organizer that displays the sequence of events from the beginning to the end. The first event can be listed on the bottom left corner of the page and all subsequent events are written indented up to the top right corner of the page (stairsteps). By drawing an arrow from the bottom left to the top right, the direction of how to read the page is clarified. Another possible format is to display the events on a timeline going from left to right. This same technique can be used for expository text that relates to historical events.

13-11: Main Idea

Brief Description

Students learn how to summarize and state the main idea in a few words.

Materials Needed

None

Detailed Description

The instructor models how to state what the story is about. After students begin to learn how to state what the main idea of the passage is about, you can ask them to try to state the main idea in 15 words or less.

Commercially Available Products for Developing Comprehension (RTF)

The first place to check for additional materials is your core reading curriculum. Many core reading programs have activities and curriculum materials for teaching comprehension strategies. A list of some commercially available products is included in Table 13.2.

Table 13.2

Recommended Commercially Available Materials for Improving Comprehension

Name	Description	Contact Information
Comprehension Programs		
Collaborative Strategic Reading: Strategies for Improving Comprehension	Manual written by Janette Klingner, Sharon Vaughn, Joseph A. Dimino, J. Schumm, and D. Bryant. Contains variety of strategies for teaching comprehension strategies.	Sopris West www.sopriswest.com 128 pages $25
Strategies to Achieve Reading Success (STARS)	By Isabel Beck, Margaret McKeown, R. Hamilton, and Linda Kucan. Series of grade-level workbooks to practice comprehension strategies.	Curriculum Associates www.curriculumassociates.com 1-800-225-0248 WS8845, WS7932–38 $3.95–5.95
Resources for Teachers		
Questioning the Author: An Approach for Enhancing Student Engagement with Text	By Isabel Beck, Margaret McKeown, and Linda Kucan. Practical teacher-friendly book.	International Reading Association (1997)
Improving Reading Comprehension: Research-Based Principles and Practices	Book by Joanne Carlisle and M. Rice. Provides research background on comprehension instruction.	York Press (2002) ISBN 0-912752-70-X
Visualizing and Verbalizing for Language Comprehension and Thinking	By Nanci Bell. Explains techniques to help students make images while reading.	Gander Educational Publishing (1991) 1-800-554-1819

Note: Prices at time of printing. Please contact vendor for current information.

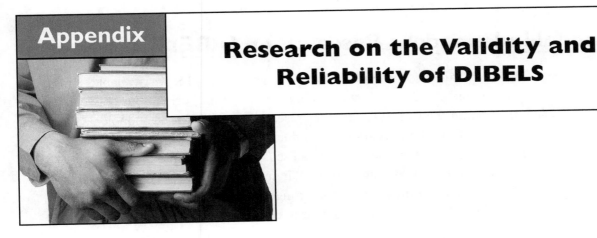

Research on the Validity and Reliability of DIBELS

Norms and Test Score Reports

DIBELS is a nationally norm-referenced test. Technical Report #7, *Technical Adequacy and Decision Making Utility of DIBELS,* describes a longitudinal study of children in two elementary school districts in Oregon over four years, from 1997 through 2001 (Good, Kaminski, Shinn, Bratten, and Laimon 2003). The ethnicity and socio-economic status of the students studied mirrors that of the United States fairly closely. By the fourth year of the study, approximately 320 students were followed in one school and 350 in the second school. Not only were these children tracked to see how well the DIBELS indicators predicted the students who would struggle in learning to read, but results also were correlated against three criterion-related measures (Woodcock-Johnson Readiness Cluster, and the Stanford-Binet Verbal Reasoning and Abstract-Visual Reasoning Scores).

More recently, as the DIBELS use has increased, norms have been calculated using a much larger pool of scores available to the researchers through the Internet-provided data management system. According to Good and colleagues in Technical Report #9, scores from over 37,000 children were used to determine the benchmarks for the middle of the year for kindergarten and first grade students. Up until a few months ago, only end-of-the-year benchmarks were published.

Validity and Reliability

According to Good, Gruba, and Kaminski, evidence of reliability, validity and sensitivity for DIBELS has been investigated in a series of studies (2001). Alternate form reliability of the DIBELS measures is generally considered adequate, ranging from .72 to .94 for the various indicators. The lowest reliability measure is for the ISF at .72. By repeating this measure five times on five days using multiple alternative forms, the resulting average score would have a reliability of above .90.

Additional Independent Research on DIBELS

Two field studies on the technical adequacy of DIBELS are available. Hintze et al. completed a study showing "moderate to strong correlations between the DIBELS and the C-TOPP," another research-derived test of phonological processing (2003). The second study, conducted by Shaw and Shaw (2002), showed that the correlation of the DIBELS fall score to the Colorado State test was .73, winter was .73, and spring was .80. Therefore the authors concluded that the DIBELS fall and winter scores are strong predictors of how well a student will do on the Colorado State Assessment in the spring of their third grade year.

Summary of Reliability and Validity Data on DIBELS

Measure	Type of Reliability or Validity	Research Result
ISF	Alternate-form reliability	.72 in Jan of Kindergarten Repeating 4 times–.91
	Concurrent criterion validity	ISF with DIBELS PSF is .48 in Jan of K .36 with the W-J Psycho-Educ. Total Reading Cluster
PSF	Alternate-form Reliability	2-week–.88 1-month–.79 in May of K
	Concurrent Criterion Validity	With W-J Psycho-Educ. Battery readiness cluster–.54
	Predictive Validity	Spring K PSF with Winter 1st grade NWF–.62 Spring 1st grade W-J Total Reading Cluster–.68 Spring 1st grade CBM ORF–.62
NWF	Alternate-form Reliability	1-month–Jan. of 1st grade–.83
	Concurrent Criterion Validity	Jan. of 1st grade–with W-J Revised reading cluster–.36 Feb of 1st grade–with W-J Revised reading cluster–.59
	Predictive Validity	Jan of 1st grade with ORF in May of 1st grade–.82 Jan of 1st grade with ORF in May of 2nd grade–.60 With W-J Total Reading Cluster–.66
LNF	Alternate-form Reliability	1-month–.88 in K
	Median Criterion Validity	With W-J Revised Reading Cluster–.70 in K
	Predictive Validity	K LNF with 1st grade W-J Revised reading cluster–.65 K LNF with 1st grade CBM reading–.71
ORF	Median Alternate-form Rel.	2nd grade passages–.94
	Concurrent Validity	2nd grade passages–.95

Source: Good, Wallin, Simmons, Kame'enui, & Kaminski 2002.

Works Cited

Adams, Marilyn, Barbara Foorman, Ingvar Lindberg, and Terri Beeler. 1999. *Phonemic Awareness in Young Children.* Baltimore: Paul H. Brookes.

Allen, Kay, and Marilyn Beckwith. 1999. "Alphabet Knowledge: Letter Recognition, Naming, and Sequencing." In *Multisensory Teaching of Basic Language Skills,* edited by Judith R. Birsh, 85–117. Baltimore: Paul H. Brookes.

American Federation of Teachers, editors. 2004. *Preventing Early Reading Failure.* Washington, DC: American Federation of Teachers.

Archer, Anita, James Flood, Diane Lapp, and Linda Lungren. 2002. *Phonics for Reading.* North Billerica, MA: Curriculum Associates.

Armbruster, Bonnie, Fran Lehr, and Jean Osborn. 2001. *Put Reading First: The Research Building Blocks for Teaching Children to Read.* Washington, DC: Partnership for Reading.

Baumann, J. F., Edward J. Kame'enui, and G. Ash. 2003. "Research on Vocabulary Instruction: Voltaire Redux." In *Handbook of Research on Teaching the English Language Arts,* 2nd ed., edited by James Flood, Diane Lapp, James R. Squire, and Julie M. Jensen, 752–758. Mahwah, NJ: Lawrence Erlbaum.

Bear, Donald, Marcia Invernizzi, Shane Templeton, and Francine Johnston. 2004. *Words Their Way: Word Study for Phonics, Vocabulary, and Spelling Instruction.* Upper Saddle River, NJ: Pearson Education.

Beck, Isabel L., Margaret G. McKeown, R. Hamilton, and Linda Kucan. 1997. *Questioning the Author: An Approach for Enhancing Student Engagement with Text.* Newark, DE: International Reading Association.

Beck, Isabel L., Margaret G. McKeown, and Linda Kucan. 2002. *Bringing Words to Life: Robust Vocabulary Instruction.* New York: Guilford Press.

Bell, Nanci. 1991. *Visualizing and Verbalizing for Language Comprehension and Thinking.* San Luis Obispo, CA: Gander Educational Publishing.

Biemiller, Andrew. 1999. *"Language and Reading Success."* In *From Reading Research to Practice: A Series for Teachers,* edited by J. Chall. Newton Upper Falls, MA: Brookline Books.

Birsh, Judith R. 1999. *Multisensory Teaching of Basic Language Skills.* Baltimore: Paul H. Brookes.

Blachman, Benita, Eileen Whynne Ball, Rochella Black, and Darlene M. Tangel. 2000. *Road to the Code.* Baltimore: Paul H. Brookes.

Blevins, Wiley. 1997. *Phonemic Awareness Activities for Early Reading Success.* New York: Scholastic.

Blevins, Wiley. 1998. *Phonics from A to Z.* New York: Scholastic.

Carlisle, Joanne, and Melinda Rice. 2002. *Improving Reading Comprehension: Research-Based Principles and Practices.* Baltimore: York Press.

Catts, Hugh, and Tina Olsen. 1993. *Sounds Abound: Listening Rhyming and Reading.* East Moline, IL: Linguisystems.

Davidson, Marcia, and J. Towner. 2001. "The Reliability, Validity, and Applications of Oral Reading Fluency Measures." Paper presented at the Society for the Scientific Study of Reading, Boulder, CO.

Denton, Carolyn, and Patricia Mathes. 2003. "Intervention for Struggling Readers: Possibilities and Challenges." In *Preventing and Remediating Reading Difficulties: Bringing Science to Scale,* edited by Barbara K. Foorman. Baltimore: York Press.

Ehri, Linnea, and L. S. Wilce. 1979. "The Mnemonic Value of Orthography among Beginning Readers." *Journal of Educational Psychology* 71: 26–40.

Fagen, Michele, and Vicki Prouty. 1998. *Language Strategies for Little Ones.* Eau Claire, WI: Thinking Publications.

Felton, Rebecca. 1993. "Effects of Instruction on the Decoding Skills of Children With Phonological-Processing Problems." *Journal of Learning Disabilities* 26: 583–589.

Fitzpatrick, Jo. 1997. *Phonemic Awareness: Playing with Sounds to Strengthen Beginning Reading Skills.* Cypress, CA: Creative Teaching Press.

Fitzpatrick, Jo. 2002. *Getting Ready to Read: Independent Phonemic Awareness Centers for Emergent Readers.* Cypress, CA: Creative Teaching Press.

Francis, David J., Sally Shaywitz, K. K. Stuebing, Bennett Shaywitz, and Jack Fletcher. 1996. "Developmental Lag versus Deficit Models of Reading Disability: A Longitudinal Individual Growth Curves Analysis." *Journal of Educational Psychology* 88: 3–17.

Gillon, Gail. 2003. *Phonological Awareness: From Research to Practice.* New York: Guilford Publications.

Glaser, Deborah. 2005. *ParaReading: A Training Guide for Tutors.* Longmont, CO: Sopris West.

Good, Roland H., J. Gruba, and Ruth A. Kaminski. 2001. "Best Practices in Using Dynamic Indicators of Basic Early Literacy Skills (DIBELS) in an Outcomes-Driven Model." *Best Practices in School Psychology* IV: 679–700.

Good, Roland H., Edward J. Kame'enui, Deborah C. Simmons, and David Chard. 2002. "Focus and Nature of Primary, Secondary, and Tertiary Prevention: The Circuits Model." Technical Report 1. College of Education, Institute for the Development of Educational Achievement. Eugene, OR: University of Oregon.

Good, Roland H., Ruth A. Kaminski, M. Shinn, J. Bratten, and L. Laimon. 2003. *Technical Adequacy and Decision Making Utility of DIBELS.* Technical Report 7. Eugene, OR: University of Oregon.

Good, Roland H., Ruth A. Kaminski, S. Smith, Deborah C. Simmons, Edward J. Kame'enui, and J. Wallin. 2003. "Reviewing Outcomes: Using DIBELS to Evaluate Kindergarten Curricula and Interventions." In *Reading in the Classroom: Systems for the Observation of Teaching and Learning,* edited by Sharon Vaughn and Kerri L. Briggs, 221–259. Baltimore: Paul H. Brookes.

Good, Roland H., Joshua U. Wallin, Deborah C. Simmons, Edward J. Kame'enui, and Ruth A. Kaminski. 2002. *System-wide Percentile Ranks for DIBELS Benchmark Assessment.* Technical Report #9. Eugene, OR: University of Oregon. Available: dibels.uoregon.edu/techreports/DIBELS_Percentiles.pdf (accessed May 5, 2005).

Hall, Susan L. 2004. "Embedding Practices through Professional Development: Establishing an Early Intervention Program to Prevent Reading Difficulties." Ed.D. dissertation. National-Louis University, Evanston, IL.

Hart, B., and T. Risley. 1995. *Meaningful Differences in the Everyday Experience of Young American Children.* Baltimore: Paul H. Brookes.

Hintze, John M., Amanda L. Ryan, and Gary Stoner. 2003. "Concurrent Validity and Diagnostic Accuracy of the Dynamic Indicators of Basic Early Literacy Skills and the Comprehensive Test of Phonological Processing." *School Psychology Review* 32(4): 541–557.

Ihnot, Candyce. 2005. *Read Naturally Master's Edition.* Saint Paul, MN: Read Naturally.

Jordano, Kimberley, and Trisha Callella. 1998. *Phonemic Awareness Songs and Rhymes.* Cypress, CA: Creative Teaching Press.

Juel, Connie. 1988. "Learning to Read and Write: A Longitudinal Study of 54 Children from First through Fourth Grades." *Journal of Educational Psychology* 80: 437–447.

Klingner, Janette K., Sharon Vaughn, Joseph A. Dimino, J. Schumm, and D. Bryant. 2001. *Collaborative Strategic Reading: Strategies for Improving Comprehension.* Longmont, CO: Sopris West.

Lacey, Karen, and Wendy Baird. 2005. *WatchWord: A MultiSensory Reading and Writing Program.* Longmont, CO: Sopris West.

Lenchner, Orna, and Blanche Podhajski. 1998. *The Sounds Abound Program.* East Moline, IL: LinguiSystems.

Lyon, G. Reid, and Jack Fletcher. 2001. "Early Warning System." *Education Matters* 2001 (Summer): 23–29.

Mathes, Patricia, Jill Howard Allor, Joseph K. Torgesen, and Shelley H. Allen. 2001. *Teacher-Directed PALS: Paths to Achieving Literacy Success.* Longmont, CO: Sopris West.

Moats, Louisa C. 2002. *Language Essentials for Teachers of Reading and Spelling (LETRS). Module 2.* Longmont, CO: Sopris West.

Montgomery, J. K. 2002. *Building Phonological Awareness Skills for Early Readers.* Orange, CA: Chapman University Reading Instruction Course Handbook.

National Assessment of Educational Progress. 1992. *National Association of Educational Progress Report.* Washington, DC: National Center for Education Statistics.

National Reading Panel. 2000. *National Reading Panel Report.* Washington, DC: National Center for Literacy.

Neuhaus Education Center. 2000. *Language Enrichment.* Houston, TX: Neuhaus Education Center.

Neuhaus Education Center. 2000. *Practices for Developing Accuracy and Fluency.* Houston, TX: Neuhaus Education Center.

Neuhaus Education Center. 2000. *The Colors and Shapes of Language.* Houston, TX: Neuhaus Education Center.

Neuhaus Education Center. 2002. *Reading Readiness Manual.* Houston, TX: Neuhaus Education Center.

O'Conner, Rollanda, Angela Notari-Syverson, and Patricia F. Vadasy. 1998. *Ladders to Literacy: A Kindergarten Activity Book.* Baltimore: Paul H. Brookes.

Ogle, Donna. 1986. "K-W-L: A Teaching Model that Develops Active Reading of Expository Text." *The Reading Teacher* 39: 564–570.

RAND Reading Study Group. 2002. "Reading for Understanding: Toward a Research and Development Program in Reading Comprehension." Available: www.rand.org/multi/achievementforall/reading/readreport.html (accessed May 5, 2005).

Reading First Academy Assessment Committee. 2002. *The Reading Leadership Academy Guidebook.* Washington, DC: U. S. Department of Education.

Reading First Leadership Academy. 2002. *The Reading Leadership Academy Guidebook.* Washington, DC: U. S. Department of Education. //Au: These two references appear to be for the same publication? Which is correct?//

Scott, Judith, and William E. Nagy. 2004. "Developing Word Consciousness." In *Vocabulary Instruction: Research to Practice,* edited by J. Baumann and Edward Kame'enui, 201–217. New York: Guilford Press.

Shaw, D., and R. Shaw. 2002. "DIBELS Oral Reading Fluency-Based Indicators of Third Grade Reading Skills for Colorado State Assessment Program (CSAP)." (Technical Report). Eugene, OR: University of Oregon.

Shaywitz, Sally E. . 1996. "Dyslexia." *Scientific American* Vol. 275, No. 5 (November): 98–104.

Simmons, Deborah C., and Ed Kame'enui. 2003. *Scott Foresman Early Reading Intervention.* Lebanon, IN: Scott Foresman.

Texas Education Agency. 2003–2004. *Intervention Activities Guide.*

Torgesen, Joseph K. 2004. "Avoiding the Devastating Downward Spiral: The Evidence That Early Intervention Prevents Reading Failure." *American Educator* Vol. 28, No. 3 (Fall): 6–19.

Torgesen, Joseph, and Brian Bryant. 2004. *Phonological Awareness Training for Reading.* Austin, TX: ProEd.

Torgesen, Joseph K., Patricia M. Mathes, and M. L. Grek. 2002. "Effectiveness of an Early Intervention Curriculum That is Closely Coordinated with the Regular Classroom Reading Curriculum." Paper presented at the Pacific Coast Research Conference, San Diego, CA, February.

Torgesen, Joseph K., Richard K. Wagner, Carol A. Rashotte, and J. Herron. (Manuscript in preparation). "A Comparison of Two Computer Assisted Approaches to the Prevention of Reading Disabilities in Young Children." Unpublished paper. Tallahassee, FL: Florida State University.

Torgesen, Joseph K., Richard K. Wagner, Carol A. Rashotte, E. Rose., Pat Lindamood, T. Conway, and C. Garvin. 1999. "Preventing Reading Failure in Young Children with Phonological Processing Disabilities: Group and Individual Responses to Instruction." *Journal of Educational Psychology* 91: 579–594.

United States Department of Education. 2002. *The Reading Leadership Academy Guidebook.* Washington, DC: United States Department of Education.

University of Texas and Texas Education Agency. 2002. *First Grade Teacher Reading Academy, Vocabulary.* Austin, TX: University of Texas and Texas Education Agency.

University of Texas Center for Reading and Language Arts. 2003. *Three-Tier Reading Model: Reducing Reading Difficulties for Kindergarten through Third Grade Students.* Austin, TX: University of Texas Center for Reading and Language Arts.

University of Virginia, Curry School of Education. PALS website.

Vaughn, Sharon, and Sylvia Linan-Thompson. 2003. "Group Size and Time Allotted to Intervention: Effects for Students with Reading Difficulties." In *Preventing and Remediating Reading Difficulties: Bringing Science to Scale,* edited by Barbara K. Foorman. Baltimore: York Press.

Vellutino, Frank R., D. M. Scanlon, and G. Reid Lyon. 2000. "Differentiating between Difficult-to-Remediate and Readily Remediated Poor Readers: More Evidence Against the IQ-Achievement Discrepancy Definition for Reading Disability." *Journal of Learning Disabilities* 33: 223–238.

Vellutino, Frank R., D. M. Scanlon, E. R. Sipay, S.G. Small, A. Pratt, R. Chen, and N. B. Denckla. 1996. "Cognitive Profiles of Difficult-to-Remediate and Readily Remediated Poor Readers: Early Intervention as a Vehicle for Distinguishing between Cognitive and Experiential Deficits as Basic Causes of Specific Reading Disability." *Journal of Educational Psychology* 88: 601–638.

World's Best Teachers. 2001. *Colleague in the Classroom.* Boise, ID: Wide Eye Productions.

Yopp, Hallie Kay, and Ruth Helen Yopp. (1996). *Oo-pples and Boo-noo-noos: Songs and Activities for Phonemic Awareness.* Orlando, FL: Harcourt Brace School Publishers.

Zgonc, Yvette. 2000. *Sounds in Action: Phonological Awareness Activities and Assessment.* Peterborough, NH: Crystal Springs Books.